NAMING SILENCED LIVES

Personal Narratives and
Processes of Educational Change

Daniel McLaughlin
and
William G. Tierney

ROUTLEDGE

NEW YORK AND LONDON

Published in 1993 by

Routledge
29 West 35 Street
New York, NY 10001

Published in Great Britain by
Routledge
11 New Fetter Lane
London EC4P 4EE

Copyright © 1993 by Routledge

Printed in the United States of America on acid free paper.

Library of Congress Cataloging-in-Publication Data

Naming silenced lives : personal narratives and the process of educational
    change / [edited by] Daniel McLaughlin and William G. Tierney.
        p. cm.
    Includes bibliographical references and index.
    ISBN 0-415-90516-8. — ISBN 0-415-90517-6 (pbk.)
    1. Discrimination in education—United States. 2. Education—Political
Aspects—United States. 3. Minorities—United States—Biography. 4.
Minorities—Education—United States. 5. Oral history. I. McLaughlin,
Daniel, 1951– . II. Tierney, William G.
LC212.2.N36 1993
370.19'34—dc20   93-20361
                                                                        CIP

Contents

Introduction
Developing Archives of Resistance:
Speak, Memory

William G. Tierney

Here's a memory of the times:

Charles, a forty-year-old African American who works as a librarian, is helped down the stairs by Kevin. It is early morning and I stand in Kevin's living room awaiting Charles. I have spilled the remnants of coffee on my blue sweater and silently dab at it as Charles slowly approaches. He reaches out to me as much to gain my support on his unsteady feet as to offer a greeting. I give him a hug and we sit down on the white couch.

Charles is leaving. Going home. I detect a certain resignation in Charles's voice as he says, "I guess I'm ready." We have been plotting his departure for a month now, perhaps two. Or perhaps I have been silently counting the time, unsure of when, at what point, but certain nonetheless, that when I first visited him a year ago in the hospital that it would eventually get him. AIDS does as it pleases.

Charles has grown sicker, and I have watched him. I have tried to help, but too often I have felt helpless. One is supposed to grow inured to death so that when one watches a second friend die, or a third, or a fourth, or a fifth, it should be easier than the first. But that is not the case. I see Charles and think not of numbers—the "third" or "fourth" or "fifth"—but of names Don, Bill, Robert. And I see Charles.

Yesterday Charles watched all of his belongings packaged and loaded on the truck that will take him home to his mother's in North Carolina. Imagine how difficult it must be to see one's life loaded on a U-Haul laden with cartons of memories that will be stored in some vault and never retrieved.

There goes my high school yearbook with pictures of friends long forgotten. There goes my rug that I bought when I went to Europe with my first lover. These memories are points of existence, testimony to a lived past and a possible future. But more importantly, these memories also define the present.

Memories are also collective. They offer definition and meaning to our lives, what we value, what we mean as community, family. My memory, for example, of Charles will be the final image of him standing in a blue bathrobe, sort of a black Gandhi. The chemotherapy has made him bald, and his rimless glasses make his head appear larger than it is. His face is gaunt. His legs have become pathetically thin and he has a crawl step since he has grown so weak. His friends swirled around him yesterday as they tried to box up his life and put it on the truck. Some people spoke animatedly with one another, uncomfortable with the silence, and others surreptitiously wiped their eyes between armloads of boxes. His mother sat in the living room silently watching this flurry of activity and waited to take him home. His house was eventually emptied and everyone left.

My memory returns me to Kevin's living room. Charles holds a Bible now and says he will soon be sitting in Charlotte's sunshine, away from the cold of my town. We laugh and I mention that I will have to visit. A final hug good-bye and I walk out the door.

This is a memory that I lived today. It will stay with me forever, and involves how I define this moment. It speaks of society, of community, of me, and of Charles.

Naming Silenced Lives

I offer my memory of Charles as a way to begin a discussion about the purpose of this book. By telling Charles's story I move the memory beyond merely my own private reflection, and involve others in the retelling. Individuals attach significance to an event and it becomes a memory. When we speak our memories and document them, we are engaged in an act of construction of our present worlds. Our individual and collective memories help construct the reality of our present.

In this book we offer a range of narratives for people who work in schools and colleges. Through a series of autobiographies, we demonstrate how educational organizations often marginalize and silence different groups. Each chapter examines how an individual or group is silenced by different educational arrangements, and the authors then consider the import of using autobiographies and other narrative methods to alter individuals' received circumstances. Our aim is to call attention to the experiences of people who have traditionally been left out of the educational mainstream, and to describe how their naming of silenced lives and relationships to educational institutions have propounded change.

We suggest that education's participants and organizations operate within ongoing patterns of struggle that embody competing conceptions of what counts for knowledge. The value of this approach is that it refuses to remain mired in modes of analysis that examine educational life from the singular perspective of effectiveness and efficiency. Theory and method act in a dialectical nature with policy and practice.

Throughout the book we highlight how theory mediates between education's constituencies and the larger social reality. Seen in this light, education is investigated not merely as a functionalist tool of effectiveness, but rather as a cacophony of voices mediated within different layers of reality and shaped by an interaction of dominant and subordinate forms of power. We observe not only the constraints placed on the human will, but also the possibilities for change and action. At the core of this approach is the recognition that power, knowledge, ideology, and culture are inextricably linked to one another in constantly changing patterns and relationships-

In the chapters in part one, the authors set the stage for a discussion of personal narrative, oral history, and critical theory in the study of educational institutions. Margaret LeCompte develops in chapter 1 the theoretical scaffolding for the book. She highlights how the ensuing chapters utilize life-history methodology and critical theory as a way to change some of the oppressive characteristics that we find in society. In chapter 2 Yvonna Lincoln continues the dialogue about how life-history research might operate in a dialectical manner to bring about change. In particular, Lincoln suggests that doing this kind of research fundamentally alters the relationship between the researcher and the researched, and also brings into question how one creates a text and the criteria for judging it.

Part two is composed of seven chapters that utilize the theoretical and methodological constructs developed in part one in order to ground in concrete practice the development of personal narratives for influencing change in schools and colleges. Andrew Gitlin and Beth Myers, for example, discuss the importance of dialogical encounters that enable school teachers to speak out in the public domain. In doing so, they argue, life-history research becomes a political act that inevitably contests narrow and limiting forms of education. Ivor Goodson and Ardra Cole follow in similar fashion; they argue that educational research must begin by listening to those people at whom the research is aimed. In effect, they argue against hierarchical models or top-down research agendas that seek to find the solutions to the myriad of problems that schools face without first involving teachers in the definitions of those problems. Daniel McLaughlin then provides a case study based on his work with Navajo elementary-school teachers. He points out how the development of life histories enable individuals to reflect on their own lives and at the same time incorporate their sense of identity into pedagogic encounters with one's own students.

My chapter is a discussion of a faculty member who died of AIDS. It revolves around an analysis of how we define "identity" in a postmodern world, and what the implications are for the role of the author if one does the kind of research advocated in this book. Patricia Gumport offers three life-history interviews of fired faculty at one university. She, too, uses postmodernism as a lens through which to filter the words of the faculty. Her purpose is to use the individual stories as a means to understand larger currents within society and how these dynamics get played out in the organization.

Michèle Foster first analyzes how race has been used in the discourse about teaching to essentialize "white pedagogy" and she then examines the lives and careers of nineteen experienced Black teachers in order to portray the dynamically different relationship they have to their communities and their beliefs about teaching. Finally, Grace Szepkouski has undertaken a life history with an elderly woman labeled moderately mentally retarded. By keying in on one individual's experiences with institutionalization, the author opens up a larger focus that highlights the struggles and challenges that pertain to social misplacement, and social support systems.

By way of concluding, part three analyzes what we mean by active, critical citizenship. Peter McLaren sketches an emergent topology of life histories that enable teachers, students, educational researchers, and the researched to analyze and transform, rather than merely serve, prevailing logic in educational institutions and the wider social order. Daniel McLaughlin then summarizes the chapters and points out tasks that await us.

Archives of Resistance

Archives are repositories of public records. Memory is the faculty through which one remembers. The argument in this book is that individual memory must be preserved not simply for some romantic future where people will be able to see how we lived in the late twentieth century, but rather, we collect life histories as a way to document how we live now so that we might change how we live now. Archives are not static hermetically sealed museums; they are active commentaries about our lives.

Further, because the individuals whose lives are documented in this book are often the ones who are forgotten and overlooked—Native Americans, gay men, fired faculty, or the mentally retarded—we are not simply suggesting that our task is to develop a "catalogue of silenced lives" as if the simple act of recording individual lives absolves us of any further activity. To be sure, one purpose here is to uncover narratives that most often are lost or forgotten. Yet essentially, we are arguing that critical research needs to challenge the oppressive structures that create the conditions for silencing. The collection of these texts and our engagement with those whose lives we have recorded, then, is one act of resistance. And our individual work with the people whose lives account for the stories also must involve more than simply recording what someone has to say.

Research in the postmodern world maintains traditional social-science standards of accuracy and representation, but it must also break down the shibboleths of disengagement and objectivity. Instead, postmodern research demands that the researcher be involved both with the "research subject" and with changing those conditions that seek to silence and marginalize.

We name Charles life. In doing so, we honor his memory and struggle to ensure that he will not be forgotten. In our struggle, we also try to create the conditions that enable others to gain voice and to resist.

PART I

1

A Framework for Hearing Silence:
What Does Telling Stories Mean
When We Are Supposed to Be Doing Science?

Margaret D. LeCompte

The purpose of this chapter is to establish a common theoretical framework for interpreting the studies in this book. To do so is difficult. The empirical studies herein borrow from two time-honored, but not necessarily harmonious, traditions. The first is storytelling, in the form of oral history, narrative biography, or life-history ethnography; the second is that of social activism and critique. Storytelling and biography are research-oriented activities whose purpose is discovery and analysis; they may be, but are not always, put at the service of social activism. Social activism is intended to alleviate or at least to ameliorate oppressive conditions under which specific groups labor; however, neither storytelling, the services of a researcher, nor the results of his or her work are required for its execution. Researchers who combine the two traditions often confuse theoretical or epistemological concerns with concerns about methods and ethics. In this chapter, I will attempt to distinguish among these concerns and examine their consequences. Then, I will propose theoretical guidelines for framing what the authors term emancipatory life-history narratives.

Epistemologies and Ethics

The title of this book, *Naming Silenced Lives*, implies that a certain political stance has been taken toward the individuals whose lives are described.

I am deeply grateful to Shelby Wolf for making me aware of this aspect of Bateson's work, and to Donna Deyhle, Elias Martinez, Dan McLaughlin, Barbara Medina, and Mary Ellen Wiertelak for their editorial assistance and substantive advice.

That their lives are defined as silenced implies that the individuals involved have been deprived of voice without their consent—that they are victims of oppression. The very fact that these silenced lives must be *named* implies that those who live them may lack consciousness of their own oppression, or, if they once *were* conscious of oppression, that they have suppressed that knowledge. The purpose of the authors of this book (see also Delpit 1988; Weis and Fine, 1992a; Weis and Fine 1992b) is to give voice to people who have not been heard because their points of view are believed to be unimportant or difficult to access by those in power. Their voices are silenced because of social stigma or inferior status; they include children, the disabled, women, members of minority groups, homosexuals, and lower participants in formal organizations. The focus of this book is to elicit these voices, permitting the informants to speak in ways not heard before. The vehicle by which this is accomplished is the mediation of a researcher.

Researchers seek out the silenced because their perspectives often are counter-hegemonic. Their voices serve to critique the canon of existing social structure, relationships of production, aesthetics, and even scientific theories. In this sense, research on the silenced is part of the postmodern tradition. In another sense, studies of the silenced and the unheard become problematic with the very act of sampling or selection, or defining the population to be studied. The purported voicelessness of the silenced, the key variable which interests a researcher, is an issue of relative status. Scholars who study the unheard—anthropologists, sociologists, educators, political scientists, literary critics, and even social activists—define them as silenced to and by those in power. While the subjects of such research may, in fact, come to share the researcher's definition, being selected for participation in such research creates a new set of frames through which and by which participants are defined, frames created by the researcher and not by the informants themselves.

In some cases, silenced individuals may, in fact, be quite vocal about their life situations among peers. In others they may be silent even to themselves. Under these circumstances, researchers may give name to a condition the informant may not even be aware of possessing, or may attribute to a people circumstances or conditions which they cannot or do not want to hear about. They may also uncover conditions which dominant groups would prefer to remain hidden.

The initial job of the researcher or participant observer/narrator is to define the powerlessness (within a specific context) of a group of individuals, and then to identify members of that group whose story "begs to be told." The researcher then elicits their story and translates it for those who have not heard it. In this way the researcher becomes a hermeneut—an interpreter—whose task is to render the voices of the unheard in a language accessible both to them and to a wider and presumably more powerful audience. The hermeneutic stance mandates an interpretive framework for elicitation of the narrative (Erickson 1986). The techniques for eliciting such narratives are well known; see for example, Spradley (1979) or Mishler (1986). It also requires that the ethnographer, or hermeneut, be a culture broker, especially insofar as the ethnographer represents a liaison between the cultures of higher- and lower-status people.

However, ethical research on the disempowered, whether in a social activist or a scholarly tradition, obliges researchers to consider how informants will participate in the disclosure of their situations and secrets, as well as how researchers will participate in the future life and destiny of the people they study. None of these issues are matters which can be unilaterally decided by the researcher, or even by the researcher in consultation with colleagues, disciplinary codes of conduct, or guidelines for the ethical treatment of human subjects. (See Deyhle, Hess, and LeCompte 1992, for a discussion of such codes and their development and use in the human sciences.) Rather, they are a matter for open and egalitarian discussion and negotiation between researchers and the researched. They also are the subject of possible veto by the researched.

Naming something may make it real; that reality becomes more apparent when the naming is done by those for whom it has become salient. However, if the naming is done by an outsider—even a sympathetic researcher— the appellation may not feel entirely authentic to the individual or group to which it is affixed. The names may lack authenticity altogether if researchers affix them to people who do not share the researcher's characterization or people who have not been told—either during the process of the research or in a later write-up—how the researcher characterized them. Because naming people or concepts links their new—or researcher-determined—identity to their original identity, it inevitably involves a degree of disclosure. For this reason, researchers have an ethical imperative to operate under strictures of informed consent.

Narrative as a Critique of Positivism

Narrative storytelling, such as that found in this text, is a reaction to the strictures of positivism. Critical, feminist and poststructural researchers such as Roman (1992), Lather (1986), Ellsworth (1989), Harding (1987), and others have suggested that positivistic science imposes a false distance between researchers and the researched by mandating that the researcher maintain an artificially impersonal stance toward the people studied. As a consequence, research informants are treated as mere objects of investigation. This type of relationship not only impedes the development of cathexis between participants in the research act, but also results in data that present a partial and therefore false, and an elitist and therefore biased, reality.

The poststructural remedy to the positivistic canon of conventional science is to overturn old dichotomies between research/practice, author/text, subject/object, knower/known, method/procedure, and theory/practice. Critical researchers blur the boundaries between all concepts such as these and often go even farther, eschewing traditional analytic and conceptual frames altogether. The resulting stories or narratives are presented almost in the form of raw data, letting the informants "speak for themselves." This mode of presentation presumably frees the informant voices from interpretation by the researcher. However, the discourse reported still is one selected by the ethnographer; it may be powerful, and it may seem truthful and authentic. But it is, in fact, still a partial discourse, one that presents whatever perspective emerges from those parts of the story the ethnographer includes in the text, and that often leaves the researcher as an "absent presence." This partiality derives from those aspects of life upon which the ethnographer concentrates; in critical ethnography, for example, conditions of oppression can form the focus of a narrative—to the exclusion of a wide range of other issues. Thus, even critical ethnographic discourse still is embedded in historical context and social conventions (McLaren 1992, 80); It cannot be presented without considering the power relations inherent in the research context, each of which defines truth in its own terms (Foucault 1980).

Relativism and the Trivializing of Oppression

A key issue for critical researchers is that in rejecting the alienating aspects of positivism, they often create two other problems. The first is that the lives of their subjects are cast within a completely relativistic frame. The stories told are situated only in the here and now and they emphasize only that reality constructed during interaction within small groups or dyads. By presenting the stories devoid of external context, the relativistic stance of researchers trivializes the concerns of participants because it limits them only to the time or set of circumstances addressed in the study. Under such conditions, poverty, for example, can be justified as functional for the context, or simply treated as a state of mind. The lack of context ignores the fact that, while the subjective experience of poverty may to some extent be relative to individual contexts, its actual experience is no more a state of mind than is biological pregnancy and the subsequent act of giving birth.

Extreme relativism functions in the end to justify the status quo in the same way that structural functionalism does. Structural functionalism imposes a false consensus that all is well; relativism justifies the status quo by measuring it only against *internal* conditions rather than permitting its assessment against possible external sets of standards and material conditions.

A Problem of Imposition

The second problem created by eschewing old frameworks is that critical researchers can create new and often idiosyncratic frameworks which are as doctrinaire and orthodox as those they discard. Often the success of these frameworks, and the research they inspire, demands the emancipation of the "subject" in ways which are sanctioned by the researcher, but which may not take into full consideration the structural constraints within which informants live, or believe they live. An initial blindness on the part of researchers is an understandable consequence of their status as outsiders. In the first place, they cannot fully participate in or understand all of the circumstances of informant life. In the second place, they can leave the field when the study is finished or if conditions become too uncomfortable. However, it is contradictory in what purports to be interpretive research, whose overriding goal is to frame the study in terms of the constructs used by those who are studied (Bennett and LeCompte 1990; Clifford and Marcus 1986; Erickson 1986; Geertz 1989; Marcus and Fisher 1986). In fact, the "other" *can* get lost in research whose stated purpose is exploration of this foreign territory on its own terms. This is because, by the very act of engaging in critical, emancipatory, empowering research, researchers take a particular ethical stance toward their informants, defining them as disempowered or oppressed, regardless of how the informants define themselves. McLaren refers to this as the "evangelizing tendency of critical ethnography," which presents itself as the "sole theoretical representative of the oppressed" (McLaren 1992, 88).

Such a definition of situation by a researcher, even if generally accepted by both scientific and indigenous communities, constrains the research. Especially insofar as definitions are imposed *in advance* of fieldwork, researchers may fail to listen adequately to feedback from the field, especially to stories which contradict their definitions. Consequently, they may silence participants who are desperately trying to "talk back," contesting what researchers say or believe. Research participants, especially those who hitherto have been silenced, should have "the first right to name reality, to articulate how social reality functions, and to decide how the issues are to be organized and defined" (Mihevc 1989, cited in McLaren 1992). Without this right, the stance taken by critical researchers toward informants may be just as dogmatic and objectifying as it would be in a positivistic frame. Notwithstanding their use of constructivist or interpretive theoretical frames, critical researchers run the risk of entering a setting not to find out what informants think is there, but what researchers already know is there. This limits the scope of their research to a portrayal of nuance—an examination of how individuals under study express their particular relationship to oppression and how it affects them. It also leaves unchanged the status asymmetry between researcher and researched. While the role of researcher-as-liberator is perhaps a more comfortable one to assume than that of researcher-as-equal-partner, the researcher who leaves the field with his or her data intact often benefits more than the informant who remains behind.

Naming vs. Empowerment

Creating a name for a condition is not the same as changing it. In order to create change, researchers must do more than to posit that "ye shall know the truth, and the truth shall set you free." In fact, informants may decide that, given the web of intergroup relations in which they are caught, the researcher's definition of their oppression may be true, but inescapable, at least in the short run. In those cases, the only option remaining to a researcher is simply to pack up and go home. There is, in other words, a critical link missing in much purportedly emancipatory research. It begins and ends with the illusion that self-awareness alone is sufficient to bring about empowerment. To go beyond consciousness-raising requires a greater commitment. If researchers truly wish to empower those whom they study, they must redefine informants to be those *with* whom they study, and redefine their own activities far beyond production of a document describing events experienced, recorded, and analyzed. This is why, at the risk of seeming merely to be reinventing a materialist or Marxist perspective, I emphasize the need to frame narrative within a social, economic, political, and historical context. Furthermore, as Gore (1990) points out, empowerment is not just a discourse or a state of mind. Empowerment requires the acquisition of the property of power and its exercise in the accomplishment of some vision or desired future condition. That vision cannot simply be the construction of a text to be published.

A Problem of Means vs. Ends

Critical researchers speak often of the need for struggle in the service of liberation. Most frequently, the stated purpose of struggle is to permit participants to break free from oppressive conditions which blind them to power asymmetries among individuals created by differences of race, class, status, and gender. Critical ethnography often loses focus when the beneficiary of the struggle is unclear. In a well-intended attempt to address the biases of the researcher as well as the oppression of participants, critical ethnographers have broadened the struggle for enlightenment to involve both the researcher and the researched; no longer are false consciousness and praxis for the informant alone. Judith Stacey (1988) notes that too often, critical ethnographers dominate their own narratives; *they* become the natives to be understood, and the ethnography itself becomes the territory to be explored. Naive researchers confuse their own means to achieve a study—the struggle to be accepted by informants or to get the informants to listen, or just to survive in the informants' world—with the informants' struggle for emancipation. Indeed, the former *is* a genuine struggle, but it is one shared by all fieldworkers in the course of their activity. The process of struggling may and usually does result in enlightenment for the fieldworker, and it always conduces to better storytelling. It is the grist for thousands of war stories, those "tales from the field" with which all ethnographies begin. Yet it is not necessarily linked, if it has anything at all to do with the *enlightenment* of informants. It is only incidentally related to their struggle to *act* upon any awareness created in the course of activities in which the fieldworker might have induced informants to participate.

Further, the struggle of researchers to translate the world of the informant into language intelligible to outsiders can be mistaken for a struggle to achieve empowerment. Like the struggle for acceptance by the researcher described above, accurate translation often is confused with empowerment of informants. However, empowering people requires more than making each person aware of the other's life situation. Actual empowerment requires a second act of translation: from awareness to activism. Someone in the equation, someone *other than the researcher,* has to want to change the situation, take action, and define the change as both possible and worthwhile.

Too often, the struggle for emancipation gets lost in the research procedures. *Real* empowerment requires *real* participant observation, wherein the researcher is a participant for the long term, with no ability to run away from the trials, petty tribulations, and real dangers that their informants suffer. Real participant observation may even mean a lifetime of collaboration. Real collaboration may mean getting roughed up, losing battles and projects, and sometimes even losing one's life. Few of us achieve this; such participation is more the province of social activists such as the Catholic religious activists of Latin America (Cleary 1985; Lernoux 1982) and Miles Horton and the Highlander Folk School in the United States (Adams 1980).

Bringing about change is not a quiet academic pursuit; to empower is to get into trouble. If one really is engaged in research meant to be empowering, one should never expect to reconcile warring constituencies or stakeholders; rather, one should expect continual conflict with informants and the Establishment. This is because by its nature, true empowering, rare though it may be, is a revolutionary activity that requires wrenching privileges away from entrenched interests—even those privileges without which members of the Establishment feel they cannot survive. In these terms, the problem of empowerment becomes a problem of life—or death. Given this reframing, it is important to examine the rhetoric within which research is cast, and to be somewhat modest as to its purposes and achievements. In the pages that follow, I will discuss an approach to doing and interpreting

narrative research that is both more sensitive to the needs and lives of informants and realistic in terms of the fieldwork commitments that academic
researchers generally can make.

Finding a Theoretical Frame for Research on Silence

As the preceding pages have made clear, critical researchers face a double
burden. On the one hand, they need to portray the inner reality of their informants. On the other hand, they also need to frame that reality within a context of meaning external to the reality experienced by informants. On the one
hand, they must present the socially constructed—and therefore completely
unique—experience of the people studied. On the other hand, they must situate that experience within relatively predictable sociohistorical patterns and
regularities. While all of this must be done in the context of commitment described earlier, from a methodological point of view, there is nothing particularly radical about the kinds of actual data needed to address both sets of
needs. Careful researchers will not only elicit the perspective of the informant
with regard to the phenomena under consideration, but also will document
their own reactions to and impact upon both informants and their life situations. Critical researchers will elicit the social constructions of all participants,
and also will be conscious of the larger context in which the study is
framed—in ways quite similar to those of conventional science. The radical
difference between critical research and conventional scientific practice relates
to the stance taken toward truth, toward informants (especially in terms of
the longevity of relationships with informants), toward the analysis of data,
and toward the generalizability and presentation of results. In these aspects of
the research process, two conceptual frameworks provide guidance: an elabo-
ration on Bateson's (1982) notion of "double description," and the concept of
chaos (Gleick 1987; Prigogine and Stengers 1984).

Double Description

Double description is a way of looking at and understanding the world involving binocular vision. Bateson (1982) asserts that using only one eye delivers to the brain phenomenological perceptions which lack the depth perception which results from integration of perceptions from both eyes. Depth perception comes from "a combination of two versions of the outside universe
very slightly different from each other" (Bateson 1982, 3), versions that differ
from each other in logical type. These differences arise because monocular vision sends to the brain only data from the report of *one* eye. Binocular vision,
by contrast, involves seeing a phenomenon with both eyes so that, in effect,
the researcher has two or more descriptions rather than one. Bateson points
out that double description creates a boundary problem because it is constituted by the blurring of two or more distinct and different visions. Because

only single vision can produce the image of a discrete unit, double description blurs the clear boundaries between units such as "self," "other," "mind," "body," "object," "subject," "researcher," and "researched." This blurring is what actually creates binocular vision. While it is less clear, nonetheless it is a much more adequate portrayal of phenomena, because the blurring of differences between the images (or data) projected to the brain by each eye creates depth perception, or a picture located in contexts of time, place, and belief.

What is unique to Bateson's conception (and important for collaborative and emancipatory research) is the importance which Bateson ascribes to the idea of difference. Rather than holding out for the achievement of a single unitary vision, Bateson celebrates diversity and difference, because it provides not only greater accuracy within a single dimension, but also adds dimensions to the vision. In the same way, researchers in the tradition of emancipatory narrative also require binocular vision. With one "eye," they record what they "see" the subject doing, creating a record of the participant's activities—often in the participant's own words. With the other, they record a whole range of other data, including what they themselves are doing and what everyone involved in the research setting is feeling and doing. Thus, in the practice of the project, the boundaries between research-as-reporter and researcher-as-participant become blurred. Just as the researcher tries to "make sense" of what is going on in the project, other participants try to "make sense" of what the researcher is doing to, for and with them (Gadamer 1975).

Double Description and Double Consciousness

Double description involves more than simply trying to understand unilaterally how subjects make sense of the world (Gadamer 1975). Simply adding more and more versions of reality does not change the relationship between researcher and researched, nor does it necessarily de-center attention from the researcher-constructed text. Rather, double description in collaborative research involves the development of double consciousness. It is not enough to see, and not even enough to understand. Collaboration requires the consciousness, or embrace, of the "other" in ways that change researchers and those they study so that their destinies are inextricably linked and shared. Such consciousness must transcend the self-consciousness customarily called for in critical and collaborative research. It is required for the ethical presentation of personal narrative because the researcher's notes usually constitute the only data, construction of reality, text to be interpreted, or story to be told. Without double consciousness, the power asymmetries between researcher and researched, and the consequences of those asymmetries, can be ignored or set aside when the researcher leaves the field with his or her data. Given double consciousness, participants (including the researcher) struggle on an equal basis over what

each could—or would—do to or for the other, as well as the kinds of participation necessary and possible, the stakes involved in participating by all par-
ties, and the risks which failure to participate would entail. In addition, participants struggle to achieve understanding of what researchers could—or
could be forced to—do to or for the participants—and the risks that such activities would entail for both, including the risks to the research project.

Double consciousness makes a relativistic stance impossible, because it
necessitates links to an external context. No act can be justified simply
within its own context. The text created within the study, whether by the
researcher alone or in collaboration with participants, and the sense of
reality it conveys, is mediated by and situated not just within itself, but
within constraining networks of time, place, beliefs, and historical context.

Achieving Double Consciousness

The practice of double description requires three kinds of learning.
The first is of details; the second is learning the patterns and contexts in
which relationships occur, and the third is learning to change. Metaphor-
ically, detail learning involves monocular vision; it is achieved with one eye
and creates a description of one thing at a time. The second kind of learning
requires two eyes. Binocular vision permits recording information about
more than one person or phenomenon; it also is required in order to learn
the ongoing patterns and contexts within which relationships occur. Bateson
suggests that learning these contexts of life "is a matter which cannot be considered to be internal, as if you were talking about something happening inside the organism. [Rather] it is a matter of external relationship" (Bateson
1982, 5). It is impossible to understand the internal states of human beings
without learning about both the details pertinent to individuals and the external differences between individuals in the study (including the researcher)
and their respective experiences of each other, their history, their beliefs, and
their participation in the environment.

The third kind of learning—how people engage in the process of change
—Bateson called "deutero-learning." It stimulates double consciousness,
because it forces "interactants to change so as to fit themselves to the ongoing pattern of relationships . . . between two creatures or between a
creature and a mountain or an environment of some sort" (Bateson 1982,
5). It is a precondition for understanding how participants "make sense" of
their world, and is the catalyst both for praxis and the subsequent achievement of double consciousness.

Double Description and Postmodern Portrayal

One task of double description is to render the autobiography of a person
as mirror exemplar of his or her place, time, and context (Mason, 1988, 45).

Often this means rendering individuals in ways that are antithetical to canons of method and portrayal. For example Brodzki and Schenck (1988) point out that the autobiographies of women almost never follow the same pattern that autobiographies of men do. The latter are oriented around Western Eurocentric notions of the unquestioned right of the individual to celebrate his unique and undivided contribution to the world without taking into account place, time, and context. By contrast, female autobiographies present divided selves that always are more complex, mediated, and negotiated. While women autobiographers do proclaim the right to tell their story and assert its interest and value to future generations, the life of the speaker is not presented as undivided. It is always framed in terms of relationships with others. Therefore, its production or presentation requires some sort of binocular vision and double description.

From a feminist perspective, double description constitutes a good model for the uniquely feminine experience. The perspective of women is the only human perspective which is inevitably at least divided in two, whether or not the woman in question has privileged status. The lives of women always are divided and mediated by the imposition of an Other. Woman has a Self, but it is defined in terms of its negotiation with the Other. Men, even ethnic minority men who experience oppression outside their community, can arrogate the power of undisputed kings in their own castles, with dominion over their own mates and children. However, women, regardless of their achieved or even ascribed status, remain prisoners to their gender, held hostage by threats of degradation and trivialization, as well as of disbelief, simply because they are women. This is true even in contemporary matriarchial societies, because of the colonization of matriarchy by contemporary patriarchal capitalist practice. This is not to say that all women are conscious of their double status. Rather, it is to suggest that in this universally divided condition of women exists a foothold or an opportunity for new strategies for understanding and for engaging in critical emancipatory research.

Double Description and Validity

Double description creates a real problem for researchers confined by traditional notions of reliability and validity. Conventional science strives toward one indisputable truth; this in turn requires objectification of the research subject, a detached presentation of the results, and replicability of the project for the truth value of the research to be considered adequate. Postmodern science of the kind represented in this text finds it impossible to adhere to such strictures because of the intimacy of relationships and the praxis required in collaborative and even emancipatory research. Further, the uniqueness of each person's discourse and text, as well as its constructed nature, make replicability unfeasible. The double description required by such research delivers at least two versions of reality or truth which often cannot be reconciled or synthesized. As a consequence, under conventional canons of science, binocular (or multi-ocular, multilensed) research is rendered suspect, both in terms of its content and the methods that it uses.

The validity or truth of accounts by marginal people is questioned because it contests or at least is not congruent with the accepted canons of truth or reality. Women's narrative, for example, is dismissed first as trivial. When these narratives turn out to be powerful ones, such as the prophecies of Jeanne d'Arc or the testimony of Anita Hill, they are attacked as untruthful and their perpetrators are burned, literally or figuratively, at the stake.

This suggests a need for the generator of critical personal narratives to be doubly sensitive to issues of the audiences their finished work might encounter. The write-up of a study reestablishes to some degree the boundaries between researcher/subject and local knowledge/external knowledge. While the issue of authorial voice may be forgotten during the data-collection phases of the study, the publication phase raises a critical ontological question: whose "being" is being reflected? How does the reality constructed during the research process get presented in a way which preserves the authenticity of all who experienced it and the collaboration which generated it? Critical research, even more than traditional research, plays to multiple audiences. Researchers must consider, then, the consumer of the research and what is to be consumed. Too often, the consumer is defined only as a disinterested outside reader and the only consumable is considered to be the written text itself. Lost is how informants themselves can be consumed if sensitive materials about their lives fall into unfriendly hands, or if those same materials—hitherto unseen by participants-constitute a devastating portrayal and a ghastly surprise. Writers of personal narratives must, as a consequence, maintain the stance of double consciousness which identifies with their informants' condition even after they leave the field, so that they do not publish works which might harm their informants.

The Validity of Method

Double description has great power, and this power poses great danger to vested interests. The depth of vision which it creates is not seen simply as a contrast to accepted notions; rather, it is redefined as a confrontation. Even the call for alternative epistemologies—those used to implement double description—has exploded from a minor debate over technique into a full-blown "paradigm war." In the process, both the content of silence and the methods used to hear it have been discredited; conversations between the canon and its critics have been redefined as a battle to be joined and won. The canon of conventional positivistic science posits a world in which some visions or renditions of experience must be excluded. It renders invisible the voice and role of the interlocutor or researcher, and makes inaudible the voice of the person portrayed, because that person is denied institutional or procedural means to contest the portrait. Further, positivistic science does not actively seek out, within the given experiment, alternative explanations, descriptions, and critiques. It is self-contained, self-limiting; alternatives have to await the development of a new project. The field cannot "talk back." This view of science and the version of truth it legitimates now has been revealed by feminists and other critical theorists to be incomplete and biased. However, equally partial are visions based upon any attempt to elicit a more complete vision by imposing an alternative canon. In fact, the necessity for double description necessarily elicits visions that are partial— at least within a given study.

Double Consciousness/Partial Consciousness

In the preceding pages, I am arguing neither for some unitary form of feminist objectivity or truth, nor that all women possess a unique clarity of vision which should be emulated by critical and collaborative researchers. Nor am I suggesting that researchers should utilize double description to strive for some new kind of higher—or schizophrenic—reality. Rather, like Haraway (1991), I suggest that truth derives from double and partial consciousness; it should be recognized as consisting of situated, and therefore partial, knowledge. This stance does not reject conceptions of truth altogether; rather, it admits of a knowledge that, because it has known and confessed limitations, invites further inquiry. This invitation must go beyond anemic recommendations for further study to encourage contestation and critique from totally unknown, and currently unimaginable, quarters.

In Haraway's view, such a version of knowledge is neither passive, fuzzy, nor uncertain.

> Rational knowledge does not pretend to be disengagement; to be from everywhere and so nowhere—to be free from interpretation, from being represented, to be fully self-contained or fully formalizable. Rational knowledge is a process of ongoing critical interpretation among "fields" of interpreters and decoders. (1991, 197)

Such a stance requires "passionate detachment" (Kuhn 1982, cited in Haraway 1991). Passionate detachment means both the intensity of immersion and praxis *and* the recognition that both of the pictures one sees with two eyes are real and valid, as are their locations within constraining contexts as well as their synthesis. Passionate detachment furthermore means that just as researchers cannot remain immune to participants, so also are they barred from "going native" or completely identifying with those under study. This is the essence of double consciousness. Simply put, one cannot "be" and simultaneously be critical of that being. A step outside, a disengagement, is necessary to prevent the researcher from so strongly identifying with participants or so completely rejecting analysis and theory that the story told is related only from the perspective of the researcher's one eye. As I have indicated earlier, such presentation is not honest because it is not possible; moreover, it is not ethical because it trivializes the experiences recounted and subordinates all accounts to that of the researcher.

The product of the kind of rational inquiry advocated by Haraway is not uncertainty. Letting go of the need for unitary truth, in fact, is itself liberating. As subatomic physicists have reassured us, all knowledge, even in physics, is partial. If we know where a particle is at this moment, we cannot know its velocity and vector. However, if we accept that we know *now* where the particle *was* at several time points in the past, we may know something a great deal more important than mere location, such as what direction the particle is traveling, even if we do not know where it ultimately may end up (Zukav 1979). Thus, though possession of one piece of information may permit us the luxury of an illusory certainty, we must recognize the consequences of such a choice. Not only does the delusion of certainty which monocular vision produces prevent us from knowing much more about a given phenomenon, but it is a choice for stasis, for stopping the inquiry.

"Our Viewpoints are Too Small"[1]: An Introduction to Chaos Theory

Personal narratives are much like clinical case studies. They can be lovely stories by themselves, but as isolated texts, they tell us little about the human condition. Furthermore, a tension exists between the uniqueness of the case—which characterizes the content of a story as a random occurrence—and the temptation to seek generalizable patterns from it. One resolution to the tension is to escape into relativism—a stance which I have rejected. Another is methodological; groups of cases can be treated comparatively. In this way, they can generate profound insights about our existence. None of these solutions, however, provides a new vantage point or a framework within which to address the idiosyncrasies or vagaries of the individual case. Chaos theory (Gleick 1987), however, provides a response to the relativism implied in misplaced assertions of uniqueness, or to the inability of researchers to discover patterns or common themes among discrete studies.

Chaos theory is a theory of order within apparent disorder (Prigogine and Stengers 1984). Chaos theory rejects the Newtonian predictability and uniformity of, for example, the classical physics upon which most positivistic social science has been modeled (Dobbert and Kurth-Schai 1992). However, it does not reject regularity altogether. It does assume that all aspects of the

---

[1]Acknowledgment is owed to Marion Dobbert and Ruthanne Kurth-Schai, from whose 1992 publication this phrase is borrowed.

universe are patterned in some way, and that relationships among all living beings in the universe reflect, in some way, subsets of those patterns. It looks for underlying simplicities, principles, or regularities in what otherwise appear to be random, unpredictable, and even wild events. Chaos theory permits the general shape of a process to be determined, but not its specific individual parts or happenings.

Dobbert and Kurth-Schai (1992) suggest that two kinds of chaotic order have particular importance to the social sciences. The first is what Lorenz (described in Gleick 1987, 48) describes as stable, aperiodic order, which describes phenomena, like cycles of weather, which are locally unpredictable but globally stable. Weather cycles, like individual human behaviors, are unpredictable. While individual events may closely resemble each other, they never are duplicates. They recur over a period of time with some regularity until some small variation suddenly leads to a major shift in the behavior of the whole system. This shift, however, does not remove the system from within fixed boundaries of a well-defined complex track (Dobbert and Kurth-Schai 1992, 132).

The second form of chaotic order useful to the social sciences is the geometric type of fractal order which explains Newtonian boundaryless mapping. This kind of order, seen in Escher and Mandelbrot diagrams, is found in complex shapes that infinitely *almost* repeat themselves on a smaller and smaller scale, creating as they do boundaries of infinite lengths within finite space. These extremely complex and infinitely variable shapes are constituted from a few extremely simple mathematical rules, hidden in the apparent complexity of the forms they can create. Both of these forms of order—apparent randomness within a pattern, and infinite variety generated by finite principles—facilitate a search for underlying simplicity within the complexity of human life without eliminating its unpredictability and uniqueness (Dobbert and Kurth-Schai 1992). They do so by looking at phenomena from a different vantage point. They suggest that phenomena which ordinarily are seen as random, erratic, unpredictable, and wild when viewed close up or treated in isolation—as is the case in experimental or case studies—often actually exist within somewhat predictable or orderly systems when analyzed with different lenses, such as on a larger scale or on a longer time frame. It also suggests that the regularity and predictability which scientists once sought as the most elegant and parsimonious explanation for events often is, in fact, a delusion and based upon very specialized problems which scientists chose to study because they yielded to existing scientific tools (Gleick 1987; Prigogine and Stengers 1984).

Randomness within a system provides a better model for more and more naturally occurring phenomena than does regularity within a system. A good example is that of the human heart; medical treatment of heart patients has tried to achieve a perfectly regularly heartbeat. However, the perfectly regularized heart cannot respond spontaneously or adapt quickly to external stimuli. In fact, studies of pathology indicate the heart becomes perfectly regular just *before* it experiences a cardiac arrest (Langreth 1991). If regularity, predictability, or stasis can be an unhealthy state for biological organisms, it may also be a poor model for social organisms. If this is the case, then the casting out of nonconforming cases and rejection of the unique and random may be poor social science.

The creators of personal narratives may, in fact, be collecting the multiple random points whose variability masks underlying patterns of human behavior and belief. Radcliffe-Brown (1957, quoted in Dobbert and Kurth-Schai 1992, 150) notes that systemic regularity or patterns cannot be found by direct examination of field notes. This is because the viewpoints they represent are too small, too close to the data. A search for regularity and explanations in social science research, as in mathematics, involves a search for basic principles that generate larger social systems and subsystems.

This does not mean that personal narratives must be reduced to mathematical formulae for ease of manipulation. However, looking at each narrative in relation to the body of such literature permits us to elicit basic principles not only about how to do personal narratives, but what they may mean for human behavior and belief. It permits their situation within Batesonian contexts of time, place, and belief, and facilitates identification of processes and leverage points for change. Rather than viewing them simply as part of an idiosyncratic, anecdotal genre, it permits them to be appreciated in a more appropriately rigorous—even scientific—context. It remains for researchers and collaborators such as those presented in this text to begin the search for meaning, patterns, regularities, and principles hidden within the rich uniqueness of these stories.

References

Adams, Frank (with Miles Horton). 1980. *Unearthing seeds of fire: The idea of Highlander.* Winston-Salem, N.C.: John F. Blair.

Bateson, Gregory. 1982. Difference, double description and the interactive designation of the self. In *Studies in Symbolism and Cultural Communication,* edited by F. Allan Hanson, 3–8. Lawrence, Kan.: University of Kansas Publications in Anthropology.

Bennett, Kathleen G., and LeCompte, Margaret D. 1990. *The way schools work: A sociological analysis of education.* White Plains, N.Y.: Longman.

Brodzki, Bella, and Schenck, Celeste. 1988. *Life/lines: Theorizing women's autobiography*. Ithaca, N.Y.: Cornell University Press.

Cleary, Edward N. 1985. *Crisis and change: The church in Latin America today*. Maryknoll, N.Y.: Orbis Books.

Clifford, James & Marcus, George E. (Eds) 1986. *Writing Culture: The Poetics and politics of ethnography*. Berkeley, CA: University of California Press.

Delpit, Lisa. 1988. The silenced dialogue: Power and pedagogy in educating other people's children. *Harvard Educational Review* 58, no 3: 280–98.

Deyhle, Donna, Hess, G. Alfred, and LeCompte, Margaret D. 1992. Approaching ethical issues for qualitative researchers in education. In *The handbook of qualitative research in education,* edited by M. D. LeCompte, W. Millroy, and J. Preissle, 597–642. San Diego, Cal.: Academic Press.

Dobbert, Marion, and Kurth-Schai, Ruthanne. 1992. Systematic ethnography: Toward an evolutionary science of education and culture. In *The handbook of qualitative research in education,* edited by M. D. LeCompte, W. Millroy, and J. Preissle, 93–154. San Diego, Cal: Academic Press.

Ellsworth, Elizabeth. 1989. Why doesn't this feel empowering? Working through the repressive myths of critical pedagogy. *Harvard Educational Review* 59, no 3: 297–324.

Erickson, Frederick. 1986. Qualitative methods in research on teaching. In *The handbook of research in teaching,* edited by Merle Wittrock, 119–62. New York: Macmillan.

Foucault, M. 1980. Truth and power. In *Power/knowledges: Selected interviews and other writings 1972–77,* edited by C. Gordon, 109–33. New York: Pantheon.

Gadamer, M. G. 1975. *Truth and method*. New York: Continuum Books.

Geertz, Clifford. 1973. Thick description: Toward an interpretive theory of culture. In *The interpretation of cultures: Selected essays by Clifford Geertz*. New York, Basic Books.

Geertz, Clifford. 1989. *Works and lives: The anthropologist as author*. Stanford, CA: Stanford University Press.

Gleick, James. 1987. *Chaos: Making a new science*. New York: Viking Press.

Gore, Jennifer M. 1990. What can we do for you! What can "we" do for "you"?: Struggling over empowerment in critical and feminist pedagogy. *Educational Foundations* 4, no 3: 5–27.

Haraway, Donna. 1991. Situated knowledges: The science question in feminism and the privilege of partial perspective. In *Simians, cyborgs and women: The reinvention of nature,* edited by Donna J. Haraway, 83–203. New York: Routledge.

Harding, Sandra. 1987. *Feminism and methodology*. Bloomington and Indianapolis: Indiana University Press.

Keller, Evelyn. 1983. Gender and science. In *Discovering reality: Feminist perspectives on epistemology, metaphysics, methodology, and philosophy of science*, edited by Sandra Harding and Merrill B. Hintikka, 187–207. Boston, Mass.: D. Reidel.

Kuhn, Annette. 1982. *Women's pictures: Feminism and cinema*. London: Routledge and Kegan Paul.

Langreth, Robert. 1991. Engineering dogma gives way to chaos. *Science* Vol. 252, 10 May, 776–728.

Lather, Patti, 1986. Research as praxis. *Harvard Educational Review* 56: 257–77.

Lernoux, Penny. 1982. *Cry of the people: The struggle for human rights in Latin America*. New York: Viking.

McLaren, P. 1992. Collisions with otherness: "Travelling" theory, post-colonial criticism, and the politics of ethnographic practice—the mission of the wounded ethnographer. *Qualitative Studies in Education* 5, no. 1: 77–92.

Marcus, George E. & Fischer, Michael M. 1986. *Anthropology as cultural critique: An experimental moment in the human sciences*. Chicago: University of Chicago Press.

Mason, Mary G. 1988. The other voice: Autobiographies of women writers. In *Life/lines: Theorizing women's autobiographies,* edited by Bella Brodzki and Celeste Schenck, 19–44. Ithaca, N.Y.: Cornell University Press.

Mead, Margaret. 1978. *Culture and commitment: The new relationships between the generations in the 1970s*. Garden City, N.Y.: Anchor Press/Doubleday.

Mishler, Elliot. 1986;. *Research interviewing: Context and narrative*. Cambridge, Mass.: Harvard University Press.

Radcliffe-Brown, A. R. 1957. *A natural science of society*. Glencoe, Ill.: Free Press.

Roman, Leslie G. 1992. The political significance of other ways of narrating ethnography: A feminist materialist approach. In *The handbook of qualitative research in education*, edited by Margaret D. LeCompte, Wendy L. Millroy, and Judith Preissle, 555–95. San Diego, Cal.: Academic Press.

Spradley, James P. 1979. *The ethnographic interview*. New York: Holt, Rinehart and Winston.

Stacey, J. 1988. Can there be a feminist ethnography? *Women's Studies International Forum* 11: 21–27.

Weis, Lois, and Fine, Michelle. 1992a. The need for research on "silencing." In *The Division G—Social Context of Education—Newsletter,* (Washington: American Educational Research Association) (Winter): 6–8.

Weis, Lois, and Fine, Michelle. 1992b. *Beyond Silenced Voices: Class, Race, and Gender in United States Schools.* Albany, N.Y.: SUNY Press.

Zukav, Gary. 1979. *The dancing Wu-Li masters: An overview of the new physics.* New York: Morrow.

2

I and Thou:
Method, Voice, and Roles
in Research with the Silenced

Yvonna S. Lincoln

Although the research literature has begun to reflect increasing interest in, and attention to, nonmainstream concerns and issues, nevertheless, there is still a paucity of research on those whose voices have been silent. Typically, the "silent" as a research category has been broadly defined to include non-mainstream gender, classes, and races (Weis 1988; Giroux 1991), although they may be more specifically described as women, racial and ethnic minorities, Native Americans, the poor, and gay and lesbian persons. Such individuals and groups are described as marginal, living at the margins, or existing at the "borders" (Giroux 1991). Individuals and groups "at the borders" have had their lives defined and circumscribed by texts which take as their point of departure the "normal" concerns of science and the social world: white, male, middle-aged preoccupations (Bleier 1984, 1986).

Historical texts do exist, but social science, and particularly education, is "at a point now where [it] need[s] the interpretive texts, . . . [because] it's time for theory building" (Catapano 1991, 14). It has been argued that "traditional epistemologies . . . systematically exclude the possibility that women could be [either] 'knowers' or *agents of knowledge*; . . . that the voice of science is a masculine one; . . . that history is written from only the point of view of men (of the dominant class and race)" (Harding 1987, 3), but the same could be said of others who have been silenced, not simply women. The views which permeate social science, from the perspectives of the silenced, are *etic* views: the views of those with the power and access to control the naming process, even while being outsiders to marginal lives. As

Brown, commenting about the American Psychological Association, noticed, "'Psychology,' the official entity, values those experiences that are white, male, heterosexual, young, middle class, ablebodied, and North American: thus has the universe of 'human behavior' been defined" (1989, 446).

Not only have definitions of "the world" (or "normal" science) tended to be white and androcentric, but both the roots and rules of discourse have been constructed to reflect these "deeply internalized structures of Western thinking" (Brown 1989, 446–47). As a result, systematic exclusion from social and scientific discourse has occurred for women, nonheterosexual individuals, and racial and ethnic minorities. Maynard argues, for example, that anthropology has been so disadvantageous to the Native American communities it has studied that now "the motivations of anthropologists, the dissemination of research results, and the [proposed] benefits of research to Indians" (1974, 402) are suspect, and further, that "non-Indian social scientists . . . are viewed as intruders" (Trimble 1977, 160).

Given the paucity of authentic texts, the white, androcentric, and peculiarly "Western" flavor of the texts which exist, and the general suspicion with which traditional social scientists are viewed, what instruction does that provide for the future of social-science research on and with the silenced? Several issues emerge at the intersection of method and the marginalized. Each issue suggests that emergent approaches to research (Van Maanen 1988; Marcus and Fischer 1986)—often regarded as marginal, exotic, or nonmainstream themselves—may provide the authentic texts and grounded theories essential to the naming and description of lives lived in silence.

This chapter will embrace four separate considerations. The first is a springboard for the three subsequent discussions, and provides additional justifications for entertaining alternative conceptions of research, researchers, and research roles. The second, third, and fourth discussions will probe new roles for researchers, new demands placed on texts, and new roles for the silenced-as-researchers. The conclusion advances several speculations regarding what new forms of texts and narratives might "offer worthwhile and interesting critiques of our own society; enlighten us about other human possibilities, . . . make accessible the normally unexamined assumptions by which we operate and through which we encounter members of other cultures . . . [and] use . . . cultural richness for self-reflection and self-growth" (Marcus and Fischer 1986, ix–x).

Alternative Conceptions of Research and Research Roles

Dominant paradigm research, in directing both research antecedents and potential research outcomes toward mainstream questions and concerns and etically normative findings, has communicated a singular ontology (philosophy of reality) and epistemology (philosophy of knowing and relating to the intended known, the "other"). Such science is synoptic, in that it presumes a singularity of values, views, historicity, and accounts (Lincoln and Guba 1985; Guba and Lincoln 1981, 1989; Fay 1987; Tuana 1989; Jones and Jonasdottir 1988; Weis 1988). Elizabeth Fee notes that "We have been used to a virtual male monopoly on the production of scientific knowledge and discourses about science, its history and meaning" (1986, 43).

One clue to the problem may be found in the contemporary controversies surrounding the construction of texts (ethnographies) in social science. Anthropologists have been contending with the questions of etic (or realist) texts, the texts created from the perspective of anthropologists only. Van Maanen observed dryly that

> What, precisely might be called the native's point of view is indeed subject to much debate in fieldwork circles. But rest assured, realist ethnographies all claim to have located it and tamed it sufficiently so that it can be represented in the fieldwork report. Whether this is done by simply allowing some natives to have their say (*through the author's pen*) or by various formal elicitation techniques, indigenous meaning systems have claimed a place in realist tales. *In a sense the debate concerning the native's point of view now turns on how such a perspective is to be rendered in the text rather than whether or not it belongs in one.* (1988, 50-51, emphases added)

As anthropologists (archetypical fieldworkers) come to terms with etic versus emic (insider) perspectives, they must also come to terms with the ahistoricity of their accounts (Van Maanen 1988, 68-72). Texts presented in the present tense suggest that the way things were is the way things are, and deny the essential evolution of groups, while simultaneously ignoring both the likelihood of change and the possibilities for radical social transformation. As Van Maanen points out, present-tense texts consider primarily the question of "What is this?" rather than the question "How did this come to be?" (1988, 72). The central issue here might well be the criticalist's question of how things came to be, since an examination of social circumstance and existence is essential to any research on silenced lives.

But other possibilities exist. Social science could recreate itself in ways which are simultaneously critical of the status quo and multivocal. In the first instance, I intend to imply that an emergent social science might shed its seeming ahistoricity and presumed objectivity in favor of the commitment to change, empowerment, and social transformation. In the latter instance, I mean to suggest the creation of narratives in multiple forms (which I shall take up later) with multiple voices represented. Epistemologies could be expanded to include criticalist theories (Fay 1987); feminist epistemologies and methodologies (Harding 1987); standpoint epistemologies for racial and ethnic groups; participant and cooperative methodologies (Woodill 1992; Reason 1988) and constructivist and interpretive paradigms and meth-

ods (Lincoln and Guba 1985; Denzin 1989). Each of these stances, paradigms, or epistemologies, however, suggests that the roles of the researcher,
researched, and text will change radically. The force and direction of those
changes, however, remain the least systematically explored arena in the contemporary literature on method.

Roles of the Researcher

The "crisis of representation" in ethnography (Marcus and Fischer 1986)
directly addresses the question of silence, posing as it does the issue of how
we create adequate and authentic accounts of those we study. This is especially true because "the relation between the knower and the known . . . [is]
a most problematic one and anything but independent in cultural studies
. . . [and] there is no way of hearing, seeing, or representing the world of
others that is absolutely, universally valid or correct" (Van Maanen 1988,
35). It is also true because silence is created when those who are the subjects
of research have little or no power in the construction of accounts about
them, no access to texts, and no avenues into the corridors of knowledge-
production power. The silenced are silenced precisely because they share
few if any mainstream characteristics.

Researchers face a new set of imperatives in conducting research on and
with the silenced. At least four responsibilities are implicit in the sparse literature on researching the underrepresented, and a number of new criteria
may be posed for establishing the soundness of such accounts above and beyond those suggested either for conventional research (criteria of rigor) or
phenomenological research (criteria for authenticity; see, for instance, Guba
and Lincoln 1989, for a complete discussion of such criteria).

Alternative Methods

First, inquirers are obliged to seek out alternatives for conducting research on, and with, the underrepresented. This means there will be no
"business as usual" in designing and conducting such research. At a minimum, inquirers will be obliged to study carefully, and adapt strategies developed for researching women's lives, and will need to explore a small but
growing literature on research with racial and ethnic minorities (De Vos
and Suarez-Orozco 1990; Kahana and Felton 1977; Maykovich 1977; Montero 1977; Morrison and Von Glinow 1990; Myers 1977; Shosteck 1977;
Weiss 1977). Alternative epistemologies and methods will become the standard for engaging in such research. Traditional epistemologies and methods
grounded in white androcentric concerns, and rooted in values which are
understood to be inimical to the interests of the silenced, will fail to capture
the voices needed. The methods which will be appropriate are both fore-
shadowed and explicated by ongoing debates in ethnographic circles, where

newer experimental forms selfconsciously consider problems of the "native" point of view, the ahistoricity of texts created by certain narrative conventions, characterizations (a classic case of which would be the characterization of the single, individual life experiences known as the "biography" or "life history"), the interconnectedness of the knower and the known (the collapse of dualist, objectivist epistemology), and a certain open-endedness with respect to authority, interpretation, reinterpretation and finality of findings (Van Maanen 1988; Marcus and Fischer 1986).

Producing Knowledge

Several of the more radical experimental forms will be based on conflictual notions of social theory rather than on consensual forms (Brown and Tandon 1983), on theories of ownership and creation of social knowledge (Woodill 1992), and/or on theories of social transformation wherein knowledge is generated specifically for the purposes of addressing and ameliorating conditions of oppression, poverty, or deprivation (Latapi 1988). All such theories specifically deny the assertion that the role of science is to create disinterested knowledge, and assume instead that the purpose of knowledge generation is the transformation of social life toward its improvement. Further, these theories, based in liberation theologies and rural education, seek to root their efforts specifically and openly in ideologies connected to the poorer classes and to the politics of knowledge. In their most radical form (typically criticalist and neo-Marxist), such theories of knowledge and knowledge production share certain other assumptions: (1) that knowledge "monopolies" have been created by privileged classes; (2) that knowledge should, and can, be produced, "owned," and used by ordinary people; (3) that useful social knowledge—that is, knowledge directed at social transformation—is created within a political context which aids the "other" in achieving solidarity, which is mutual and nonhierarchical rather than characterized by relations of superordinate/subordinate power structures, and which is marked by high participation; and (4) that knowledge so generated is marked by collective analysis of issues and problems (Woodill 1992).

Open Ideologies

When the conditions for producing social science are themselves so radically transformed, issues which formerly assumed primacy (ownership of research data, for instance) become unimportant or irrelevant, while at the same time, issues which were formerly tangential (e.g., questions of ethics and morality) will assume center stage. Other issues, presumed by mainstream social scientists to be the especial province of critical theorists, neo-Marxists, or others who engaged in "openly ideological" social science, become central issues for the social-science community to engage. The role of social science in either contributing to a genuine transformation of social life for the silenced, or contributing to the maintenance of a status quo, will create a potential cleavage between practitioners of various paradigms. The senior researcher who commented that if one "scratches a naturalist, one finds a moralist" (Patti Gumport, personal communication, April 1991) missed the point. "Most crucially," Van Maanen points out (1988, 5), "ethnography irrevocably influences the interests and lives of the people represented in them—individually and collectively, for better or for worse." Since the representation of people does indeed act to change their lives, then it is the writer's obligation to ask hard questions about the morality and ethics of his or her work. Those questions themselves become a part of the methods used to investigate, and therefore a part of the eventual text.

Researchers working with the silenced, attentive to participative methods designed to elicit and display the multiple perspectives of the silenced, would likewise be attentive to criticisms of the ahistoricity and acontextuality of texts. The implications of tense and narrative convention for "creating" the culture or individual one is studying become more apparent, since "a culture or a cultural practice is as much created by the writing . . . as it determines the writing itself" (Wagner, cited in Van Maanen 1988, 6). Method which explicitly takes account of narrative form, that is, which demands narrative experiments and writing forms deliberately unlike older ethnographies, will be demanded of researchers. Such narrative forms, when they are constructed at all (a point to which I shall return later) will be dictated as much by the needs and nominations of the studied as by the interests, desires, or biases of the studier, or of the current concerns of a funding agency. Epistemologies which deny or collapse the distinction between knowers and known will emerge, and the construction of texts will proceed from nonobjectivist standpoints. Finally, methods which contribute to understanding openness and uncertainty, which prevent "closure" on the text, and which prompt and invite multiple interpretations and reinterpretations will be called for. The implication of these alternative methods and narrative strategies is that they will increasingly lean toward the constructivist, the critical, the feminist, and the action-oriented, the participative, and standpoint methodologies.

The Search for Stories

Second, it will be the inquirer's role to seek out stories, and to engage in listening both active and patient. As women discovered in the consciousness-raising groups of the 1970s, it sometimes takes an extended amount of time for the silenced to seek and find their voices, and to frame their stories. Many of the stories which the silent could tell remain at the tacit level: they have never been spoken aloud. The search for such stories must involve active seeking, active listening, and patient probing, since would-be narrators may have to find the shape and form of such stories, and a language and imagery for telling them.

Listener/researchers need not be entirely passive, but their roles must never be understood as "putting words into the mouths" of respondents. Rather, researchers can provide active counterpoint by describing historical and social contexts in which silenced groups have traditionally found themselves. Presenting "situational," historical, or case data can often help respondents and research collaborators identify ways in which they have been marginalized, silenced, or discriminated against. But the choice of story, example, language, and timing must be at the discretion of those providing the stories.

Increasingly, the stories which inquirers seek and tell will be the stories rooted in problems, issues, and concerns nominated or framed by the former "subjects" of the research process. As social scientists encounter the loss of "exotic" research settings (Marcus and Fischer 1986), the increasing sophistication of the silenced regarding the conditions of their own existence (Florin and Wandersman 1990), and disciplinary presses for socially useful critiques from "the underside" (Holman and Maltz 1987), they will likely find the stories they seek identified by research participants acting in their own emancipatory and problem-solving interests. The ethnographer has always been her own best "instrument" (Lincoln and Guba 1985; Guba and Lincoln 1981), but may discover that the range of instrumentation may be expanded (Guba and Lincoln 1989) to include that of storyteller, imagery conveyer, explicator of social issues, or conduit, for stories not of her choice or framing.

The Creation of "Text"

Third, it is the researcher's responsibility to take part in faithfully reproducing stories. While the trickle of minorities, women, gays, lesbians, Native Americans, or the poor who make it through higher education often turn back to their own communities to do research, and have provided research examples which are not suspect to the communities themselves, there are nevertheless too few such individuals to conduct all the inquiries which need to be conducted. This suggests that mainstream researchers will continue to play a strong role in research for the near future, and therefore, will have a role in policy formation. It is also the case that those silenced do not themselves typically have access to research outlets and policy circles. It will therefore rest with the social-science community to tell the stories and present the narratives of nonmainstream, "border" individuals. Until the structure of the research community changes to include representatives of silenced groups, providing accounts which speak to the interests of the silenced will be accomplished partially by individuals who may not be members of such groups. Such individuals must take responsibility for altering the premises of their inquiries, and for sharing responsibility with research participants in presenting the narratives of their existence. Only by taking part in reproducing these narratives for public consumption will the research community be able to redress the systematic imbalance of perspectives embedded in previous research.

Assuring Texts with Rigor

Fourth, it is also the responsibility of the researcher to create narratives of fidelity (validity) and rigor. Narratives which are sought and presented must fulfill the criterion of *persuasiveness* not only to those who have provided such accounts as representative of their lives, but also to the social/science, educational/research, and policy communities. The implications of the rigor and validity question are that narratives no longer have a single, disciplinary, audience. They must continue to speak to disciplinary and policy communities, of course; but increasingly, such accounts will also serve the interests and aspirations of the silenced themselves. Among those interests and aspirations, and therefore intimately tied to judgments of rigor and validity, are concerns regarding the educative functions of the research methods and processes; questions of how collective research knowledge was produced and analyzed; whether its display and ordering facilitates interrogating social realities; and whether or not such research promotes solidarity and group problem solving (Woodill 1992).

Narrow disciplinary conceptions of rigor will only be one facet of consideration for scholars, as a result. The disciplinary communities of social science will want to educate themselves regarding how and in what forms they can best respond to mandates for social criticism (Marcus and Fischer 1986). Narratives which are faithful to the lives of those they represent, and persuasive to the various communities which are consumers of such narratives (especially as policy documents), create a convincing environment for those who might otherwise continue to ignore and silence groups.

Beyond new roles and responsibilities of the researchers themselves, the narratives and life histories will have characteristics not commonly considered critical in more conventional research. These characteristics might be thought of as the roles of accounts, narratives, and texts.

Roles of the Narratives

Texts provided in collaboration with the silenced are formulated under different guidelines than those produced by researchers alone, since "action research projects automatically enlarge the circle of relevant constituencies, and scrutiny of the research activity is no longer limited to a disciplinary peer group" (Bengston *et al* 1977, 89). This enlargement of scrutiny demands narratives which are also subject to the scrutiny, inspection, and assent of the researched. Texts which are not only assented to, but co-created with researchers, will have characteristics unlike earlier ethnographies.

Isomorphism

First, such texts will exhibit a closer one-to-one correspondence with the lives of the researched. Such correspondence is termed isomorphism. As a criterion of internal validity, such correspondence has previously been the province of narrators alone, ethnographers who belonged to and interacted with the disciplinary community. In new texts from the silent, it is the silent who will determine whether or not texts concerning their lives are valid or faithful to the stories, whether they are authentic or possess isomorphism. Some of the criteria for such a determination have been suggested in an earlier section.

In addition to correspondence, texts will have to exhibit authenticity. Authenticity in this sense implies that a text is not only faithful to the story lines provided by respondents, but also that texts convey the "feeling tone" (Terkel 1984) of the lives. This feeling tone is best conveyed when the text itself admits and invites the reader into a vicarious experience (however brief) of the life or lives described. It is an experience of the lives "in the round"—with a range of mood, feeling, experience, situational variety, and language. The reader should come away from such texts with heightened sensitivity to the lives being depicted, and with some flavor of the kinds of events, characters, and social circumstances which circumscribe those lives.

Narrative Conventions

In addition, the text itself must move away from traditional narrative conventions by displaying rhetorical elements not ordinarily found in such kinds of reports. Among those nonconventional elements would be power and elegance, grace and precision, creativity, independence (of the researcher from disciplinary strictures and conventions), openness and the problematic quality of the lives under discussion, courage—(in the sense of extending the case beyond "safe" boundaries or disciplinary limits), egalitarianism toward respondents, participant, and collaborators, and passion (Lincoln and Guba 1990). Assuredly, the senior researcher who was repulsed by the idea of finding a moralist under the skin of a naturalist would be even more dismayed to discover an egalitarian, courageous, and passionate researcher, deeply concerned about the problematic nature of texts and representation of the "other."

Analysis Discussions

Third, an appropriate and meaningful text about the silenced would be careful to explicate the analytic processes (as well as the methodological) in arriving at the text. Cronbach and Suppes (1969) define inquiry by noting that

> the report of a disciplined inquiry has a texture that displays the raw materials entering the argument and the logical processes by which they were compressed and rearranged to make the conclusion credible (1969, 16)

If emergent textual strategies are to be taken seriously by the research and policy communities, they also must fulfill the criterion of being disciplined inquiries. At a minimum, this means that the researcher must provide narratives with auditable methodological and analytic "trails," so that data can be checked, tracked, and verified by other social scientists wishing to understand how data and conclusions were captured, compressed, and presented.

In the past, comments on method, design strategy, and analytic processes were often missing, or merely appended, to ethnographies (Van Maanen 1988). In emergent research on the silent and silenced, however, method, strategy, and analysis may comprise a more forthright and integral part of texts. How data were elicited, from whom, under what circumstances, how analyses were carried out, who drafted the text, who read and member-checked the stories, and the roles of collaborators in the community, will need to be more explicitly spelled out than has previously been the case. When inquirers share responsibility for design and method, a concomitant sharing of responsibility for results and conclusions occurs. The shape and form of that responsibility will have to be made transparent to consumers of the narrative—including those who themselves may soon be solicited for research participation. The frankness and clarity with which analytic processes are handled in any text will serve either to open or close further venues for research. As I noted earlier, Native American communities sometimes view social scientists and their research with suspicion; clearly explicated co-directed research could reverse that situation in these and other minority communities.

Ethical Considerations

Fourth, the text must make clear the ethical and political considerations in doing such research. Federal guidelines for treatment of research subjects are clearly inadequate. A simple "deconstruction" of the language should make transparent why this is so. "Treatment" suggests that the researcher is doing something to the research participant, or that the participants are part of an experiment—designed by researchers, approved by an anonymous institutional review board. "Research subjects" suggests disparities in power relationships surrounding the inquiry itself, with scientists possessing the power to make subjects (i.e., subordinates, victims, dependents) of other human beings. Rights to dignity, agency, and individual control are often displaced or suspended in favor of the scientist's right to know.

Each criterion thus far advanced suggests that guidelines which ensure only that "subjects" are not harmed permanently or deceived without adequate institutional review are inadequate for seeking to engage the silenced in research on themselves. Deep and abiding suspicion of the social-science community has been engendered by just such guidelines. Baumrind (1979, 1985) and others (Lincoln and Guba 1989; Bulmer 1980; Reinharz 1978) have commented extensively on the damage done not only to the "researched," but to the social-science community more broadly, when scientists act solely from self-interest, with deception, or even merely within federal regulations and guidelines. New ethical and political stances will have to be sought if such research is not to further erode the rights of, alienate, and indeed silence, the silenced (Callan and McElwain 1980; Kayal 1976; Jules-Rosette, 1988; Guba and Lincoln 1989).

Assumption Reversals

Fifth, texts will have to embody several assumptions and presumptions which are missing from "normal science." First, it will be critical to generate texts which presume silenced persons are individuals representing "ethnicity, plurality, and anti-assimilationist thought" in contemporary social life (Kayal 1976). This means that racial and ethnic minorities, the poor, women, and nonheterosexual individuals cannot be treated as though they were deviant since to continue to do so ignores the recognition that their lives provide social diversity and cultural richness. The presumption that marginalization and silence are appropriate responses to those who do not participate in the knowledge monopoly robs the body politic of texture, variety, and wholeness. The diminution of civic life which occurs in marginalization impoverishes not only the silenced, marginalization's known victims, but also the mainstream, whose lives are constricted and abridged by virtue of ignorance and the absence of a meaningful social critique. The stigma which has been attached to nonmainstream individuals, and to those who have conducted research with them (Warren 1977), acts as a barrier both to those who would engage in such research, and to those whose lives should be the center of a collaborative inquiry effort. Only when such research is viewed as contributing to a larger understanding of social richness, pluralism, heterodoxy, and texture, to critiques of social structure, and to the creation of texts which celebrate such diversity, will it have authority in policy circles.

Another presumption of texts will be that of dialecticalism in social life and research. Researchers and respondent-collaborators alike will presume that all social life is characterized by some forms of conflict, and that an entirely cooperative model of social research is both unreasonable and unreflective of social realities. The expanded nature of the community with which one must negotiate in order to conduct such research implies conflict (multiple interests and agendas, multiple constituencies), and the very fact that silenced individuals and groups are marginalized by mainstream society already implies conflict between majority and minority. At a minimum, texts and narratives must reflect upon these forms and sources of conflict; at best, texts will relate such conflict to historical roots and social arrangements which create and perpetuate such conflict and which act to institutionalize conflicts arising from injustice and misunderstanding.

Is There a "Text" At All?

Not only will the shape, form and intent of texts change, but there exists the possibility that no text will be created, or that texts will be created secondarily to research or community processes. As Woodill points out

> most participatory research is a group effort, and community building among the participants is one of the objectives of participatory research. Group discussions, public meetings, community seminars, open-ended surveys, the forming of research teams, fact-finding tours, collective production of audio-visual materials, popular theater, group mapping and drawing exercises, group writing, and educational camps, can all be part of the process. (1992)

In such contexts, texts may be the central, necessary, or desired product for researchers, but only an ancillary concern for the community with which the inquiry occurs.

Queries to the Social Science Community

Finally, a role of any text might be to demonstrate the hermeneutic and interactive role of social science. There are three ways in which this might be done: by describing the interactive roles of researcher and researched in creating the stories, texts, and narratives; by providing texts which are narratively dense, rich, and elaborative; and by directing queries to the social-science community more broadly regarding its role in the creation of social realities (just and unjust) and its part in redressing injustice.

The preceding criteria are probably not final criteria for judging the utility, rigor, or possibility of change in narratives on the silenced, but they are suggestive of the direction in which textual construction needs to be headed. Further, they are all completely resonant with the basic assumptions underlying research on and with those whose voices have been silenced, namely that in order for their voices to be heard, different strategies must be adopted by researcher and researched alike, and that the products of such research—typically case studies, life histories, biographies, or ethnographies—must go beyond traditional and conventional narrative forms to achieve their ends. Changes not only in form, but also in rhetoric, must accompany such inquiries.

Yet another alteration in research style, however, attends such inquiry.

Changes are demanded of researchers, and of the texts which they present, but little difference will be noted if there are not concomitant changes in the roles of the researched, and in the interaction between researchers and those from whom we need to hear more.

Roles of the Researched

Normal science has typically cast research respondents as subjects, individuals whose sole purpose in social science is the provision of specific data desired by researchers. Emergent forms of research cast the role of respondent in very different terms. These new forms of research can be considered as existing on a continuum, with roles of the respondent ranging from active coparticipants in the research process (phenomenological and constructivist research) to full research collaborators, nominating issues of salience, specifying dignity-protecting methods, engaging in dialogue with researchers regarding appropriate analyses, and shaping, framing, and producing the texts which represent their lives (criticalist, feminist, dialectic and/or hermeneutic methodologies). All of these postures along the continuum may be thought of as forms of action research, with varying levels of participation with and from respondents.

But higher levels of participation from those who are the focus of the research implies responsibilities which many have never undertaken. Sometimes, the silenced may have to be "coached" in how to be collaborators in their own histories, much as patients in a doctor's office have to be coached in being oriented to wellness and health promotion rather than behaving as passive agents waiting to be "cured." The significance of this statement is that many groups have grown more accustomed to finessing social scientists than to creating active roles for themselves in the research process. This situation has been reinforced over time by researchers who neither want to engage in action-oriented inquiry—it is too troublesome, ill-respected in academic circles, takes nearly double the amount of time of traditional studies, and courts conflict—nor have any training in community collaboration (Bengston et al. 1977). The logical outcome of such a situation has been the creation of cadres of individuals, and indeed, whole communities, who are much more savvy about how to torpedo social research than how to facilitate, shape it, produce, and own it.

But research participants who want and need to engage in collaboration regarding the purposes and proposed outcomes of research have responsibilities for their own behavior. And those responsibilities dictate both alterations in the role of the researched, and alterations in the relationship between the researched and those who would research them.

The researched are those who provide the raw material for the narratives of silence. Whatever else may be said, the silenced are the only ones who can tell their stories with any fidelity. Therefore, those who are silenced must agree to tell those stories, and in agreeing, consummate a social contract to help reinvent the world in a less androcentric or unjust form and shape.

In recognizing they are the ones who own the stories by virtue of having lived them, the researched must be open to taking a role in narrating the events and the meanings of their own lives. It is not unusual for those who have been silenced to learn to wait in silence, patient until the social scientist has moved on to greener pastures, and left the scene to settle into its more routine events and rhythms. But the pattern of holding back, enculturated then reinforced by the profound suspicion that social science is no servant to the silenced, has to be broken if the silenced are ever to have voice. Openness, trust, and reciprocity between researcher and researched may involve unlearning and relearning old habits and behaviors and most certainly mandates new relationships between the two.

The silenced who agree to participate in research must also be willing to take the several and profound risks of acting as collaborators in this research. This will mean, at a minimum, a dialogic partnership of equal involvement in nominating and setting research agendas, discussing the weaknesses and strengths of various data-collection methods for their communities, negotiating the overall design strategy of any study, inviting participation from others in their vicinity, conducting analyses of data alongside social scientists, and outlining, framing, writing, and assenting to the narratives and texts which represent their lives.

In the latter two instances in particular—the analytic stage and the text-creation stage—participants-as-collaborators will need to commit to active learning. In some instances, their roles will involve moving to new and perhaps unfamiliar levels of abstraction in order to analyze the meanings of events surrounding their lives, and to connect their personal, individual, and group histories to larger social and historical contexts and issues. The connections between history and social circumstance are the responsibility of the researcher, but the meanings which are made of those connections, and the transformations and liberations which may be enacted, are the responsibility of the silenced, the researched. Learning to move between the historical, the political, and the personal is risky business—but the business, nevertheless, of individuals who would be full and legitimate collaborators with social scientists, educational researchers, and the policy community.

Finally, the researched must share in learning about dialogue and dialogic processes, querying first the researcher, then the community, then the text, and finally, society. Such processes can be taught; but they are best and most efficiently taught via modeling. This suggests that researchers must make explicit the role of dialectic and criticism, largely by living it. Only with dialogue, dialectic, and criticism will collaborators in research come to a new understanding, both more sophisticated and more informed, about the circumstances of their lives. Such a reconstruction is the end product, indeed, of a hermeneutic and/or critical method.

Some means must be provided whereby the silenced can come to terms with the social, historical, and cultural contexts in which the research effort is embedded. That is an essential function to be served in the relationship between researcher and researched. Researchers, in accomplishing this, can take an activist stance, forgo the "disinterested observer" role demanded by traditional research, and undertake consciousness-raising activities (community seminars, community-building activities, public meetings, group research design work, and the like) which enable the silenced to come to terms with their own historicity and personal locations. Researcher and researched together can explore and possibly create new ways to develop reliable, trustworthy data of high fidelity which both empower the silenced and which prove persuasive to the social science, education, and policy communities. This step will involve creating new forms and new formats for narratives and texts, and a conscious rejection of more conventional "realist tales" from the field. Researcher and researched can engage themselves together in formulating questions which have high salience for the community which is the context of the study. In this way, the silenced, in becoming producers, analysts, and presenters of their own narratives, cease to be the objects of their histories and knowledge. They are enabled instead to become the agents of the stories which are produced and consumed about them, and the agents and instruments of their own change processes.

Conclusion

Why would anyone consider such radical changes in the way social and educational research is designed and conducted? And why would any researcher consider relinquishing such control? There is the argument of social justice, but this argument is rarely compelling to the policy community. Indeed, Warren cites the cynicism regarding research on gays:

> Some sociologists assert that research findings on the gay world can be used to develop policies related to gays which might prove harmful to them. It does not, however, appear that policymakers are notably attending to or influenced by sociological field research—particularly field research—and, even if they are interested in using research, they will undoubtedly be able to use it in any way they desire, for ill or well. (1977, 96).

But other interesting, heuristic, and important rationales exist for conducting research with radically altered roles for researcher, researched, and texts. Since so few descriptive studies exist on those who are silenced, and even fewer exist which are told from the perspectives of the silenced, and further, since theories of human behavior and social circumstance are built on majority concerns, rather than growing out of the the concerns of the unasked, it behooves both research and policy communities to consider building grounded theories. Grounded theories are those which are derived from comprehensive and vivid description of personal and community lives, from narratives and life histories. If social science is to build either policy or theory on the silenced, and thereby balance "grand narratives" with narratives of the ordinary, the description which underpins such theory will be assembled solely or largely from the silenced themselves. At present, we have only a small body of such descriptive research, and it is wholly inadequate for redesigning social or educational policy, or social services, or for redressing injustice.

A second powerful rationale revolves about ongoing social-science concerns. By training the silenced to engage in research on and about themselves, and to engage in construction of their own narratives, we achieve several interesting by-products. One, access to hidden and silenced lives is more readily obtained, and the difficulty in accessing hidden lives is readily substantiated by social scientists, regardless of discipline. Two, an "authority" in voice and narrative is achieved. This first-person authority is largely absent from most literatures on minorities and other "invisible" subcultures in the Western world. Only in the feminist literature is there currently a strong set of "voices of authority," predominantly as a result of female scholars and researchers framing questions and attacking persistent problems systematically and from their own experiential and scholarly base. The example of the feminist scholars is instructive. The feminist literature is polyvocal; certainly not all feminist scholars see the world in the same terms, nor is there adherence expected to some "party line." Further, problems were "found," or named, by that community; the critique of normal science was not undertaken by practitioners of normal science. Further, solutions to the problems posed by science for women were nominated by those who were its experiential and social victims.

Until we have such a literature from the silenced, we will probably not have a full critique of the social order from their perspectives. Nor will we have their proposed solutions, or the means of sharing their daily worlds.

References

Baumrind, Diane. 1979. IRBs and social science research: The costs of deception. *IRB: A Review of Human Subjects Research* 6: 1–4.

———. 1985. Research using intentional deception: Ethical issues revisited. *American Psychologist* 40: 165–174.

Bengtson, Vern L., Grigsby, Eugene, Corry, Elaine M. and Hruby, Mary. 1977. Relating academic research to community concerns: A case study in collaborative effort. *Journal of Social Issues,* 4: 75–92.

Bleier, Ruth. 1984. *Science and gender.* New York: Pergamon Press.

———. 1986. *Feminist approaches to science.* New York: Pergamon Press.

Brown, L. David, and Tandon, Rajesh. 1983. Ideology and political economy in inquiry: Action research and participatory research. *Journal of Applied Behavioral Science* 19, no 3: 277–94.

Brown, Laura S. 1989. New voices, new visions: Toward a lesbian/gay paradigm for psychology. *Psychology of Women Quarterly* 13: 445–58.

Bulmer, Martin. 1980. The impact of ethical concerns upon sociological research. *Sociology: The Journal of the British Sociological Association* 40: 125–30.

Callan, Vic, and McElwain, O. 1980. General consideration in the research of ethnic minorities. *Australian Psychologist* 15, no. 2: 1981–87.

Catapano, Joan. 1991. What do editors really want? *Lingua Franca* 1: 12–15.

Cronbach, Lee J. and Suppes, Patrick. 1969. *Research for tomorrow's schools: Disciplined inquiry in education.* New York: Macmillan.

Denzin, Norman K. 1989. *Interpretive interactionism.* Applied Social Research Methods Series, vol. 16. Newbury Park, Cal.: Sage.

De Vos, George A., and Suarez-Orozco, Marcelo. 1990. *Status inequality: The self in culture.* Newbury Park, Cal: Sage.

Fay, Brian. 1987. *Critical social science.* Ithaca, N.Y.: Cornell University Press.

Fee, Elizabeth. 1986. Critiques of modern science: The relationship of feminism to other radical epistemologies. In *Feminist approaches to science,* edited by Ruth Bleier, 42–56. New York: Pergamon Press.

Florin, Paul and Wandersman, Abraham. 1990. An introduction to citizen participation, voluntary organizations, and community development: Insights for empowerment through research. *American Journal of Community Psychology* 18: 41–54.

Giroux, Henry A. 1991. *Postmodernism, feminism, and cultural politics: Redrawing educational boundaries.* Albany, N.Y.: State University of New York Press.

Guba, Egon G., and Lincoln, Yvonna S. 1981. *Effective evaluation*. San Francisco: Jossey-Bass.

———. 1989. *Fourth generation evaluation*. Newbury Park, Cal.: Sage.

Harding, Sandra, ed. 1987. *Feminism and Methodology*. Bloomington, Ind.: Indiana University Press.

Holman, Beverly and Maltz, Wendy. 1987. *Incest and sexuality: A guide to understanding and healing*. Lexington, Mass.: Lexington Books.

Jones, Kathleen B., and Jonasdottir, Anna G. 1988. *The political interests of gender: Developing theory and research with a feminist face*. London: Sage.

Jules-Rosette, Benetta. 1986. The dual vision: Insights and applications of cross-cultural research. *Journal of Negro Education* 55, no. 2: 125–41.

Kahana, Eva, and Felton, Barbara J. 1977. Social context and personal need: A study of Polish and Jewish aged. *Journal of Social Issues* 33, no. 4: 56–74.

Kayal, Phillip M. 1976. Researching behavior: Sociological objectivity and homosexual analysis. *Corrective and Social Psychiatry and Journal of Behavior Technology* 22, no. 2: 25–31.

Latapi, Pablo. 1988. Participatory research: A new research paradigm? *Alberta Journal of Educational Research* 34, no. 3 (September): 310–19.

Leavy, Richard L., and Adams, Eve M. 1986. Feminism as a correlate of self-esteem, self-acceptance, and social support among lesbians. *Psychology of Women Quarterly* 10: 321–26.

Lincoln, Yvonna S., and Guba, Egon G. 1985. *Naturalistic inquiry*. Newbury Park, Cal.: Sage.

———. 1989. Ethics: The failure of positivist science. *Review of Higher Education* 12, no. 3: 221–40.

———. 1990. Judging the quality of case study reports. *International Journal of Qualitative Studies in Education* 3, no. 1: 53–60.

Marcus, George E., and Fischer, Michael M. J. 1986. *Anthropology as cultural critique: An experimental moment in the human sciences*. Chicago: University of Chicago Press.

Maykovich, Minako Kurokawa. 1977. The difficulties of a minority researcher in minority communities. *Journal of Social Issues* 33, no. 4: 108–19.

Maynard, Edward. 1974. The growing negative image of the anthropologist among American Indians. *Human Organization* 33: 402–03.

Montero, Darrel. 1977. Research among racial and cultural minorities: An overview. *Journal of Social Issues* 33, no. 4: 1–10.

Morrison, Ann M., and Von Glinow, Mary Ann. 1990. Minorities in management. *American Psychologist* 45, no. 2: 200–08.

Myers, Vincent. 1977. Survey methods for minority populations. *Journal of Social Issues* 33, no. 4: 11–19.

Reason, Peter, ed. 1988. *Human inquiry in action: Developments in new paradigm research*. London: Sage.

Reinharz, Shulamit. 1978. *On becoming a social scientist*. San Francisco: Jossey-Bass.

Shosteck, Herschel. 1977. Respondent militancy as a control variable for interviewer effect. *Journal of Social Issues* 33, no 4: 36–45.

Terkel, Studs. 1984. Interview by Robert Wolf. Bloomington, Ind.: Indiana University, Audiovisual Center. Videotape.

Trimble, Joseph E. 1977. The sojourner in the American Indian community: Methodological issues and concerns. *Journal of Social Issues* 33, no 4: 159–74.

Tuana, Nancy, ed. 1989. *Feminism and science*. Bloomington, Ind.: Indiana University Press.

Van Maanen, John. 1988. *Tales of the field: On writing ethnography*. Chicago: University of Chicago Press.

Warren, Carol A. B. 1977. Fieldwork in the gay world: Issues in phenomenological research. *Journal of Social Issues* 33, no. 4: 93–107.

Weeks, Michael F., and R. Paul Moore. 1981. Ethnicity-of-interviewer effects on ethnic respondents. *Public Opinion Quarterly* 45: 245–49.

Weis, Lois, ed. 1988. *Class, race and gender in American education*. Albany, N.Y.: State University of New York Press.

Weiss, Carol H. 1977. Survey researchers and minority communities. *Journal of Social Issues* 33, no. 4: 20–35.

Woodill, Gary, 1992. Empowering adolescents through participatory research. Ontario Ministry of Health, Toronto, Canada, 1991.

Zusman, Marty E., and Olson, Arnold O. 1977. Gathering complete response from Mexican-Americans by personal interview. *Journal of Social Issues* 33, no. 4: 46–55.

PART II

3

Beth's Story:
The Search for the Mother/Teacher

Andrew Gitlin and Beth Myers

This is a story about stories. It is about the making, telling, and the returning to a story. The making of the story began in a class situation that brought together Andrew, a professor at the University of Utah, and Beth, a student in a master's class. Andrew was interested in alternative forms of research and structured the class around a method—Educative Research—that he was trying to develop. Beth's story, emerging out of the Educative Research process, traces her quest to find the mother/teacher, a way of teaching that uses and values maternal knowledge. Once this text was produced, Beth and Andrew revisited this story to consider its meaning and significance. Before we begin, however, it is important that we make clear why we would want to tell this story in the first place.

For reasons both of ideology and material circumstances, certain groups have historically been silenced. Teachers are a case in point. Because we live in a patriarchical society that devalues women and the work they typically do, teachers, who are for the most part women, tend to be ignored in policy debates and decisions. The Holmes Group, a group trying to reform schooling, for example, is made up primarily of deans of schools of education. None of the original founding members of this group were practicing teachers (Holmes Group 1986). What this suggests is that while teachers have stories to tell about educational policy and practice, these stories are rarely given a forum in the public domain. Furthermore, teachers' work is structured such that it is difficult if not impossible for them to construct a story that is based on a careful examination of practice and school issues (Apple 1986). This is not particularly surprising given that teachers often are not expected to formulate policy or influence the direction of educational practice but rather are expected to take the wisdom of others and find ways to put these theories into practice. Even in the now-popular site-based management approaches, the role of teachers is often restricted primarily to "how-to questions" that are constrained by district goals and guidelines (Gitlin, Margonis, and Brunjes1990).

One reason, therefore, for the telling of stories is that they give those who have been historically disenfranchised a voice, an opportunity to speak out. The opportunity to speak out does not assure that one's voice will be heard, but it does have the immediate effect of providing groups with a potential source of power that can enable them to participate more fully in educational discussions. Speaking out and telling one's story, however, even if it is the story of a group member who has been silenced, does little to offset how all stories are distorted by material conditions and prejudgments in narrow and confining ways. To confront this limitation, the stories told can include a protest of the contextual factors and beliefs that shape them and a challenge to the way we act in the world. Stories that incorporate this notion of protest enable those who have been silenced to speak out, rewrite their stories and act, based on inward protests that scrutinize the values and perspectives of the author and outward protests that examine the structures and wider ideologies that constrain our goals and actions. The central importance of storytelling, for us, is that it can provide an opportunity for silenced groups to enter into policy debates and remake their own history. Put simply, our aim is to develop voice as a form of protest.

Making the Story

Our attempt to further this aim occurred within the context of a cooperative master's program. While typical in many regards, this program differed from others in that it limited enrollment to practicing teachers, allowed a group of teachers to take the majority of classes together and had a very open-ended curriculum. Because the curriculum was flexible, Andrew could focus the program around Educative Research. Educative Research, therefore, was pivotal in shaping how the members of this cooperative master's class developed their stories. To gain some understanding of this approach to story making, it is necessary to describe the central aspects of Educative Research. In particular, we will focus on two aspects of this process: the creation of personal and school history texts.

Personal histories, as one might imagine, focus on the individual, revealing how past experiences, circumstances, and significant events may be related to the perspectives teachers bring to the classroom, how they act in particular situations and what they see as problems or questions to be asked about their work and the functioning of schools. School histories, on the other hand, center more directly on context, illuminating both the structures and norms of a local school as well as widely held beliefs about schooling. What follows is our attempt to create these histories.

The intent of the first draft, for both school and personal histories, is to describe, as opposed to analyze, aspects of self and context. Although all descriptions embody the roots of analysis because they reflect a particular slant on the events told, this form of analysis is not emphasized in the beginning. While largely open-ended, these descriptions are focused around particular themes in teaching and schooling. These themes direct participants to ask educational questions, reflect on their behavior in the classroom, and examine the ethos of the school.

Once these descriptions of self and context are drafted, participants can engage in a reflective process where the intent is to rework the descriptions by considering what is left out as well as clarifying the events and circumstances explained in the text. To facilitate this type of reflectivity, texts are exchanged and commented on by others. When it is thought to be appropriate, this phase of the process ends and the focus switches from description to analysis. To do so, participants can look for recurring themes or categories that seem to capture their stories.

To further this type of analysis, texts written by others can be brought into the process. In part, the purpose is to make it possible for those writing their histories to look at the relation between their own understandings of teaching and schooling and others' understandings. It would be deceptive, however, to suggest that the sole purpose of utilizing texts written by others is to compare one point of view with another. Instead, these texts also are a way to expose the political. While it would be antithetical to our position to argue that all personal and school histories must use a particular set of "political" readings, if voice as a form of protest is the aim, one criteria for selection should be the potential of readings to clarify and disclose oppressive formations related to schooling.

With readings of this type in mind, the analysis proceeds in a free-flowing way with participants using the three sets of texts—personal history, school history, and those written by others—to create a "plot" that imposes meaning on a set of events. In some cases the analysis of context helps participants rethink their personal histories. For others, the outside readings can help them rethink their understanding of context and vice versa. In either case, the outside readings did not obtain a privileged status; it is not assumed that this form of knowing is more valuable, worthwhile, or legitimate than the knowledge produced in the personal and school histories. Instead, value is placed on different ways of knowing that are likely to illuminate angles and shades of the question or issue not initially considered.

Once these analyses reach a point where the participants feel satisfied about their authenticity and power, the final stage of the process is to look across school and personal histories to identify common themes and differences. This comparative process enhances the possibility of identifying constraints and limitations held in common, and raises questions about what is still taken for granted or deemed impossible to change at the school level.

Telling the Story

The creation of personal and school histories helped shape the story that Beth would tell. What follows is an abbreviated version of this story in which Beth describes aspects of self and context.

Self

Fear accompanied me to school for most of my early years. In the classroom I rarely spoke and was always afraid to raise my hand. I was a child that was easy to "school," though, because I was quiet and compliant. I learned quickly to follow rules and to avoid drawing attention to myself. Follow the rules, don't take any risks, don't express opinions, better yet, don't even form them. These themes seemed to repeat themselves throughout my elementary years. Neither school nor home were places where I ever felt free to express myself.

Throughout high school [early 1970s] I maintained the "good girl" image—never skipped class, always did assignments, obeyed curfews, etc. Because of high grades, I was in a few advanced placement classes which I found stimulating and rewarding. I was still very insecure about speaking up, however, and felt intimidated by my classmates and teachers who could express themselves and defend their ideas. The fact that I had never been encouraged to participate in discussions at home, while being told my ideas were wrong or incomplete on the rare occasions when I did try, kept me from developing an external voice. There was an inner voice, but rarely could I bring it forth.

When it came time to leave the student role and choose a career, teaching seemed a suitable choice given my family socialization. Of the women in my immediate family, five were teachers and one was a nurse. I believe it was partially this history that both repelled and later induced me to become a teacher. Although I wanted to see myself in a less traditional role, the extent to which I internalized these familial and societal expectations is quite revealing in retrospect.

My role as a teacher began to be shaped during my first student teaching experience in 1976. The cooperating teacher was very authoritarian with her students and filled the day with workbook practice. Every night she took home mounds of workbooks to correct and, as her student teacher, I did the same. As I look back, I feel that she cared about her students mostly in terms of what they could produce. She insisted that they work hard, but the nature of the work had very little personal relevance, and I do not recall any emphasis on cognitive development.

By the conclusion of my student-teaching experience, my assumptions about the teacher role had been solidified. These assumptions revolved around the appropriateness of teachers being in control. What had been modeled for me was a teacher-centered instructional approach with just a glimmer of student involvement. I left student teaching feeling like teaching was definitely not for me. I was overwhelmed by the tremendous amount of paperwork, and the stress of managing the behavior of thirty-five children. I did not want to assume power over students the way it had been modeled, but my reluctance was based on more than just what I had observed in this classroom. It came from a pervasive feeling that I sensed about schools in general: they were places where little bodies came to be filled with knowledge that someone else had determined would be good for them. It was this assumption, that while not wanting to claim as my own, I was willing to condone as normal and let go unchallenged.

After student teaching, I completed a music-therapy internship at a psycho-educational center for severely emotionally disturbed children. My approach to discipline had additional roots in the training I received during this internship. I was taught to be consistent, follow through, and to portray a sense of control and calm in the face of any disruption. Group decision making and group formulation of rules and consequences were important skills for these children to acquire. In this respect, the orientation was much more student-centered than was my student-teaching experience. However, I found it difficult to implement this student-centered approach because the students I was working with were extremely volatile, hostile, and both physically and verbally aggressive. To try to support them as they learned how to take control of their lives was frightening. I was quite intimidated by their behavior, but felt that I had to hide and overcome my feelings at all cost.

These fears, although I tried to downplay them, later followed me into my first few years of teaching in the public schools. They added fuel to my sense that it was just too difficult for me to avoid a teacher-controlled classroom. I believed in a student-centered approach, but I had not seen it work. I had not seen students successfully manage their behavior, their time, or their choices. Instead, I had observed disruption and chaos. Although it was contrary to the atmosphere for which I yearned and wanted to establish, it was safer and quicker for me to assume control.

I have always struggled with the issue of control. At this point in my career, the struggle revolved around three aspects. First, I wanted something that I didn't know how to achieve—a student centered classroom. Second, I felt safer taking charge in order to avoid chaos. Third, assuming that the controlling I had observed during student teaching was part of a "normal" teaching role, then the way I was structuring my teaching was appropriate. Following the commonsense notion that the teacher should be in charge, I adopted the role, but I still knew that I was ill-prepared for the realities of teaching. I took a job as an aide in a resource room, planning to observe, ask questions, and essentially fill in the gaps created by my student-teaching experience.

My "apprenticeship" was short lived. In October of 1980, I was offered a full-time position in a fifth-grade classroom. I was apprehensive, especially when I learned that this particular group of students had already been taught by three contract teachers, and two long-term substitutes. There were various reasons given for their resignations, but the last teacher clearly stated that the class was quite out of control.

I assumed this position with determination and a lot of energy. How bad could it be? I had worked with children with behavioral problems, I knew how to set limits, I knew how to take control. I tried to apply what I had learned from the internship. I was consistent, firm, and calm. It didn't work. I had inherited a group of students that, even now, after seven additional years of teaching, I would find exhaustive and challenging. One group of students in the class had high academic capabilities, and another very low academic skills. Both groups were unmotivated, unruly, and used to doing whatever they wanted. Somehow, we all survived, and actually ended the year on a fairly positive note. Even though I fell into many traps of teacher control, I still managed to communicate to my students a genuine respect for them, and for what went on in our classroom. I believe they knew I cared about them as people. I'd like to think that my *desire* to teach in a way that encouraged student empowerment came through in subtle ways of spirit, if not in fact.

This tentative reach toward student empowerment was contested by the introduction of a research study developed at the district and school level which would reinforce appropriate, on-task behavior in my class. The idea promoted by these researchers was that in order to get students to work, it was appropriate to use reinforcers such as points and tokens. After the study ended, I continued to use reinforcers, not exclusively, but fairly substantially, in order to survive. Although I had mixed feelings about their appropriateness, "experts" had set up the program, and it was effective. The stress of teaching was significant, and I was certainly open to suggestions. I therefore put aside my hesitancies in favor of something that seemed to work.

My colleagues at the school were of little or no help. Many had been teaching in the same grade and the same building for many years and were simply waiting to retire. Teaching took place behind closed doors and was marked by a climate of conservatism. The "old guard" at the school had tremendous power. These teachers did not want to take any risks toward change and fought hard to maintain the status quo. As a beginning teacher, my socialization was furthered by these educators. I did not intentionally pattern my own teaching style after their stagnant methods, but I had little encouragement and virtually no models upon which to develop a more innovative or progressive way of teaching.

My first three years of teaching were characterized by unresolved tensions. From my internship experience, I carried with me a great fear of what can happen when students are out of control. Because of this fear, I felt it was necessary to be in control, and to be seen as the authority figure in the classroom at all times. However, this role actually contradicted the basic nature of my personality. With each year of teaching, I felt a longing to nurture my students' ability to take control and assume responsibility for their learning. Even so, I continued to use teacher-centered methods. Feeling the pressure to adhere to a time schedule, and to bring all of the students to a certain level of academic success, I was not confident that I knew how to make a student-centered approach work.

At this point, I was worn-out and dissatisfied. I felt stifled and did not see this school as an intellectual community in which I could look forward to growth and change. I decided to transfer to a new school in hopes of renewing my enthusiasm and aligning myself with more enlightened colleagues. At this second school, I did find a more innovative and supportive staff, but also a greater teaching challenge. One third of my class was functioning considerably below grade level and another third had limited or no English-speaking ability.

The pressure to bring all students up to grade level was ever strong. I had no idea how to deal with so many students who were so far below this standard, let alone how to help those without a knowledge of English. I went home daily feeling pulled in every possible direction, trying to meet everyone else's needs, with no time for my own. I felt like I was giving all I had and still it was never enough. It was the situation of giving without getting which Sarason so aptly describes.

> Inherent in teaching is giving, that is the teacher is required to give of himself intellectually and emotionally.
>
> . . . Constant giving in the context of constant vigilance required by the presence of many children is a demanding, draining, taxing affair that cannot be easily sustained.
>
> . . . To sustain the giving at a high level requires that the teacher experi-

ence **getting**. The sources for getting are surprisingly infrequent and indi-
rect (1971, 167).

After two more years, I decided I'd had enough of teaching. I knew that I
had given a lot of myself to my students. I knew that students, parents, and
colleagues considered me to be an excellent teacher, but I could only think
about getting out. I felt my life was completely ruled by school bells and
children. I was tired of feeling like I was on stage from 7:30 a.m. to 4:00
p.m. and I wanted to spend more of my day involved with adults. I was
tired of giving all I had and still needing to give more. I didn't know how to
make my job easier, less stressful, and still be effective. In fact, I seriously
doubted that this was possible.

I took a leave of absence for a year and worked as an associate librarian for
the city library system. During this year, I realized, for perhaps the first time,
some of the positive aspects of teaching. When my library duties became te-
dious, I realized that rarely while teaching did I watch the clock. I had often
been exhausted by teaching, and yet, it was also stimulating. As I shelved the
children's books, I missed being able to share them with my students. I
missed the creative energy that went into planning a teaching unit that truly
excited and interested me. I realized that there are many other jobs which are
more routinized than teaching and lack the spontaneity and unpredictability
that teaching does offer. These factors drew me back into teaching and when
the school year began, I accepted a position in a different school.

After two years, I again felt disillusioned with teaching. At this point, I was
aware of a pattern in my love/hate relationship with teaching. At each of
the schools where I had taught, I had been respected by colleagues, and well
liked by students and parents. Nevertheless, I could maintain a tolerance
level for the constraints of teaching for only two or three years at a time.
After the first three years I had tried a new school and new grade. Two
years later I had tried a new profession, only to return to teaching. Now,
after two more years, I was again searching for more satisfaction. The constraints of teaching under a mandated curriculum, with large numbers of
very diverse students, made me feel that my own philosophy of teaching
was continually getting lost and failing to solidify. I still wanted to shift the
focus of my classroom from being teacher-centered to student-centered, and
to assume a more cognitive approach to curriculum. In hopes of expanding
my theoretical knowledge and finding a more effective and personally satis-
fying way of working with my students, I decided to take another leave of
absence, this time to pursue a master's degree.

***

After providing this text on self, Beth turned her attention to the context of her work, the school. What follows is a brief description of her school history.

Context

The School: Richmond Elementary (fictitious name) serves a population of about 680 students, the majority of whom are considered to be "at risk." Seventy per cent of the student body come from low-income families and many of these are single-parent homes. Forty percent of the students are minorities, primarily Hispanic and Pacific Islanders. The students are typically achieving from one to two years below grade level. Over the past ten years, our academic achievement scores on national tests have dropped from the 60th percentile and now range between the 20th and 30th percentile. They are currently the lowest in the district. Our mobility rate is 48 percent and our attendance figures again place the school at the bottom of the district.

Our students have considerable difficulty with time-on-task and with exhibiting appropriate behavior. Playground difficulties and fighting have been continual problems. Students have, however, learned to be very accepting and supportive of the handicapped population at our school. Many classes adopt the special education classes and involve them in their activities. Older students often volunteer to be tutors and aides in the handicapped classes.

Our faculty is dedicated and hardworking. Teachers come early and stay late. Cars begin arriving between 6:30 and 7:00 a.m. and the parking lot is rarely empty before 6:00 p.m. Teachers demonstrate initiative and those that hold leadership positions devote even more time and energy. Although we are diverse in our educational philosophies, most teachers tend to utilize an effectiveness orientation to curriculum making. Nevertheless, from its very beginnings, the school has attracted teachers who also favor a cognitive approach that stresses personal relevance.

The principal reports that in terms of instruction and educational aims, we have been fragmented and without a central focus. This problem has been compounded by the number and variety of programs where students are taken out of the classroom for remedial instruction. Many students have participated in one and often two programs of this kind. This has led to considerable inconsistency with regard to educational goals and accountability. At times, a certain amount of resentment and intolerance for the variety of curriculum orientations can be observed among teachers in our school. Many of the students in the school are such low achievers that the tendency is to shift the blame for school failure.

In terms of support for new teachers and for those who want to examine their teaching methods, several teachers formed a literacy support group and have met, on their own time, for the past two years. The purpose of the group has been for teachers to raise educational concerns, ask for help, clarify aims, and share ideas.

Our present principal has provided direction and consistency for the school. She is a highly visible person in the building. Her level of interaction lets both students and teachers know she is available and aware of day-to-day problems. Teachers are becoming more open in discussing problems with the principal. She observes, gives suggestions, and lends support. At the same time, she is not intrusive and allows teachers the freedom to teach their classes in the manner in which they are most comfortable. She deals with our diverse faculty with sensitivity and openmindedness. She listens to teachers and incorporates their ideas into the vision that she has for the school.

School History: When our school began to receive funding for students who were behind grade level, there was a new emphasis placed upon the basic skills, almost to the exclusion of everything else. In addition, there seemed to be an influx of "at-risk" students. Burn-out began to strike everyone, tension was high, and morale was low. Behavior problems began to escalate, and the community was extremely unhappy. Several suspensions occurred daily and there was essentially little positive reinforcement for students or teachers.

A major staff change occurred during the summer of 1986. Nine teachers transferred and the principal left to assume a new position. I was one of ten new teachers placed at the school. Our new principal had the task of pulling together the newly hired faculty with an established faculty that was basically discouraged and worn out.

One of her first major decisions in this regard was to implement a discipline policy based on Canter's (1976) Assertive Discipline model. We received training and were encouraged, but not required, to follow the constructs of Assertive Discipline, which included putting teachers in charge, and using positive reinforcement techniques. Rules were posted throughout the building and both rewards and consequences were specifically stated. There was a replacement of home suspension with in-school suspension and detention. Our primary focus in using the Assertive Discipline plan, however, was to emphasize the positive. There were monthly behavior reward activities, "Good Note Home" rewards, lunchroom behavior rewards, and "Citizen of the Month" honors. In general, the plan was well accepted and the school climate began to change for the better.

At the end of her first year, the principal then introduced a three-year plan to improve the school. The challenge was stated as follows:

To mobilize students, staff, and parents around a school in which students are expected to achieve. We will set and enforce standards to make the school environment orderly, safe, and academically demanding.

Even though there were fewer suspensions and fights under the reward system, the student body as a whole continued to have difficulty with three major areas: following directions, staying on task, and accepting correction from an authority. The reward system seemed to be effective in motivating the average students with minor behavior problems, but there were many students with severe behavior problems who were not significantly influenced by this discipline policy. The principal concluded that we were spending a lot of time focusing on positive and negative consequences, but little time teaching these identified types of behavior. As a way of enhancing our existing disciplinary techniques, we began to use the Administrative Intervention program. Administrative Intervention is a term used to identify a set of procedures developed from the Teaching Family model (a group home and residential treatment program for troubled children and for youth who experience behavior deficits) and adapted to educational settings.

Administrative Intervention operates on the philosophy that when students misbehave, they must be retaught in much the same way they would be retaught had they made a mistake on a math problem. Given the fact that there is not enough time in the day for teachers to teach the core curriculum, let alone social skills, a major strength of the program is that the intervention is done by the administrator. Initially, teachers are responsible for teaching the "social skills," such as staying on task, to their entire class. When a disruptive event occurs, however, the principal steps in to provide the necessary reteaching and intervention strategy. The reteaching strategy combines empathetic response, positive and negative consequences, and detailed record-keeping, with the reteaching of specific behaviors. During the first year of implementation, our principal spent 90 percent of her day involved in interventions. It was clear that our students truly did not know how to perform many of the behaviors that are termed social skills. As the program's effectiveness became apparent, even those teachers who had not participated began to become involved. In the second year of use, the principal reported that the percentage of her day devoted to interventions had decreased from 90 percent to 50 percent.

Following the Administrative Intervention program, the focus switched to the development of school-wide teaming and ability grouping in reading and math. Within this approach, teachers are encouraged to group across grade levels, but most choose to group within their own grade. Each grade contains four groupings from severely low to high abilities. There is now a school-wide block scheduling, consisting of a two-hour block for reading, followed by a one-hour block for math. At the conclusion of the math block, the students return to their heterogeneously grouped home rooms for science, social studies, health, music, and art. Team meetings, held weekly, allow for discussion about individual students and the sharing of instructional strategies. Each team has a person who acts as a liaison between the team and the principal.

Another part of the reform is the creation of a time-on-task room and the hiring of a supervisory aide. Students who are unable to stay on task are sent by the teacher to T.O.T. for instruction on the identified social skills and the completion of their work in isolation.

Revisiting the Story

Beth's story not only gave her an opportunity to speak out, but also provided an opportunity to consider the import of the text. What follows is our attempt to examine this story. We do so by drawing on Beth's words and insights that were produced as part of the analysis phase of her personal and school histories.

The mere writing of personal and school histories is a step towards enabling silenced groups to speak out. However, if voice is to be more than a solipsistic endeavor, the story not only has to be heard, but also must be seen as valuable. Ironically, even those groups who have been silenced often do not value their experiential or practical knowledge. This is not surprising, given their lack of power and the dominant view about what counts as legitimate knowledge. An important part of developing voice, therefore, is seeing stories of the self as valuable. For Beth this process occurred during the sharing of personal histories.

I continually learned by listening to other teachers' personal histories, and by having my own history listened to and valued. It gave me the incentive to keep searching for a way to fulfill my dreams of the teacher I wanted to be. And yet, as I wrote, I sometimes had the uneasy feeling, "But this is just my story." I found myself wondering at times, "Is this real academic work, does it count?" When my paper was returned I was still awed by the fact that my story had been read, heard, and responded to seriously. Myself as text; it was such an incredibly empowering experience for me. I had never developed a sense of voice. On the contrary, I had grown up in classrooms that deposited information in the heads of students just like the one to which, as a teacher, I sadly realized I had succumbed.

Speaking out, especially when one has been historically silenced, is an essential part of altering power relations. The fact that a particular group no longer has the exclusive privilege to speak alters to a degree the decision-making process of a culture, community, or even a society. However, if voice is to be more than speaking out, if it is to be a form of protest that enables groups to contest structures and to recognize their own part in fostering narrow and limiting forms of schooling, then part of the process involves contesting conformity and valuing difference. In Beth's description of her history it is clear that her past was one of following rules and not taking risks. With the writing of her personal and school history, however, the old patterns of compliance became obvious and Beth began to speak out about the school district's policies and challenge her acceptance of those policies.

I had deliberately built into my curriculum times of choice, times where there were no right answers, no put-downs, times when students were free to express any and all opinions. These were some of the most sacred moments to me in teaching, the times I was most fulfilled. There was a sense of being able to give to kids what I had been denied. Yet, these experiences could not be easily measured or standardized. They did not fit the mold of the district's basic skill requirements. Therefore, I had let them slip away, and let the skills I was required to teach take precedence. There was a glaring contradiction between what I wanted to accomplish and what I felt compelled to accomplish and teach.

By identifying tensions between policy and practice, Beth also gained confidence that she could raise questions instead of depending on others to pose these queries. She was more willing to take a critical stance toward her own history and the knowledge presented by others.

My ability to formulate ideas and to raise questions began to expand while my self-doubt began to diminish. I began to listen less and less to my self-imposed censor, and to risk sharing my perceptions with others. I noticed that not only was I able to think critically about my own ideas, but also about the knowledge that others communicated. The writing of these texts also gave me the opportunity to think carefully about my own history and how it might interact with the history of my students.

Once Beth was willing to confront her history and look critically at the arguments posed by others, she had the foundation to direct her protest both inward at self and outward at context. These came together in her analysis of the Administrative Intervention program being implemented in her school. Her first concerns were directed at the policy itself.

As Apple (1979) points out, schools tend to devalue conflict in favor of compliance. They also develop student roles that will contribute to the maintenance of society. The specific content of social skills taught through Administrative Intervention supports this idea that schools prepare students to become good workers who will uphold the work ethic of their society. While the social skills teach children to be respectful and to work hard, these same skills also encourage passivity and place considerable value on order and routine. Consider the components of the rules "follow directions and 'stay on task'":

Follow Directions	*Stay on Task*
1. Eye contact	1. Self start
2. Say O.K.	2. Work steadily for required time
3. Do task immediately	3. Do not make distractions
4. No arguing	4. Ignore others distractions

These behaviors are the very ones that are seen as desirable in industry. They are the behaviors a supervisor looks for in factory workers, but are they the ones we should be emphasizing in schools? How much do they contribute to the intellectual growth of the student?

While Beth has not come to any conclusions, she has raised a number of questions which enable her to examine how the implementation of policy acts to serve particular interests, those of producing good workers, while fostering overly narrow forms of education. Her protest, however, is not limited to the context in which she works; she also looks inward at her role as teacher.

At times, I lose my balance. Working with "at-risk" students, it is easy to fall into the trap of an over-reliance on teacher authority, but this is not the answer. To find the answer we need to go beyond our classroom walls. We need to look at the cultural values that such students bring with them to school in order to determine how to help them succeed. For example, in the descriptive part of this history I made the statement that our students "truly did not know how to follow directions, stay on task etc." Why do they now know how? Is it that the values we teach in school are not those that are applicable to them at home? Is it possible that their parents do not have the same white, middle-class values that the school espouses? What do our parents value and hope for, in terms of their children's education? Are students able to use the strategies we teach to help them solve problems at home? Do they agree with these strategies and with these values? Is it that our students do not know how to implement the expected behaviors of the school or do they just not care? If they do not care, might it also be due to a long history of irrelevant curriculum and rigid teaching practices that do not allow them to be involved in their own education?

As Beth continued to pose a number of questions about self and context, her insights about her silence in the past held the key to what she wanted for students.

In the cooperative master's program each of us had been guided and supported in finding, developing, and expressing our voice. But how had "voice" been protected and nurtured? The answer lay not with finding a student-centered approach, but with achieving a sense of mutuality and reciprocity between teacher and student. Freire has said that education begins "with the resolution of the teacher/student contradiction, by reconciling the poles of the contradiction so that both are simultaneously teacher and student" (1970, 59). The environment that I now envisioned for my class was one based on a truly reciprocal community where all involved would be considered teacher-learners. No longer was I willing to deposit the information into the heads of my students, thereby setting up a subject-object dualism. Essentially, I wanted to provide them with the same sense of empowerment that I gained from learning to produce, rather than simply receive knowledge.

The articulation of the need for reciprocal community of teacher-learners led Beth to consider what she might want to do in the classroom. This action plan revolved around an examination of the words *instruct* and *educate*.

How was I to begin to make these changes I now envisioned? Turning to the etymology of the words *instruct* and *educate*, I found both clues and contradictions. The word *instruct* comes from the Latin, *in* + *stuere*, meaning "to build." In my classroom rarely had students and I been able to concentrate on building or creating. Instead, we had been required to follow the practices common to instrumental rationality which encouraged us to reproduce rather than to build. I had deposited information; they had reproduced and memorized facts, knowledge from others, which more often than not, had little connection to their own lives. To confront this type of education I had to find a way to introduce a process of building and creating.

When I then studied the word *educate*, I found that it comes from the Latin derivative *educare* meaning "to rear." These etymologies seemed to confirm for me a notion that I had felt for a long time, while illuminating what had been so frustrating and limiting to me as a teacher: There is a fundamental connection between educating and rearing children; however, it is a denied and devalued connection that is gender-related. When we are educating, we are rearing, but women are expected to educate in ways that contradict our ways of rearing and what we know about living and being with children. The rearing of children involves intimacy and nurturance. Home is a place of exploration, a place where the development of initiative and curiosity is carried out in the daily activities that women do with children. It is a place of continuous and evolving relationships which, if they are to succeed, are built on caring, cooperation, and the listening to and valuing of difference. School, on the other hand, is a place of control and compliance. It is a place where children, while being observed, measured, and evaluated, must master tasks that are broken down and compartmentalized. Rather than fostering intimacy and nurturance, relationships in schools center around theories of expertise and authority leading to a sense of detachment and isolation.

Although the majority of teachers are women, the culture of schooling is based on concepts that represent a denial of women's experiences. Grumet views schooling as a passage from the domestic world to the public world, and consequently, also to patriarchal institutions.

> We have required women to draw children out of the intimacy and knowl-
> edge of the family into the categorical and public world. We have bur-
> dened the teaching profession with contradictions and betrayals that have
> alienated teachers from our experiences, from our bodies, our memories,
> our dreams, from each other, from children and from the sisters who are
> mothers to those children (1988, 57)

As I looked back on my personal and school history, I began to see the part that I was playing, and being forced to play, in perpetuating this passage. I understood how the agentic school structures and my own personal history had worked together to try to separate me from a nurturing, communal approach to education. Often they had been successful. When this separation occurred, I would look for something to change—grade, school, occupation—and when it became unbearable I left teaching, twice. Yet each time something drew me back. Now I knew what it was—the need to use and value maternal knowledge. It was the desire to connect the private and public spheres which not only schooling, but also society, has forced apart.

As Beth looked for ways to make this connection, she wanted to change the metaphor of her teaching from "factory" to "family." Assertive Discipline may have gotten her through the day, but the price of using these techniques was that she was forced to use behaviors that would lead her away from intimate relationships. As the authority figure and controller, Beth had put aside the very behaviors that would nurture her students and sustain her in teaching. With these thoughts in mind, she developed the following general goals for the next year:

1. To build a community of teacher/learners based on care, concern, a connection.
2. To develop a sense of voice in my students by helping them recognize the importance of their experience. And to use this knowledge to build and create new knowledge and further their understandings of the selves and the world.
3. To bridge the gap between school and home.

Theory into Practice: Beth's Reflection

Here, Beth reflects on the effects that her participation in the Educative Research project, and her consequent reorganization of curriculum priorities, had on actual teaching practice.

I have stated that the maternal influence in teaching is energetic, resilient, resourceful, and persevering. In day-to-day work with children, however, these qualities are continually tested. My quest for developing a community of teacher-learners has not been, and seems will not be, a smooth or easy one. Although I anticipated it to some degree, I was nevertheless discouraged to see the resistance of students to my new curriculum. Despite the preliminary changes in the curriculum, the acting-out behavior has limited my initial attempts to form a community. At age seven, their lived experience has already taught them not to trust. These students are so used to fighting, ridiculing, and complaining that even personally relevant curriculum has so far had little impact. They have learned to be tough and rebellious and to think of care or concern as a sign of weakness. To cooperate or connect with others is to somehow lose face.

Although they rebel against authority, when given opportunities to make rules and decisions for themselves, many are at a loss. They look to "teacher," and consider me, as an adult figure in the room to be either the creator of their problems—in which case they rebel, or the solver of their problems—in which case they become dependent. Initially they did not respond to my efforts to establish care, concern, and connection. What they responded to were the M & Ms—those extrinsic rewards that I found myself using once again. I have been angry, frustrated, and fearful that they were going to force me back into that position of the authority and controller that I had worked so hard to escape. They have not done so, but this experience has shown me the incredible difficulty of finding the balance between giving up and holding on to my previous role.

We do not yet have a community of teacher-learners. What we have is a group of individuals struggling to discover where our voices begin and end in relation to each other. In order to be able to get to the point where we can begin to work on the development of our voices, I have done considerable talking and modeling of what it means to be a teacher-learner. As a class, we have talked about the qualities of teacher-learners and we have looked at the many people in our lives that serve as "teachers"—parents, siblings, peers, ourselves. We have examined the other environments in which we can and do learn besides our classroom.

The path to reconciliation of the contradiction between teacher and student is indeed an arduous one, but one I shall continue to follow, and invite my students to join me. Our next task, the recording and sharing of our personal histories, will be a big risk for them. But I believe that as they read and respond to their own histories, they will gradually gain the sense of empowerment that can come from using their own voice.

At this point, they must practice learning to listen to and value each others' voices, and we may yet go through more bags of M & Ms. Nevertheless, I am committed to making this change in my teaching and am encouraged by recent promising moments. Last Friday, when I asked my students, "Who is the teacher in this room?" a few fingers instantly pointed to me. But then I saw several heads shake and heard Melissa's voice indignantly retort, "Huh-uh we *all* are."

As Beth's story points out, the telling of one's story not only gives teachers an opportunity to tell their stories, but importantly, can release them from a cycle of compliance. When this occurs, they often see value in what they do and know and then can use this new confidence to take risks, to look critically at themselves and their world and to protest what is narrow and constraining about schooling. This development of voice, in turn, allows them to take some initial steps in posing questions about schools and teaching as well as to consider what actions they might take to remake the education offered students.

References

Apple, M. 1979. *Ideology and curriculum*. London: Routledge and Kegan Paul.

Canter, L. 1976. *Assertive discipline*. Santa Monica: Canter and Associates.

Freire, P. 1970. *Pedagogy of the oppressed*. New York: Seabury Press.

Gitlin, A., Margonis, F., and Brunjes, H. 1990. Dilemmas of reform: A case study of a democratic initiative. Paper presented at the annual American Education Research Association meeting, San Francisco.

Grumet, M. 1988. *Bitter milk*. Amherst: University of Massachusetts Press.

Holmes Group. 1986. *Tomorrow's teachers: A report of the Holmes Group*. East Lansing, Mich.: Michigan State University.

Sarason, S. 1971. *The culture of the school and the problem of change*. Boston: Allyn and Bacon.

4

Exploring the Teacher's
Professional Knowledge

Ivor Goodson and Ardra Cole

> But the self, whatever its age, is subject to the usual laws of optics. However peripheral we may be in the lives of others, each of us is always a central point round which the entire world whirls in radiating perspectives.
> Alison Lurie, *Foreign Affairs*

A starting point for this chapter is a belief that if we are to develop valued models of teacher development, we first need to listen closely to the teacher's voice. We need to continue, almost obsessively, that act of listening. Hence we feel that the best way to develop sensitive models of professional development is first of all to listen to the professionals at whom the development is aimed. This process of sensitive listening has been advocated at a number of levels recently. For instance, an emerging body of work has suggestively recommended the development of collaborative case studies, life stories, and narratives which seek to elicit the teacher's "personal practical knowledge" (e.g., Connelly and Clandinin 1988, 1990) or the teacher's "pedagogical content knowledge" (Shulman 1986, 1987; Grossman 1990; Gudmundsdottir 1990).

While these approaches make a valuable start in sensitizing us to the teacher's voice, they may encourage too partial a view of teachers' knowledge. The research reported herein implies that personal practical knowledge or pedagogical content knowledge is only a part of teachers' *professional knowledge*. This professional knowledge moves well beyond the personal, practical, and pedagogical. To confine it there is to speak in a voice of empowerment while ultimately disempowering. To define teachers' knowledge

This is a modified version of a paper to appear in *Teacher Education Quarterly* vol. 20.

in terms of its location within the confines of the classroom is to set limits on its potential and use.

Our work points to a range of levels at which teachers' professional knowledge can be discerned. It is certainly true that there is a range of practical and pedagogical knowledge which is of vital import in understanding the teacher's conduct in classrooms. But alongside that, we have found, there is a range of knowledge of great importance which deals with the micropolitical and contextual realities of school life. Such knowledge is critically important, not least because these micropolitical and contextual factors affect the lives and arenas in which personal, practical, and pedagogical knowledge are utilized.

Background and Context

Our study of teachers' professional knowledge and development involved seven full-time instructors newly hired to a community college in southwestern Ontario, Canada. The community college system in Canada began during the 1960s and 1970s to meet the growing demands for skilled and technical workers, and to respond to the postwar population explosion.

These community colleges are loosely defined as postsecondary, non–degree-granting institutions. They are governed by a board of representatives from the local community, and offer programs reflecting the concerns of the region. The largest college system in Canada is found in Ontario where there are twenty-three community colleges serving over one hundred thousand full-time postsecondary students and part-time enrollments of more than seven hundred thousand.

There are approximately six thousand full-time faculty employed in the community college system. As a group, college teachers are unique. Almost without exception, teaching is not their first career. Most are hired because of their practical work experience and move into the community college setting from some area of business, industry, technology, trades, or the professions. They receive no formal preparation for their teaching roles; yet, they are expected to carry out all the roles and responsibilities associated with being a teacher.

In order to gain a fuller understanding of what it means to become a teacher in a community college, we (Goodson and Cole along with Fliesser, a curriculum consultant at the college) invited a small group of newly hired full-time community college teachers to join us in a two-year exploration of their experiences, development, and socialization as community college instructors. Like most community college teachers, they joined the faculty "fresh from the field." For each, teaching in a community college represented both a career change and a change in professional venue.

The Teachers

In this chapter we focus primarily but not exclusively on Brian and Karen. Brian is an architectural technologist, and Karen is a television production technician.

Studying the socialization and development of the instructors was particularly interesting because they had not been through any conventional teacher-preparation program; hence we were able to observe their on-the-job responses to the new educational workplace. As we followed them through their first two years of teaching, we saw the teachers struggle to define their new role(s) and contexts and to understand themselves as teachers in the community college setting. Although not always articulated explicitly, they seemed to spend much of their induction period searching for answers to questions such as: What does it mean to be a teacher? What does it mean to be part of a new professional community? How do I define the boundaries of my new professional community? How do I become part of that community? To develop an understanding of their answers to these questions and to ground it in a fuller context for each person we employed the *life-history method* and particularly the *life-history interview* (for a full discussion of life-history work see, e.g., Goodson 1981).

A Note on Method

To illustrate our conception of professional knowledge and teacher development, we rely on thoughts, ideas, and observations the teachers provided us throughout the two-year period. In particular, we draw on information collected in a series of life-history interviews with each teacher and bi-weekly group discussions which took place throughout the period of the study. These group sessions were the major collective milieux for the teachers to voice their views and concerns and express their developing perspectives. Because of our commitment to sponsoring the teacher's voice and learning from what teachers have to say, much of what follows is excerpts from interviews with and discussions among the teachers. We have tried to keep our commentary to a minimum. Not all of the teachers' voices are heard individually in this paper, however. (For a more extensive life-history account of each teacher, see Goodson, Cole, and Fliesser, forthcoming.) We selected excerpts from the life-history interviews and group discussions which seemed particularly illustrative of the ideas we advance here. Because the entire group was involved in the bi-weekly discussions, all seven teachers (eight, when Linda was still part of the project) are in fact represented, although frequently as a collective voice.

***

Teacher Development, Teachers' Lives

Teacher development has been characterized in a variety of ways. Fuller and Brown (1975), for example, propose that new teachers progress through a series of concerns-based developmental stages beginning with actions based on self-centered concerns about survival through to actions based on concerns about students and curricular issues. Ryan (1986) suggests that beginning teachers move through stages of "fantasy," "survival," "mastery," and "impact." Burke, Fessler, and Christensen (1984) characterize teacher development in a model of career cycles. Huberman reflects our own and others' dissatisfaction with such generalized characterizations when he states

> Modal trends such as these are suspect. Put together, they would probably describe no single individual in [a] sample, and only pieces of subgroups. They are, in fact, normative constructs enabling us to keep analytic order in our minds until we can handle more differentiation and complexity. (1989, 53)

A more recent focus on teachers' lives and personal biographies consequently has led to conceptualizations of teacher development rooted in the "personal" (e.g., Bullough, Knowles, and Crow 1991; Butt and Raymond 1987; Clandinin 1986; Connelly and Clandinin 1990; Knowles, 1992; Knowles and Holt-Reynolds 1991). Other studies have argued for a personal mode linked to broader contextual parameters (e.g., Apple 1986; Ball and Goodson 1985; Britzman 1986; Cole 1990, 1991; Goodson 1981, 1988, 1989, 1990, 1991; Zeichner and Grant 1981; Zeichner and Tabachnick 1985). This chapter seeks to extend this latter view and to provide a story of action within a theory of context.

Toward a Broadened Perspective in Teacher Development

Our concept of teacher development is rooted both in the personal and professional. We consider teachers as persons and professionals whose lives and work are shaped by conditions inside and outside of school. Events and experiences, both past and present, that take place at home, school, and in the broader social sphere help to shape teachers' lives and careers. How teachers construe their professional realities and how they carry out their lives in classrooms is an ongoing process of personal and contextual interpretation. In this chapter, we further develop this concept. We move beyond the primarily personal, practical, and pedagogical notions to define a broader conception of professional knowledge and teacher development, one that places teachers in the broader micropolitical and contextual realities of school life.

In our study of the development and socialization of seven new community college teachers, a pattern of teacher development emerged which clearly reflects a transitional quality in the teachers' perceptions of their experiences. We characterize the personal aspect of their development as a struggle to establish professional identity; the context, we characterize in terms of defining boundaries of professional community. Personal/professional development within that personally defined context we describe in terms of belonging.

Two interlinked analytic foci are employed as we examine these issues of professional development:

1. Constructing professional identities
2. Constructing professional communities

Articulating the Link between Identity and Community

To rehearse the interlinked nature of our two analytic themes, we begin with a lengthy passage from an interview with Karen who, at the time of the interview, had recently left her job in technical production at a national television station and joined the community college faculty to teach in her area of practical expertise. We quote at length to capture the essence of the link between conceptions of professional identity and professional community.

Karen: I started [at the television station] in '78, and four years later was married. [My husband and I] were friends first because we ran in a crew. He was an editor. Everybody on that crew I knew on a first-name basis. I was the one supplying them with the tapes—the gofer. And we would go for lunch together, all of us, so I got to know all of these guys.

Ivor: You were the only female there at the time?

Karen: Yeah, except for the service secretaries who worked in the scheduling office and who would schedule the shows in the different suites. During the evening shifts we'd go for lunch and then for a beer after the shifts were over at 11:00. [The crew members] became my friends. Some of them had girlfriends, and we sort of got a group going. I started dating Jim. We were married in '82 and bought our house in '83. We had our daughter in '84.

Right after we got married, I switched from videotape to production. I applied to the woman who was in charge of production services, said I would be happy in videotape but I wanted to learn something else and that I would like to get into production. I think I wanted to use more creativity. The videotape was creative but you were also pushing the buttons for somebody beside you. They would assign a producer to come in who would say, "Okay, cut this item and edit this item." He/she would sit beside you and say, "Edit there. Let's put this music on." It was a little frustrating. So I thought,

"Well I'll go to [the production] side and see what that's like for awhile. Since I know the editing it might help." So I went into pro duction and was offered a job.

First of all you have to go through another training, first as a script assistant and then a production assistant. The script assistant is in the control room timing the shows.

It tended to be a little more clerical than I would have liked. I'm not a clerical type of person but I certainly learned how to time a show—I did [two news programs]—and I certainly know the feeling of going live with a new show. It is very exciting.

Everything is [trade] unions [at the station] so everything is classified at union scale. Going from videotape to production was essentially a lateral move but since there are just three [job classification] groups in production, I just moved up to the third group.

Ardra: So you were in the top group?

Karen: Yeah, the top of the script assistant group. And then, I worked on [an afternoon news and information show] where I became what they call a service producer. Because of budget cuts you didn't get any extra money for it but the job function was still there and they still trained people for it. I liked doing it so I didn't really care about the money.

I was kind of a producer who oversees the videotape department. It was a perfect setting for me because it was production; yet, I was in the videotape department with all the old guys, the gang. My job was basically organizing and coordinating the whole videotape department for that whole particular show. You were there in the morning until it was off-air and then you go back and prepare for the next day. And that's where I was when we left in June '88.

Ardra: Where was Jim?

Karen: Jim was an editor, one of the top editors. Then he started with [a national prime-time news show]. When we got married in '82, I went to production. At the same time he went to [the news show] which was, at that time, quite a separate section of videotape. Supposedly, the "elite" editors went to work on that show because it was a new show with new equipment. They had to do a lot more work and they became more production editors/directors doing a lot more than straight editing. He stayed with [that show] until we left. He was there for seven years.

It was the winter of '87 when we started thinking about leaving. I was getting sick of [the afternoon show] but there wasn't a job to go to next. It was like the ladder was chopped off, and there wasn't anything I could see to go to. I could have gone into a producer's job but the work was not any more challenging. And it wasn't a move up either. It wasn't any more money. It wasn't any more prestige. It was just another job. It didn't interest me. Management was the only other area and, since managers are a dime a dozen there, there just wasn't any little niche that I could see that I wanted to go into.

So work was getting a little depressing and we were getting just a little stagnated there. Although my husband was happy on [the news show]—the people were good, he loved the show, loved the equipment—his boss was from the old department and there was a rivalry going between him and the supervisor of the other department. So there were a lot of morale problems, back-stabbing, and some terrible things that went on that just ruined it for some of the people there.

It was just a time when Jim was getting frustrated with the politics of the corporation—mostly the politics, not anything else. And I was getting sick and tired because there wasn't anything else to go into. There weren't any new shows then. I mean a new show would have been great 'cause I would have been starting all over again. (interview, August 1989)

As is illustrated in the above case with Karen, the teachers entered the community college setting with already well-developed concepts both of professional community and professional identity—antecedents to the new notions of professional context and identity they would develop. After ten years, Karen, for example, left the community of visual broadcasting. While there she had developed strong personal and professional ties, gained considerable knowledge of the political workings of the corporation, and acquired experience and expertise in her area of work. Beginning at the bottom rung, she had worked her way up the corporate ladder until it "was chopped off." In her reading of her work context, she did not see further possibilities for the kind of creative expression and professional autonomy she needed. And so, yearning for a new challenge, Karen opted for a change and to become part of a new professional community of community college teachers.

Changing professional roles and career and moving into a new professional community initiated a process of redefinition. In a period of transition and adjustment, Karen and the others had to reconstruct their notions of professional self-identity and develop new understandings about their new workplace community. As we followed them through this process, trying to make sense of the personal/professional reconstruction which took place, an image of expanding concentric circles presented itself to us. As we listened to and talked with the teachers we picked up a clear sense of outward movement, both conceptually in terms of how they defined their new role(s) within the new work context and, physically, as they became more involved in activities outside their own classrooms. They seemed to keep pushing back the boundaries of their thinking about what it means to be a teacher in a community college, as well as the boundaries that defined their work community.

The boundaries which initially defined the teachers' personal conceptions of community were narrow and tight. In the beginning, the professional milieu was the classroom. Over time, this notion was broadened to encompass an increasing amount of territory outside the classroom until finally, the teachers' concept of community included the community college venue in a broad sense. Similarly, the process of redefining professional self-identity first involved a gradual shift from seeing oneself as primarily defined by the previous occupation to seeing oneself as a teacher. And within the new conceptual frame, the teachers gradually expanded their ideas about what it means to be a teacher. For the remainder of the paper we deal separately with these two analytic foci.

Constructing Professional Identities

With each teacher, qualitative shifts in self-perception occurred over time. They entered the community college not thinking of themselves as teachers. Each had an antecedent professional identity rooted in a previous professional context. A progressive change both in breadth and depth was evidenced in the individual interviews and in the group discussions as the teachers came to define and redefine their roles and see themselves as teachers. Excerpts from two of the life-history interviews provide examples of how the teachers began teaching not yet "feeling like teachers," not thinking about themselves as teachers. These interviews took place prior to or very early in the first term of the first year.

Karen: The thought of teaching [at the time of a first career decision] was "Teaching what? What do I teach?" Teaching students, standing up in front of the class. I mean I just didn't see it as the job I wanted to do.

I can't think like a teacher yet. I can't look at a calendar and say: "Mid terms are worth this percentage; 25 percent have to be of written marks; and, when am I going to write a test?" I haven't put together tests yet or projects or figured out how many weeks [I have to work with]. I mean, I keep looking at the calendar and going, "How many weeks are in this semester?" I haven't thought yet in that thought process as a teacher as far as long-term planning of curriculum. . . . I think obviously after one year I'll be able to say, "Well, that didn't work. I'm throwing that out next year and I'm going to add this and shorten this and lengthen that and maybe spend more time doing this." Then I'll know, but right now it's . . . (interview, August 1989)

Brian: [When I started] I thought I felt like a teacher—a teacher of architectural technology—because I had learned [the content of] what I had to teach. I'd been in the industry for a number of years so I felt I had something. I felt confident in my position. I'm not saying I felt like a teacher yet. But I felt confident in my position [with regard to content expertise]. (interview, September 1989)

Initially, the teachers seemed to be striving toward improved practice based on a narrow and technical view of teaching, their implicit assumption being, "I have the content knowledge so I will be a teacher once I master certain technical skills for its delivery." In the early group discussions, facilitated by the curriculum consultant at the college, the teachers focused their conversations on the technical aspects of teaching. Excerpts from our field notes illustrate.

> The group explored possible ways of handling difficult students. There was further discussion on how to handle missed assignments. Brian raised a question about the appropriate use of overhead transparencies, a topic which precipitated much discussion. This led to further talk about the use of handouts and other teaching aids. (field notes, September 1989)
>
> There was almost a unanimous concern about time and organization. Lecture preparation and text construction were seen as especially time consuming. . . . Karen expressed concern about how to coordinate groups within the classroom. She is also trying to individualize instruction but is having trouble figuring out what she needs to teach them by a given time. (field notes, October 1989)

Qualitative shifts in thinking, however, occurred over time. As the following two passages indicate, changes in the nature and content of the group discussions indicated an ongoing redefinition of the teachers' ideas on what it means to teach. We can interpret a shift to a focus on curricular issues, the teaching-learning process, and discussions of different teaching philosophies as the teachers beginning to see themselves as pedagogues rather than as mere technicians. These field notes were taken during two group discussions held in the first year, one at the end of the first term and the other at the beginning of the second term.

> Ann offered to share a bit about what was going on in her class. The students were doing presentations which, she said, were going very well. But she wanted to know how to take the presentations one step further so that all the students could build on them. In other words, how could the presentations be used as a teaching-learning tool? "How can I teach *with* [the students] rather than to them?" (field notes, December 1989)

> The subject shifted to evaluating students in cooperative learning situa-
> tions. Brian offered to share some of his ideas about using peer evaluation
> as a team-building activity. A lot of suggestions about using group work
> and cooperative learning were made. Then Ann posed a question about
> the role of the teacher in an independent learning situation. The discussion
> turned to the issue of the image of the teacher—as director, teller, facilita-
> tor. They all seem to be struggling with their image of what a teacher is,
> what their classrooms should be, and what their role is in the classroom.
> Brian offered his perspective that in spite of the initial tendency to want to
> "teach," it's okay to "guide." (field notes, January 1990)

The following passages from an interview with Karen midway through
her first year are particularly illustrative of the reidentification process. She
reflects on how her thinking about teaching has changed, articulates some
of her developing conceptions about her role, and looks forward to further
change and role expansion over time.

Karen: I thought I was teaching because I was knowledgeable about television and that's what I was teaching. Whenever I'd say the word
teaching, in the back of my head I'd still think, "me teaching?"
Friends would say "You're a teacher?" Everybody thinks back to their
teachers in high school or elementary or university. And that would
throw me for a while. But then after a while I thought, "Yeah, I'm
here because I know what I'm talking about."

When I was hired I was excited. I got a job teaching in a college. [I
thought] "This is the career of a lifetime." It's something I never
imagined doing. And it was perfect. It was exactly what I needed to
do or wanted to do. I never thought of it like, "Yes, I wanted to be a
college teacher some day." Yet, it was the accumulation of my television background. . . . I'm a people person. And I like to move and
talk and generate ideas, and to get people going. I just like the whole
atmosphere [of teaching and learning]. You see a product at the end.
I like working hard but I also like to see something completely accomplished at the end. And this was the perfect job where that all
would come to be. When I started it was, "I'm a teacher! I'm a
teacher! I'm a teacher! I can't believe it!" My husband and everybody
would joke about it. It was like, "I can't believe that I got this job.
It's the chance of a lifetime!"

Now, [the idea of being a teacher] is not important to me any
more. It's important that [the students] are learning something from
me. And that it's fun and it's encouraging. Maybe I'll [change my
mind later on] but at this point every day is different. So to me that's
the ideal job.

That's what most people complain about. They come home after awhile and their job is mundane. Nothing changes. [Teaching] is something in which you see the accomplishment at the end of the day. Some days you come home and you're a little frustrated. It didn't go the way you want. The next day it's either a different group of faces or the same faces but a different situation. And one person comes up to you and says, "Yeah, I got that. I'm going to do this and this." You think, "I got to that person. I really got to that person and it meant something."

I want these students to come back after a couple of years when they get jobs and say, "You know you really helped me." I hope they will say that, "I had a good time at college and I really learned a lot. You were encouraging." So, I think that's more important now to me than it was the first couple of months. The first months I was still on that cloud about what I was doing—a little nervous, but now I'm not nervous any more.

I don't think [some of the older, more experienced teachers] get to know the students. I think they get to a point where they have a curriculum to follow and they teach to a class, not to individuals. By not getting to know the individuals—and I don't mean really personally, I just mean getting to know their irks and how they're motivated or how they're not motivated—you don't see the ones who don't think highly of themselves and that you have to give a little extra pat on the back or whatever. By not focusing on those individuals the classroom becomes "cattle going in, cattle going out."

I'm changing. I should say changing the program but I don't want to make it sound that large-scale. I mean changing things that I see haven't worked. I've been through that course [as a student at the same college] and it hasn't changed and now I'm saying, "Okay, can we update it a little bit?" And [the other instructors] are very receptive which is something I never imagined possible.

I thought that coming in as the low person on the totem pole [the implicit rules would be]: "Learn. Watch where you walk. And don't step on any toes." But it's not like that. That's exciting for me because to me, that's part of the job as well—if you have the time.

Ardra: Your involvement in the extracurricular activities, things that take you outside the classroom, is that part of your teacher role?

Karen: Some are. Some are political. When someone asks me to do something I'm the type that usually says, "Oh yeah I'll do it. "I always take on too much but I'm also in a position where I would like to do other things. Eventually, I'd like to coordinate our program so the more I learn about the different aspects—the budgeting process for programs and things like that—the more knowledge I'll have. So I'm enjoying that.

I think one of the things I'm enjoying is that our coordinator is very receptive to change. He wants to revamp the program, to keep it current. And he hasn't had a lot of feedback or encouragement from other colleagues as yet. Most of the other colleagues are close to retirement and the one I replaced actually was very resistant to change. I think [the coordinator] sees the potential for some new ideas because I'm new in the industry. And I didn't expect that.

I really thought that I would be the low person on the totem pole. "This is what we're doing. We'll help you out and show you some things but take a little bit at a time." Instead I'm getting, "Have you got any ideas? Can we do this? How do you want to change it?" There's more power there, more freedom to do things that I never thought I would be able to do. We're talking about revamping the whole year next year and they're going on my idea. I think, "Wow, this is exciting. It's very encouraging." (interview, January 1990)

Karen was clear in her initial conception of teaching as delivery of content knowledge. She was less certain about her identity as teacher. She experienced initial discomfort/confusion over having the label "teacher" attached to her—not certain that it fit. She was, however, euphoric over the opportunities for creative expression and accomplishment that she thought her new role would provide. Soon, Karen accepted the "teacher" label and began to develop her understandings about the role(s) associated with that label. She began to identify success and satisfaction in terms of her ability to facilitate students' learning. Later, she expanded the criteria to include her ability to effect program change.

Along with the expanding conceptions of teaching came increasing role complexity and a related need to develop new knowledge. Content knowledge was no longer sufficient to carry out the multiple and complex roles Karen was adopting. She also recognized the need for knowledge of: herself as teacher; the students as individuals; how to best facilitate their learning; curriculum (beyond content knowledge); and, how to effect program change in her own class and department. Essentially, she was experiencing and demonstrating a need for personal, practical, pedagogical, *and* professional knowledge of the micropolitical context.

The following passages further illustrate how the teachers changed their perceptions of their role to extend beyond the technical and pedagogical to the institutional. They began to see themselves as contributing members of a department, designing institutional strategies.

Ann: You know, personally I can do things creatively with my kids in the classroom but that's not all there is to it. It's wider than that. I feel as if we've got a stake, or I've got a stake, in looking at changing our early-childhood-education field. There's been a movement for probably about the last ten years to recognize the child as child. It's against that whole notion of "the hurried child"—the disappearance of childhood if you like. When I think of young four-month-old babies going into care, I think we need to address some of those aspects of how that affects that child long-term. "What sort of program do we want that child to be in when they're with us eight or nine hours a day? And what should that program look like?"

The expectation for the child entering grade one is that the child knows colors, and reading and writing skills for readiness. We used to talk about that for grade one. So the kindergarten then adjusts their program to meet what the grade one needs. If you look at junior kindergarten we're talking, about three-year-olds who are now being pushed into that situation for readiness. We're saying, "No, just a minute. The child at that age needs to develop in all areas. This is not just an intellectual approach."

And so here we've got almost a new movement which is child-centered. All our texts reflect it but some of our practice in the field doesn't. So we have some dissension among [the community college] people. We're trying to move from that traditional look at what the teacher knows best to what the child needs. And the reason we're looking at the child's needs is because of that potential institutionalization of children from the age of four months up.

It's scary! I think those are some of the issues that we need to deal with and we're not. There are a couple of us who are on the same wavelength. We're not saying that this is something new. This is not new. It's not that we've suddenly thought this up and we're going to try and mix the pot here. Other community colleges have a child-centered approach in place. We now want the curriculum to fit the child rather than the child to fit the curriculum. And that's where the clash is, I think.

If you really believe in child development, how can you not acknowledge the development? In the private sector, when I'm talking about education, I would have far more response to our innovative ideas than I do in the teaching institution which I anticipated would be full of innovative ideas and creativity. If we don't have it here, where is it?

And then I hear people saying, "Well, you know, we can't tell the community college what to do." Somebody has to start somewhere.

> It's not my approach [to be directive]. I'm much more persuasive. But give me a chance to persuade. Give me a forum to persuade and I'll do it [laughs]. (interview, May 1991)

As time went on, there was less and less talk about the technical aspects of teaching (other than as a term of reference for growth) and increasing attention to concerns about how to effect substantive change within and outside the classroom. Broadly stated, the teachers expanded their conceptions of teaching and themselves as teachers from an early image of teacher as classroom technician to one of teacher as agent of change.

Karen: The people in my department are very congenial. It's very small. There's only a coordinator and another full-time colleague and myself. They both were my teachers when I took the course there so it was a bit strange at first. But it's worked out very well. They're a good group and we get along very well. They were very good. They were very supportive. I just stood back and was quiet for awhile. And now of course I never shut up [laughs]. Now I try to take over [laughs].

Our coordinator is a very positive person, very enthusiastic. He's willing to take any ideas that I have and go with them. He wants the course to change but he just has no idea what to do. So that is good for me. I have to watch it too. I can be very political. But it's very enthusiastic for me because I've been able to do a lot of things and change a lot of things. A lot of people just sit back or sit on the fence but I'll go to it.

Maybe I'm having a lot more political freedom in our department than in some of the others as far as changing things, just because things haven't been changed for a long time. They want the change. They know they have to keep up but they've been there so long they don't know what to do. So, it's not just teaching, it's revamping the whole thing. In ten years they're going to be retired and there will be other new teachers coming in. I want it to go in a way that I can see working there still in fifteen years. So that's been really good for me.

Some of the things my coordinator said "we" would do, the two of us. I don't know what happened but he kind of took a step back and I was standing alone. (interview, April 1991)

To summarize the teachers' development of self-identity we once again turn to the teachers. Karen and Brian describe their development of "self as teacher" in this way:

Karen: I don't really know when it clicked or when it happened. It just seemed to assimilate. I remember that first interview the day before I went to teach the first day. I remember thinking, "I can't believe I'm a teacher." I'd pinch myself, "Gee, I'm working at a college. This is ridiculous." And then it's just kind of come about so that now it's almost like, "Oh yeah, no big deal."

[The transition to teaching is] not as scary as I thought it would be. It was a lot more stimulating than I thought it would be. You just start thinking like a teacher, talking like a teacher. Throughout the year I found I was constantly [collecting information related to teaching]. Anything I read I think, "Oh yeah, that's great. That's great I could use that. Or I could do that." [The same thing applies] if I hear about somebody using some other method. And you start automatically applying everything that comes in. You kind of put ideas about methods and things on that teaching shelf so that you can use them. And you just start thinking about making yourself a better teacher. It just kind of happens. You just kind of evolve and just start thinking that way. I never imagined it would be that easy to transform into a teacher. But it's something that just starts to come comfortably. (interview, May 1990)

Brian: I have a lot better idea of what a teacher does than I did at the beginning. At the beginning I thought, "How hard can it be?" I mean you just stand up and you talk, and you show them how it's done. How hard can that be? And now I know how hard it can be.

Ardra: It's not longer just standing up and talking?

Brian: It's just nuts. I mean there's a lot more involved in being a good teacher. [You need] to know your material and how to present the material. There are a lot of people who know their material inside out, but if they can't get it across to other people so that the people can walk away and understand it. . . . And then [you need] the ability to know how to use a classroom to its best abilities, and what works best in presenting that material. And then, after the material is presented, how to evaluate it, how to evaluate the students, and their abilities to understand.

There is a lot more to teaching than just standing up in front of people and talking. At the beginning I didn't think there was. You also can't teach something unless you understand it.

Ardra: So the complex roles of the teacher are sort of presenting themselves to you as you. . . .

Brian: And again, at the beginning, teaching was, "Oh, they're all the same. They're students. They want to learn architectural technology." They're not all the same. Some of them need more time. And there are other issues on hand for the student now that I need to take into consideration. A part-time job seems to be a big thing, a necessity these days in order to go to school.

In my first year I was saying to my students, "Well no, it's either school or work. You can't do both." I didn't mean it as an ultimatum. And now you talk to some of these people and literally the part-time job is what's putting food on their table and paying their rent, because [assistance funds] didn't come through or whatever. So I'm not as harsh about it. Now, instead of, "No, you can't have a part-time job," it's, "Okay, but just make sure you schedule your hours appropriately. Make sure you have the time to do the work." I'm more supportive of those [situations] rather than harsh and judgmental.

And now I think [teaching] is much more complex. The one and only time I walked into a classroom unprepared taught me that lesson. I was very busy and just didn't have the chance to fully prepare. I had an outline of what I wanted to do but I didn't have things down pat the way I should have. That taught me never again [to be unprepared]. It was really embarrassing and difficult. And I felt as if I really cheated the students, and that didn't sit well with me. So I never did that again.

Ardra: Since you came on full-time a couple of years ago almost, do you see that your role has changed very much?

Brian: I look at myself as a teacher and that's my job.

Ardra: You didn't in the beginning? [laughs]

Brian: No. No. But now I do. I guess my attitudes have changed. I wasn't quite sure that I was teacher. Yeah, I guess that's right, when I look back on it.

Ardra: You think of yourself as a teacher. Do you still think of yourself though as an architectural technologist?

Brian: Oh yes, but not as much. I still think of myself as an architectural technologist because that was my choice of profession. But what I'm doing now is instead of practicing it, (and I do still practice it) I'm now a teacher. So, I'm a teacher of architectural technology. And I feel a lot more comfortable now than I did two years ago. (interview, May 1991)

And so, as the teachers reflect on their transition to teaching, their metamorphosis seems complete. The initial discomfort with the idea of identifying themselves as teachers no longer exists. Brian's final comments reflect the sentiments of the entire group. With an acknowledgment of their "first choice of profession," they now talk about themselves, not in terms of their previous role in their respective fields, but as teachers. They seem to have achieved a level of comfort in the development of their professional identity as teachers which approximates that previously defined within the earlier professional/vocational context.

Constructing Professional Communities

Using a similar representational process we now turn to our second focus and, once again, rely on the teachers to illustrate the concept of "constructing professional communities." We remind the reader of our image of the ever-widening circle of development, and begin with the teachers' initial and somewhat narrowly defined view of "classroom as professional community." Returning to the discussions and interviews held at the beginning of the first year, once again we follow the teachers through their first two years. As our first passage indicates, the teachers' initial understandings of what teachers do and where roles are played out were bounded by the classroom walls. An analysis of field notes on the first two group sessions, held in the early part of the first term in the first year, reveals a focus on topics/concerns which relate intimately to the classroom: managing time; preparing lesson plans; interpreting curriculum guidelines and developing new curriculum; long-range planning; individualized instruction; lesson presentation; use of audiovisual equipment and aids.

At some point late in the first term, there was evidence of an initial qualitative shift in the nature and content of the group discussions. The following examples show how conversation began and continued to move beyond the classroom walls. Boundaries were extended; walls were pushed back; the circle widened to encompass a greater territory.

Karen: I think the answer, at least for our department, is to try to get more industry involved in community colleges whether it be sponsorship of private companies or just industries that are going to benefit from our graduates. I think it may take some marketing on our part as individuals in our divisions or in the college as a whole. But we need to try to say, "Look, we are putting these students out and we're giving you something. We need something back." And it can't just be the government. They can't be the only one funding right now.

We have to look at ourselves as public relations people and salespeople, as well as teachers, if we want our departments to keep up. To keep up with the level that we need to teach [we need] to keep up with the industry. And industry is also going to have to give back what they get out. I think we've got to get that across to them that we can't just keep churning out students. If we can't keep up, those students we're churning out are becoming less and less qualified.

Industry can afford to keep up because they have profits to prove it. We have to say, "Well, you've got to give what we give. You have to help us produce these students who are up-to-date and excellent." That way you also generate more students coming into the system— if they can see an end, if they can see something that is a goal worth going after. But I think we have to actively start doing something. (group discussion, December 1989)

Ann: There's a lot of money going in. I think that one of the problems is a question of where that money is going and what it's going for. I can see we may have a new building going up out there which is going to be very beneficial but it really depends on how the whole thing is operated. We asked if we could have our offices out there or if we would have close ties with that new building. "No, we'd have to stay up in our own building." In [another community college] the whole early-childhood department is all part of that whole building. They have direct access to the resource rooms and things like that going on right there. The sad part is that we're building that beautiful building out there and here we are still over here. (group discussion, December 1989)

As the year progressed and the teachers became more settled in their new professional milieu, we began to see increasing evidence of an interest in departmental activity.

Karen: In May and June I'm going to work on changing the evaluation. I can do whatever I want. I find [the current method] very awkward. I would prefer to do my own and have [the other instructor] go and do his own, and then take the average of the two because I happened to get to know the students earlier. He just found he didn't know all the faces. Now he does tend to let me do most of the marking but to me it's a waste of time. We have thirty students to go through and it's probably about twenty minutes per student to do this. It doesn't sit well with me. So it's been left that I can change it in May. (group discussion, March 1990)

The teachers' increasing involvement in activities outside the classroom was further evidenced in a group discussion that took place early in the second term of the first year. The topic of a pre-session conversation was of their involvement in extracurricular activities. Karen talked about her key role in the production of a video related to community-college activities to be shown on a local television station. Bill commented on some culinary competitions in which he had become involved in support of the students. Jim had taken on extra responsibilities related to the provision of in-service training on a recently implemented policy affecting work environment.

As time passed, the teachers continued to express a growing interest in life beyond the classroom walls. Another significant shift occurred during another discussion that took place early in the second term of year one where an interest was expressed in learning the micropolitics of the institution: how things work; how things get done; how to make changes. Again, we quote from our field notes:

> An interesting sequence of events took place here. Linda spoke about the "politics of the institution." She talked about the constraints, the roadblocks to change, and the need to acquire early insight into the politics of an institution in order to bring about any change. Ann shared her expertise and knowledge about collegiality in the college and issues of power and control in relation to status in program design and development. Brian brought up the notion of the need for new people to conform. "Otherwise," he said, "they're not wanted."
>
> This is the first time there has been such an informed and lively discussion around the issue of institutional politics and the need to be aware of and learn institutional norms as part of the whole socialization process. It will be interesting to watch that develop. We are halfway through year one now. Before there wasn't much interest beyond the walls of the classroom. Now we are starting to see the classroom walls being pushed back. (field notes, January 1990)

The teachers continued to ask questions which took them farther afield from the classroom—questions about budget, how to make curricular changes, and how to strengthen links with industry and the community beyond the college. As time went on there was even less, indeed very little, talk situated in or confined to the classroom. A good illustration of this point is found in the first group session of the second year. The first part of this meeting was spent planning session topics for the year. The teachers generated a list of possible topics and then placed them in order of priority. Institutional micropolitics was ranked number one and classroom-specific issues came up last!

> Karen made a request that really changed the whole nature of the discussion. She requested information or a workshop session on school-community relations, particularly on funding issues. I think this is a critical incident in her development and certainly in the development of the teachers, considering the response she received to that request. Here we see the teachers pushing back the classroom walls even further, wanting to move out into the community and trying to establish, maintain, and encourage school-community links.
>
> Karen commented, "Last year I was just worried about teaching. Now I'm interested in changing the program." A very critical statement, I think. "How do we get things to change?" she asked. Karen talked about her growing interest in learning how the system works and how to get things

done. "Perhaps," she said, "someone from [the college] could explain how [the college] works." There was a lively discussion and no more suggestions after this.

   After a rank-ordering of the five topics suggested for workshop sessions, it came down to a decision between "micropolitics" and a workshop on group work for the first to be held. There was consensus, in the end, that micropolitics was definitely the topic of interest, especially over the long term. It was perceived to be quite essential. Particularly, there was interest in budgeting—how the budget works and how decisions are made. (field notes, September 1991)

The boundaries of community continued to be extended; the circle ever widened. In most of the last individual interviews and certainly in the final group discussion of the second year, the entire talk was located in the broader community college venue. Often the teachers returned to their previous experiences of occupational community and drew parallels between the previous and present contexts. And so, after a two-year period of induction/ socialization to a new professional venue, the teachers, for the most part, had developed a concept of community that has degrees of continuity with that defined within the previous vocational context.

Karen: It makes me feel slightly disappointed. I think, at any job when you start you think, "This is going to be it. This is going to be wonderful." And, all of a sudden, reality sets in and you say, "You know, there are the same problems in every job. Whether you're a carpenter, or whether you're in the education field, or whether you're in the television field, the same problems are there. Some people do the job well and you have to work with those people."

   I'm a little surprised in that I didn't expect there to be a lack of interest [among the senior colleagues] in their own professional development. I just assumed that you would always want to be better, especially in the education field, because there are new minds coming in every year and it's such a changing field. Because you're teaching, that field is constantly growing but also because you're being challenged every year from young minds and different people. You're not around the same people. I would think that you would want to be constantly on the ball and that everybody would naturally be gung-ho. There are people who may not be as excited about [ongoing professional development]. I guess I'm surprised that there's no push for it to continue.

   When I got my first job after I graduated from college, I knew I wanted to be in television. I used to tell myself I wanted to be a producer because I like making decisions. I like organizing and I like working with a large group of people. I do like being the boss, if you'd like to put it that way, not for the title so much, but because when I have an idea I see working, I have to be the boss to see it followed through. And that's what I used to think I wanted to do.

So I saw this job—after being in television and not necessarily being the producer—as an opportunity to make decisions that had some meaning, that had some influence on other people's lives, that people could benefit from—not like with a television show where they would say, "Well, that was a good show but it's gone." But maybe someone would say, "That was a great teacher" or, "That was a great course I took." (interview, January 1991)

Facilitating Teacher Development

As we followed the teachers through their transition period, it became apparent that the process of redefining what it means to be a teacher and their developing sense of new professional identity were contextually dependent on their developing notions of professional community. This leads us to suspect that in order for teachers to have opportunities to realize their individually defined personal/professional potential, teaching and development need to be defined, interpreted, and facilitated within a broader institutional context. When, in the context of professional development, the boundaries of a teacher's professional community are pushed back to encompass the entire workplace context and attention is paid to the micropolitical and contextual realities of school life, it seems to us that then teachers have a better chance of becoming truly empowered. In other words, teacher development in its broadest sense depends on teachers having access to professional knowledge beyond just the personal, practical, and pedagogical.

It is in the broader institutional arenas that the teachers see both major frustrations and the possibilities for significant change. The frustration and anger about "the system" become a rising tide within the transcripts of the meetings. Take the following statement by Jim who describes his new job as a "dream come true."

> I love my job, I really do, but constantly institutional politics intercede. People trying to build empires with hidden agendas and all the bullshit shouldn't be getting in the way between me and the student. It ticks me right off. I've never been good at politics. I don't want to be good at politics. I just want to do the damned job. But it gets to the point where it's almost impossible to be able to do it properly.
> There are people who just do what they want to do and that's it. It keeps them happy. Sometimes it's bloody sad. In fact, to me, that's depressing because that spark of enthusiasm just gets smaller and smaller and smaller. And in the end it's going to be extinguished. What do you do? Do you

fight the system until you just end up on the floor or do you roll along with it? (discussion, May 1991)

In this quote, and indeed within the testimonies carried within this paper, we see the richness of pursuing detailed accounts of the life histories of teachers. The grounding of our data in these historical contexts, both personal and micropolitical, offers alternative insights into pedagogical and curricular rationales. At least as importantly, the eloquence of the teachers' voices exhorts us to develop new modes of teacher education which give new respect to the personal and political realities of teachers' lives.

We recognize that in exposing the reader to a good deal of unedited transcripts of teachers' voices we have imposed an extra task. So much of our research normally comprises researcher's commentary—it, therefore, may appear almost a "dereliction of duty" to provide so much "raw data" and so little commentary. But research paradigms and our expectations of them are social constructs. Moreover, they are social constructs which have, unwittingly or not, silenced teachers' voices and teachers' lives. The process of rehabilitating the teachers' voices is likely to be painstaking and contested. It is not by chance that paradigms have silenced the teacher, but without such rehabilitation we believe much of the research on teachers will continue to be as arid and decontextualized, irrelevant for the teachers it so systematically silences and disenfranchises. As we have written elsewhere

> The kind of theory we are searching for would not be the sole prerogative of the university scholar. Our educational study should be more collaborative, more broad-based, publically available. But it should be possible too for us to make it interesting, critical, vital and useful. (Goodson and Walker 1991, 203–4)

This chapter marks our tentative search for such a mode of study and reportage in work that is currently underway. We recognize we are at the first stage of a long journey. Behind this journey, however, lies a clear value position which embraces the notion of the teacher as potentially the central change in restructuring schooling. To quote from Lawrence Stenhouse's memorial plaque, "It is teachers who, in the end, will change the world of the school by understanding it."

References

Apple, M. 1986. *Teachers and texts*. London: Routledge & Kegan Paul.

Ball, S. J., and Goodson, I. F., eds. 1985. *Teachers' lives and careers*. London: Falmer Press.

Britzman, D. 1986. Cultural myths in the making of a teacher: Biography and social structure in education. *Harvard Educational Review* 56: 442–56.

Bullough, R. V., Jr., Knowles, J. G. and Crow, N. A. 1991. *Emerging as a teacher*. London: Routledge and Kegan Paul.

Burke, P. J., Fessler, R., and Christensen, J. C. 1984. *Teacher career stages: Implications for staff development*. Bloomington, Ind.: Phi Delta Kappa Educational Foundation.

Butt, R. L. and Raymond, D. 1987. Arguments for using qualitative approaches in understanding teacher thinking: The case for biography. *Journal for Curriculum Theorizing* 7, no. 2: 62–93.

Clandinin, D. J. 1986. *Classroom practice: Teacher images in action*. London: Falmer Press.

Cole, A. L. 1990. *Teachers' experienced knowledge: A continuing study*. Paper presented at the annual meeting of the American Education Research Association, April, Boston. RIE# ED318733.

———. 1991. Relationships in the workplace: Doing what comes naturally? *Teaching and Teacher Education* 7, no 5/6; 415–426.

Connelly, F. M., and Clandinin, D. J. 1988. *Teachers as curriculum planners: Narratives of experience*. New York: Teachers College Press.

Connelly, F. M. and Clandinin, D. J. 1990. Stories of experience and narrative inquiry. *Educational Researcher* 14, no 5: 2–14.

Fuller, F. F. and Brown, O. H. 1975. Becoming a teacher. In *Teacher Education*, Seventy-fourth yearbook of the National Society for the Study of Education. Chicago: University of Chicago Press.

Goodson, I. F. 1981. LIfe histories and studies of schooling. *Interchange* 11, no. 4.

———. 1988. *The making of curriculum: Collected essays*. London: Falmer Press.

———. 1989. Sponsoring the teacher's voice. *Cambridge Journal of Education* 21, no 1: 35–45.

———. 1990. Studying curriculum: Towards a social constructionist prospective. *Journal of Curriculum Studies* (July/August): 299–312.

Goodson, I. F., and Walker, R. 1991. *Biography, identity and schooling*. London: Falmer Press.

Grossman, P. 1990. What are we talking about anyway? Subject matter knowledge of secondary English teachers. In *Advancs in research on teaching*, Vol. 2: *Teachers' knowledge of subject matter as it relates to their teaching practice*, edited by J. Brophy. Greenwich, Conn.: JAI Press.

Gudmundsdottir, S. 1990. Values in pedagogical context knowledge. *Journal of Teacher Education* 41, no. 3.

Huberman, M. 1989. The professional life cycle of teachers. *Teachers College Record* 91, no. 1: 31–51.

Knowles, J. G. 1992. Models for understanding preservice and beginning teachers' biographies: Illustrations from case studies. In *Studying teachers' lives*, edited by I. Goodson. London: Routledge.

Knowles, J. G., and Holt-Reynolds, D. 1991. Shaping pedagogies through personal histories in preservice teacher education. *Teachers College Record* 93, no 1: 87–113.

Shulman, L. S. 1986. Those who understand: Knowledge growth in teaching. *Educational Researcher* 15: 4–14.

————. 1987. Knowledge and teaching: Foundations of the new reform. *Harvard Educational Review* 57, no. 1: 1–22.

Zeichner, K. M., and Grant, C. 1981. Biography and social structure in the socialization of student teachers: A reexamination of the pupil control ideologies of student teachers. *Journal of Education for Teaching* 3: 299–314.

Zeichner, K. M., and Tabachnick, B. R. 1985. The development of teacher perspectives: Social strategies and institutional control in the socialization of beginning teachers. *Journal of Education for Teaching* 11: 1–25.

5

Personal Narratives for School Change
in Navajo Settings

Daniel McLaughlin

Introduction

In the movie *Dances with Wolves* Lieutenant John Dunbar heads west during the Civil War era to discover the frontier and meet the American Indian. He settles into an abandoned fort and soon learns that he is only a short distance from a band of Sioux. Native warriors stumble across him one day, but decide that Dunbar must have special powers to be so near them. So they let him be. They are fearful but curious, as is he. In time, a relationship of mutual respect between Dunbar and the group of Sioux unfolds. Negotiating difficult cross-cultural terrain, both sides come to recognize an essential humanity in each other, in stark contrast to encroaching violence from the east that, "as multi-fold as the stars," as Dunbar knows all along and painfully reveals to his hosts, is soon to overrun the Sioux universe.

Similar notions of difference and harm are woven through the novel *Ceremony* by Leslie Marmon Silko (1977), set on the Laguna and Navajo Indian reservations immediately following World War II. Through the eyes of a half-breed war veteran, readers see the results of the Anglo conquest that Lieutenant Dunbar and the Sioux band had feared. One story line follows the veteran's quest for self-understanding—eventually to be realized through ceremony—amidst pervasive cultural conflict and psychological instability. Another story line describes parallel quests in the mythology of Laguna Pueblo. Both lines converge midway through the book when Silko describes the genesis of evil and thus of her war veteran's angst. The setting is in a

My deepest thanks go to Robin Burand, Donna Deyhle, Andrew Gitlin, William Leap, Robert W. Rhodes, and William Tierney for their helpful comments on earlier drafts of this chapter.

previous world at a conference of witches, who attempt to out-perform one another's most heinous deeds. "That was nothing," each says in turn, "watch this!" One especially dark entity steps forward with a story about Europeans' encroachment on American Indians' land. Once told, the story lets loose forces that cannot be called back:

> *They fear*
> *They fear the world.*
> *They destroy what they fear.*
> *They fear themselves . . .*
> *They will fear what they find*
> *They will fear the people*
> *They will kill what they fear.*
> *Entire villages will be wiped out*
> *They will slaughter whole tribes.* (p. 142–43)

Both *Dances with Wolves* and *Ceremony* alert Indians and non-Indians alike to a cultural politics in contemporary reservation settings. That is, on one level, they speak to culture—to differences of values, preferences, and beliefs documented in the ethnographic literature as a series of overlapping divergences that distinguish mainstream Anglo-American from American Indian societies: sacred versus positivistic thinking; interrelatedness versus compartmentalization; cyclical versus linear concepts of time; closed versus open society; contrasting views of work and economics; and contrasting views of authority, consensus, and individual autonomy (Benally 1988; Harris 1990; Lamphere 1977; and Witherspoon 1977). On another level, the movie and the book speak to social structure—to ways in which these differences shape, and are shaped by, social, political, ideological, and economic dimensions that constitute primary categories for understanding what goes on in American Indian settings. They reveal American Indian life not in terms of unitary, monolithic sets of rules and beliefs, but as an interplay of cultural values and overlapping political processes of struggle, accommodation, and resistance—a dialectical complexity of meanings generated from individuals' experience and social structures that the notion of cultural politics provides (Giroux & McLaren 1986: 228–29).

My aim is to show how a cultural politics in contemporary American Indian communities organizes perceptions of what is good, bad, true, and false about individuals' actions, beliefs, motives, morality, and intelligence. Further, the purpose is to show how these politics have failed to figure consciously in the development of curriculum and school programs for American Indian children. For, in general, the production of school knowledge and education of students in American Indian classrooms, consciously and otherwise, has served to defuse the stylized complexities of difference portrayed in *Dances with Wolves* and *Ceremony*, much less the pervasive injustices of everyday American Indian life (see, for instance, Crow Dog 1991; Dorris 1989; and Erdrich 1984). Pedagogical solutions have overwhelmingly stressed skills, to be taught one after another, sequenced according to cognitive complexity, and fundamentally removed from the politically charged contexts within which any pedagogy and curriculum development for American Indian children take place.

The work with teachers described in this chapter is premised on the need to orient American Indian students to examine in detail the social, cultural, political, ideological, and economic dimensions of life in reservation communities as a crucial first step toward the development of voice. By voice, following Andrew Gitlin, (chapter 3) I refer to a twofold process of speaking out: first, speaking out publicly; then doing so as a form of protest that leads to actions that contest marginalizing, silencing arrangements in schools in particular and society as a whole. For teachers in any setting but especially those working on American Indian reservations, the development of students' voice requires a fundamental shift away from normative school practice that tends to position students as objects, toward student- and community-focused instructional techniques that orient students as subjects—as authors of their existence and producers of knowledge and valued curriculum.

If teachers are to orient their students to produce knowledge in critically oriented fashion, it is important for them to experience processes of knowledge production firsthand and to recognize for themselves the politically charged nature of such work. They must recognize the efficacy of cultural-political approaches to understandings of schooling, language, and literacy. Rather than view culture apolitically, as functional aspects of society or as sets of values and beliefs, the goal is to see culture in terms of cultural politics; first, in terms of values, preferences, and beliefs; then in terms of the individual's interactions with dominant truths and power formations that marginalize and silence subordinate groups in society. In so doing, the meanings of education and school knowledge can be seen to form, and be formed by, political conditions that shape the functions and topics of school learning.

An important starting point for this work involves personal narratives. Through the production of these texts, educators in this project have started to reorganize literacy and language-arts instruction for Navajo students in isolated reservation settings. The teachers have used the texts to analyze their received circumstances, pose reflective questions about the nature of work in schools, chart courses for language and literacy program development, and reorient what their students do in the classroom. In these ways, personal histories and stories ground cultural politics in concrete teaching practice. They enable teachers to examine a host of contradictions inherent to personal growth, educational research, and work in schools, and encourage the use of alternative teaching strategies that facilitate the development of students' voice.

Five sections of this chapter follow. First, I outline theoretical assumptions about knowledge, power, school curriculum, and voice that underpin the project. Then I briefly describe the background setting in which the project has taken place. Next comes the heart of the chapter—personal narratives in the form of one teacher's interview and another teacher's story that work from critical understandings of cultural conflict, choice, self-identity, self-esteem, and voice. The following section measures the narratives against critical notions of cultural politics. I conclude with remarks about implications for K–12 curriculum development for Navajo and other minority language learners.

Theoretical Assumptions

The project described here works from a critical sociology of education that has sought to elucidate connections between knowledge, power, and school curriculum. In this section, I comment briefly on major contributions to this orientation and identify formative questions that its adherents have posed. I point out how the orientation scaffolds a pedagogy of cultural politics and empowerment. In so doing, I rely upon the work of Henry Giroux, Michael Apple, and other critical theorists, and explain how teachers' personal narratives present important possibilities for translating critical theory into classroom teaching practices that aim to help students whose voices have been silenced and lives have been marginalized.

Since the early 1970s, a number of alternative educational theories have taken as their starting point the problematic relationship between school knowledge and power. Henry Giroux (1981 and 1988) and Michael Apple (1982, 1987, and 1990) have been at the forefront of this work. In developing a critical sociology of education and school knowledge, each has argued against the claim of conservative and liberal educational theorists alike that school knowledge and school culture are rationally, objectively ordered. Instead, they have shown how schooling, through the hidden curriculum, is shaped by relations of dominance and subordination in the workplace that reproduce inequities in schools in particular and in society as a whole. Their work has launched formidable critiques of a still-dominant functionalist epistemology that reduces teaching and learning to the transmission of so-called objective forms of knowledge fundamentally removed from considerations of conflict and power. The framework that Giroux, Apple, and others have developed became the basis for new models of curriculum theorizing, with a new set of preliminary questions to ask about school curriculum:

- Whose knowledge counts as school curriculum?
- How is this knowledge organized?

- What are the underlying values, assumptions, and beliefs that structure school curriculum?
- What kind of cultural system does this knowledge work from and legitimate?
- Whose interests are served by the organization and legitimation of school curriculum?

These starting points have given rise to new models that analyze schools as sites that reproduce through the hidden curriculum social relations of dominance and subordination found in the workplace (Bowles & Gintis 1976) that provide different classes with the cultural capital—the requisite knowledge, values, and skills—needed for occupying stratified positions in society (Bernstein 1982; Bourdieu & Passeron 1977; Wilcox, 1982); and that subordinate minority cultures, values, and social relations to the ideological imperatives of dominant society (Grant & Sleeter 1986; MacLeod 1988; Willis 1977). What is crucial from these models is a basic notion of critique. From them comes the core understanding that dominant school culture functions not only to legitimate the interests and values of dominant social groups, but also to dis-confirm the lived experiences, values, and cultural and linguistic competencies of subordinate groups.

Underpinning this work is a dialectical understanding of power that not only provides an important descriptive lens but also points toward *what teachers can actually do* to transform classrooms from sites of cultural reproduction to arenas of resistance, empowerment, and social transformation. Functionalist accounts of power tend to understand it as an either/or proposition, one that works primarily as a negative force to dominate, inhibit, silence, and deny. In actuality, however, the processes and effects of power are infinitely more complicated than an either/or model implies. Power is not a structural, monolithic entity to be seized, shared, assigned, or denied; it represents a convergence of tactics specific to time and place and dialectically constructive of positive and negative moments. As a negative moment, power positions the individual as object and reproduces hierarchical relations of domination and subordination. But as a positive moment, power positions the individual as subject and provides for opportunities for critical reflection, resistance, struggle, and empowerment (Foucault 1980: 119; Giroux 1981: 121).

That power and social control can dialectically serve emancipatory as well as coercive purposes has important consequences for the reconceptualization of schooling, curriculum, and work as cultural politics. Power as dialectic moves us beyond reductive accounts of schooling, perceived either as an all-encompassing instrument of domination as or as an empty vessel waiting to be filled with enlightened, critically reflective praxis. The concept enables us to recognize power and knowledge as co-joined and thus always as representative of an opportunity to be seized. In so doing, it provides for school practices that allow teachers to produce curriculum as forms of speaking out that contest marginalizing, silencing forms of social control and validate the experiences that students bring with them to the classroom.

For this project, what the dialectic of power implies is the idea that schooling is all about the telling of people's stories, and that these stories, if they are to include and enable all of the students rather than a privileged few, must seek to incorporate the multiple narratives and histories that constitute difference in a minority language setting. Of crucial significance here, then, are ways that power can be transformed to uncover sedimented narratives and experiences, and that ultimately permit the silenced voices of members of nonmainstream, marginalized social groups to be used. We turn to such voices and naming strategies following a background description of the project.

Background

The project has been based at Red Gap School, a K–6 public institution that serves 240 children in a community of 1500 on the north-central Navajo Indian reservation.[1] Nearly all of the students at Red Gap are from Navajo families whose annual income is less than one-third of the state average. Against an arid red-rock landscape, area residents subsist on livestock raising, weaving, farming, and welfare. Uranium mining flourished in the 1950s and 1960s but at present, no local industry exists, and levels of unemployment are high. Estimates range from 35 to 60 percent. Beyond two restaurants, two trading posts, and one motel in an adjacent community just off the reservation, all of which cater to tourists who pass along the area's single paved highway, the nearest center of commerce on the reservation is forty-five miles to the south; "town" off the reservation with its supermarkets and malls, where prices are cheaper and many families prefer to shop, is more than 140 miles away.

The institution is not unlike many public and Bureau of Indian Affairs schools on the Navajo Reservation. The turnover rate of teachers at the end of the year is high, student achievement levels are low, and curriculum planning is at best haphazard. For instance, the attrition levels for certified teachers—who tend to be Anglos from outside of the community—for the past five years at Red Gap has averaged more than 35 percent. Within a recent three-year span, three different individuals served as principal. During this same period, Red Gap students' achievement levels on standardized tests of reading and language have been the lowest in the state. Moreover, even though one-third of the students come to school as native speakers of Navajo (while the rest come fluent in Indian English), nearly all instruction takes place in mainstream English. All of these difficulties are compounded

---

[1]Red Gap is a pseudonym.

by the fact that at Red Gap no language arts and literacy curriculum has existed whatsoever apart from the mainstream logic embedded in disconnected series of basal readers.

All the same, there has been a rich potential for change at this institution. Nearly two-thirds of all Red Gap staff members, certified and noncertified, are community-based Navajos. The average tenure of these individuals is nearly a decade. In all likelihood, many will remain at the school for the rest of their professional careers. Because of the presence of the Navajo teachers, their groundedness in the school and local community, and the consequent rich potential for bilingual-bicultural program development, in the fall of 1990, after having moved from a school principalship on the Navajo reservation into higher education at the University of Utah, I developed a research connection with Red Gap and targeted program-development efforts with this core group. I sought to affirm what these teachers already know about teaching and program development; to broaden their perspectives and abilities; and to encourage them to frame what they do critically, so that they best enable their students to develop academic skills, theories of themselves, and critical understandings of the world.

Toward these ends, in the winter of 1991, I taught an on-site introductory class on multicultural education, critical theory, and Navajo-English language curriculum development to twelve Red Gap staff members—seven Navajos, five Anglos. I began by asking class participants to develop personal histories of themselves. The assignment was to reflect upon earlier student experiences to discover how these might influence ways for teaching Red Gap children. Moves, divorces, inability to find jobs elsewhere, and altruism punctuated Anglos' personal histories; family responsibilities, family problems, difficulties with English, participation in the Mormon home placement program, and difficulties in K-12 and postsecondary schooling were themes that punctuated the Navajos' texts.[2] I then asked class members to develop "first look" statements about program development work that needed to be done at the school and in the district. Three-quarters of the teachers analyzed the unique language needs of the native language- and Indian English-speaking student body, and decried the lack of an appropriate language arts and literacy program for their students.

Groundwork was laid for curriculum development in the summer of 1991 with a team of seven Navajo teachers from Red Gap and a linguist well

---

[2] The Mormon home placement program is formally known as the Indian Student Placement Program, and has been run since 1954 by the Church of Jesus Christ of Latter-Day Saints to match American Indian youths with foster Anglo-American families, educate these children in public school settings away from their home reservation communities, and bring them spiritually into the Mormon Church. By 1985, more than 22,000 American Indian youths, a significant number of them Navajo, had participated in this program (Deyhle 1991).

versed in the descriptive and pragmatic features of American Indian English, all of whom probed further into the curriculum needs of Navajo learners at Red Gap School.[3] The work proceeded during the following school year in the form of two graduate seminars on language and literacy program development with three-quarters of the Red Gap teaching staff, along with an additional ten teachers from two other K-6 and two secondary-level schools that mainly serve Navajo learners elsewhere in the district. All together, twenty-two teachers participated in the effort.

Rather than merely read about critical theory and literacy program development, I proposed that the teachers produce narratives in ways that would not only allow for critical, iterative analysis, but also encourage them to have their students use the alternative classroom methods employed in the analysis and production of the stories. Having analyzed story-production approaches (Dewey [1938] 1963; Graves 1988a and 1988b; Harste, Short, & Burke 1988; McLaughlin 1989; and Wigginton 1986 and 1989), the teachers brainstormed what sorts of products they would create before deciding to produce a book that would include a successful in-class interview "What Teachers Need to Know about Navajo Students to Teach Them Well," successful out-of-class interviews, "My Most Powerful Experience in Schools," and self-generated fictional texts linked thematically to the first two sections of the volume. We would collect, write, and publish these texts in book form—for ourselves, our students, and our respective school communities.

I was more than a disinterested observer as the teachers wrestled with what sort of book to produce. While recognizing that the teachers ought to decide for themselves what to create, for what purposes, and for whom, I attempted to insert a critical agenda when asked for guidance on the second out-of-class assignment. I hoped that the interviews would connect to the politicized terrain in which they toil, and suggested that the teachers record and transcribe community members' thoughts on their most powerful experiences in school. I hypothesized that the teachers' interviewees would describe in graphic detail elements of the cultural and political landscape within which schooling, work, and life takes place at Red Gap and nearby reservation communities; the interviews would also provide illuminating comparisons between English- and Navajo-based story structure.[4]

To frame these efforts from a cultural-political perspective, we probed narrative aspects of *Dances with Wolves* and *Ceremony*. we developed story lines for the movie and the book; analyzed school curriculum as the telling

---

[3]See Leap & McLaughlin (1991) and Leap (1993) for descriptions of focused discussions of the language-related needs of Red Gap students with the Red Gap teachers.

[4]The idea of researching individuals' most powerful experiences in school is borrowed from Perry Gilmore, who has done similar program and curriculum development work with Native Alaskan teachers and students at the University of Alaska, Fairbanks.

of someone's story; and saw curriculum development as a process of producing stories that others tell (Egan 1986). We examined the necessity to go beyond the mere reporting of events and to appraise critically all that stories entail, especially ones that relate closely to Navajos and other American Indians. For these reasons, we compared and contrasted *Dances With Wolves* and *Ceremony* to develop criteria against which we would measure our own personal histories and the personal narratives of others. Such criteria devised by the teachers included notions that cultural conflict marks relations between the two races; that choices available to actors in the two stories are culturally determined; that Anglos' and Navajos' quests for knowledge and self-identity are culturally distinct; and that Anglos and Navajos struggle for voice in culturally unique ways. As I hope to show in the next section, these criteria figured prominently in the production of the teachers' personal texts.

Personal Narratives

The teachers produced twenty-four interviews and sixteen stories. The interviews were edited by the teachers with the input of their informants and produced along with the fictional texts, many of which were highly autobiographical, all of which connected to themes discussed throughout the two seminars pertaining to cultural conflict, choice, self-identity, and voice. Collectively, the out-of-class interviews and the stories, along with an in-class interview conducted by the whole group, formed sections of *Stories of School*, which was produced in book form and disseminated to all of the teachers and to the librarians in their respective schools.

With cultural conflict, choice, self-identity, self-esteem, and voice as analytic lenses, so that they could master interviewing, taping, and transcribing techniques before doing work out-of-class, the teachers first conducted an in-class interview with a local Navajo teacher on what teachers need to know about Navajo kids. In transcribing what this person said and noting how he expressed himself—in Indian English, the language of the home and playground for many Red Gap students—the teachers recognized a central tension to the effort: one purpose was to give voice to the informant, not to change what he said and how he said it; but another purpose was for clarity. In transcribing the interview, the teachers edited wherever the informant was not clear, but strove to measure that clarity against the need for maintaining authenticity of voice. With the criteria that underpin *Dances with Wolves* and *Ceremony* in mind, the teachers then set off individually to do the second assignment, an interview with a community person on his or her most powerful experience in school.

***

One Teacher's Interview

Rather than highlight small portions of each of the interviews and stories, I have excerpted major portions of one interview and included one whole story. I have done so to describe as thickly as possible the actual process of personal narrative development that the authors of *Stories of School* followed. My aim is not to generalize from the content of the two texts; rather, it is to show how the *process* of personal narrative writing has allowed project participants to begin making connections between knowledge, power, and school curriculum, and thus to see the work that they do with children in schools as a form of cultural politics. The selection that follows, a female Anglo teacher's interview with a Navajo woman who describes her school experiences off of the Navajo reservation, speaks powerfully to issues of cultural conflict, choice, self-identity, self-esteem, and voice that the teachers utilized to organize and publish the interviews. The text is rendered in Navajo English in verbatim fashion with minimal editing by the interviewer and me.

Important School Experiences
by Robin Burand

I interviewed Susie Burch.[5] She's of the Bit'áani and Todachíinii clans. Susie is from around Bitterwater, Arizona, but resides presently at Red Gap, Utah. As a young wife, mother of three, and a businesswoman, Susie has little spare time, but does enjoy writing stories of her childhood as well as fiction. Susie was brought up in a traditional Navajo home except for some years spent in foster homes in California. Though moving very graciously and competently in Bilagáana [Anglo] society, Susie maintains strong ties to Navajo ways and beliefs. Due to this balance she has created in her life, I was interested in what part school experiences had played in this.

Would you share maybe some of your first experiences going to school?

Well, my first deal is just getting to school. Just when you live all Navajo culture and you first start school and first see the brick buildings, you don't know what's inside them buildings. Especially when you've only been to trading post twice in your life before school. It's when you get there you see these long lines of kids with their mamas. All the kids throwin fits and cryin, hangin onto their mom. And your mom's standin there beside you sayin, "You can't be like them. You can't cry cause you're big girl now. You gotta go to school. Don't, don't shame me at the beginning. You gotta make me proud." And you see them women running around dressed so far different than your mama. . . .

They was Navajo women, but they wasn't dressed traditional. They

---

[5]At the interviewer's and interviewee's request, real personal names are used here.

didn't have squaw skirts. They didn't wear buns. They didn't smell like sheep camp. They had perfume. . . . It was the first time I've ever seen Navajo women that dressed like Bilagáanas. It was kind of very different to see Navajo women not dressed in your mind like how they should look because you've never seen it. They are different and your mama's standing there going, "I want you to be like them. I want you to have a job cause I always wanted to go to school, but my mama wouldn't let me. But I can want it for you, and you can have it for me and make me proud"

Your mother wanted you to go to school?

It was something that she wanted. She didn't get it, so as we got bigger, she wanted it for us. She wanted us to live that life. She wanted us to have things and not just have the rugs and the sheep for income. Because, back then there wasn't general assistance. Welfare were not common. I guess some women got it. I don't know who, but it wasn't her. She didn't get none of that. My dad worked. But, she stayed home with the sheep and did all that. That's a very hard life to live because you gotta go out in the cold and tend to it. Heat waves, cold, whatever, rain or shine, you gotta let them buggers out. But that's not what she wanted for us. She wanted us to have things.

So she took all of us to school, and she dropped me off there. Like I said, that was the first time I've seen inside a brick building that was not a trading post. The ceilings were so high, and the rooms so big and so empty. It was so cold. There was no warmth. Not as far as "brrrr I'm cold," but in a sense of emotional cold. Kind of an emptiness, when you're hanging onto your mom's skirt and tryin so hard not to cry. And you know it just seems so lonely and so empty. Then when you get up to your turn, she thumbprints the paper and she leaves and you watch her go out the big, metal doors. The whole thing was a cold experience. The doors were metal and they even had this big window, wires running through it. And these women didn't smile or nothin. You watch your mama go down the sidewalk, actually it's the first time I seen a sidewalk, and you see her get in the truck, walk down the sidewalks. You see her get in the truck and the truck starts moving and all the home smell goes with it. You see it all leaving.

Then them women takes you by the hand and takes you into another room and they take down your bun. And the first thing they do is cut off your bangs, and you been told the whole time that you never cut you hair because that's your life. And that's the first thing them women does is cut off your bangs. You see that long, black hair drop, and it's like, they take out your heart, and they give you this cold thing that beats inside you. Now you're gonna be just like them. You're gonna be cold. You're never gonna be happy or have that warm feeling and attitude towards life anymore. That's what it feels like, like taking your heart out and putting in a cold river pebble. It just felt empty.

And then they make you wash, take a shower. Even that was weird cause, you know, ain't never seen running water before! There's a block room, this little square room and you never seen light before. There's light and this little room that don't have no windows, then you see warm water coming out of the walls. You want to see the top of that building to see if there's a pond of water up there. Then they give you a small cup of clear stuff that you put in your hair, soap, you know. That's another deal, when the only kind of soap you've used in your hair is yucca root. And they give you a small cup of clear lookin stuff and it fills your hair up with soap, you know and you think, wow if my mama ever seen this she'd never have to beat another yucca root for the rest of her life.

Another thing was the toilets. You go squat in the boonies, you know. But then you say I gotta go potty, and you start headin for the doors. But they say, "No, no, no. Over here." And they make you go in another little room with this white bowl with clean, clear water in it, and tell you to go in there. Go potty! Dirty that pretty, white bowl and that clean water. Now, you think, guy! My momma'd spank me if I ever did that in a clean dish. And it sits so high. It's kind of fun. Your foot slips, and that grouchy woman's standin out there, she don't wanna help you even though she knows you never seen it. You don't know what it's about. It makes you wonder what the heck's wrong with mama. She wants me to be like her? You know, especially when she washed your hair, she kinda jerks you around. She don't have that nice, gentle touch. Jerks you around everywhere.

When you come out of the shower and you leave your squaw skirt and your blouse right there at the shower door, when you come out of the shower, it's gone. You don't get to see your squaw skirt again. Your hair strings gone, they cut your hair, now your squaw skirt. They take from the beginning. When you first walk in there, they just take everything that you're about. They just jerk it away from you. They don't even ask how you feel about it. They never even tell you you'll be fine. They never tell what they're gonna do, why they're doing it. They barely speak to you. They take everything away from you. Then you think, gaaah, mama must really be whackers. She wants me to be like them women? They're so rude, so cold. And then, every time you don't know what they're doing, they laugh at you. They kinda yell at you. They jerk you around. It was never what I wanted to be. I never wanted to be like them. But my mom wanted me to be like them. But as I got older, I found out that you don't have to be like them. You can have a nice world and everything that mama wanted, but you don't have to be cold.

As the year went on, I got more and more comfortable with the whole deal. And then Christmas was the best because we got to go home. All the parents came. Some of the kids' parents came before mine cause my dad worked so he couldn't come till after he got off work. It was about dark before he came, but he's never ever looked as good as he did that night. To this day I still remember what he looked like. I can just picture him, just clear as a bell like it was yesterday. That was the best he ever looked. He called me, and I ran up and he tossed me up in the air. He never ever felt so good. That was the best he ever felt, and the best he ever looked when he came to get me. He was so tall, so handsome. He had on a western-cut jacket with silver-tipped collar. And he had silver-tipped boots and silver heels. The back of the heels had silver on it. And he had on his silver hat band and this big bolo tie. Boy, did he look good. I've always thought I had the most handsome dad at that boarding school. Nobody's dad looked as good as mine.

Then when Christmas vacation was over, I wasn't ready to go back. Some kids didn't come back. I says, "I came back, why couldn't they come back?" It was lonely all over again. But it was easier to readjust than to get shocked the first go around. It wasn't quite as bad. We cried at night, but it was OK. It was easier. Then the second year was not bad at all. We knew, cause we'd lived through the whole year. Back then you didn't go home every weekend. Christmas was the only time you went home during the school year, then summer. Summer seemed so short. Second year I went back, and it was easier.

And then I went up to fourth grade at boarding school. My dad had a stroke, and my mom couldn't come pick us up on Christmas or any of that. So she sent me away on Mormon placement program. Fifth grade, I went to California, and they placed me with this Samoan family. Now I know how Bilagáanas feel when we all giggle and talk Navajo while they're around. Boy, they didn't talk English. They talked Samoan all the time. And they was big people. That's when I learned about cities cause we lived about five blocks down from Disneyland. We never went to Disneyland cause they just wasn't fun type of people. Matter of fact their house was as cold as the boarding school. And the mom acted kinda like them dorm maids.

I found out that there's all kinds of people in this world. They don't have to be them more modern Navajo women that was mean. There's all types of people. And that's when I started thinking. That's when I realized what my mom was talking about, to better your life. Because now I live in a city, and some people live in two-story houses, some are in two-story houses with basements, even three floors in one house. Then I started wanting. I seen all the things they had that you could have. It lasted longer even though they'd had it for years. They took care of it. They'd budget and save.

Anyway, my Samoan family, the mom was a nurse and the dad worked with some kinda somethin. I don't know, he was one of them blue-collar workers that wore them janitor outfit. I never asked him because he was always so grouchy. They never hardly ever talked to me. They never asked me if I did my homework, or if I studied, or if I had any homework. They just kinda ignored me. I just stayed there.

I'm sure glad that year was up and then the second year I got Bob and Nancy. I had them, they kept me all the way through my senior year. Then they had to move to Oregon during Christmas vacation, and the placement program said that they couldn't take me. I had to come home. We figured if I came home, they'd buy my bus ticket, and I'd go back up to Oregon.

Wrong! By then my mom and dad says that if we let you go you're never gonna come home. Boy, then I resented them. I thought in my mind, they made me go to school. They made me go on this placement program. I didn't have no say so about it. They didn't ask me if I wanted to go on a placement program. They just put me in and told me to do my best, that I better not just mess around and goof it all up or else they wouldn't let me go back that last year. They told me, if we let you go this time, you're never gonna come home. You're just gonna leave, and this will be the last time we see you other than maybe once every two, three years, if you visit us at all. This is the last of your childhood, they says. We're just gonna see the last little bit of your childhood cause we missed it all. And they actually did. They wasn't there when I lost my first tooth. They wasn't there when I went out on my first date. They missed out on the whole deal from when I was seven years old.

They says they did it all for me. They gave it all up just so I could better my life. That's a lot for a parent to do for a kid. What they basically done was give me up for me. At the time, I resented them and thought, they always says they done this all for me, and now they're gonna mess up my last part. They're gonna just take the last part away. I probably would have never gone home, now that I look at it. It was true, because my foster parents called me a lot the first few years after I didn't go back. We stayed in close contact. They said that after Oregon when I finished high school, they was gonna move to Salt Lake so I could go to BYU. But if I'd gone to BYU, I surely woulda never gone home. My dreams of life woulda probably been so much bigger. And I woulda wanted so much more out of life, you know. But I'm not sayin that I don't want nothin out of life.

Do you feel that this place that you have come to, this understanding, do you think this came from adjusting to these different experiences? Is that where you feel this came from, or was it just the home situations that you had to adjust to?

Actually what I think I learned out of the whole deal is, when you're a parent you try to give to your kids what you think they oughta have. I really admire my parents today for what they done for me They gave me up for me. They didn't like it, because we visit about it, you know, today. We talked about it since I've grown up and have my own, now that I have my own kids. We talk about it, and I understand now what they done. And what they done was all for me. But you know, a lot of people they look at me and they says, "Well, you're just like a Bilagáana, that's how come you have that same thought." No, it's not, you know. My parents had them thoughts. It's where it began. They had it first. They wanted, and they're the ones that told me that I can be anything I want to be. And I'm still trying to decide what I wanna be, not to screw up and make the best of every situation, you know, make the best. But I'm happy where I am. I like it. I like the people that I know. I like my friends and what not.

A lot of people just don't understand my thoughts. They says, "Well you don't even know the traditional Navajo side." I know the traditional side. Matter of fact, a lot of people my age have less tradition in their life than I do. I believe in medicine mans, I believe in witch doctor. I have a lot of Navajo superstitions that I still live by today. I'm still very much a traditional person. Only thing is, I live in a trailer with running water and heat and a stove that you turn on. I don't have to build one of them fires to cook. I don't have no sheep. I don't have no horses, but that don't make me any less traditional.

See, to me today, still today, whenever I get lonesome, I go home to mama. If I get lonesome for no reason at all, I go home, and it still feels just as good as it did when I was a kid. And I feel my mom's just as sweet.

Another Teacher's Story

Here is a story written by a secondary-level Navajo teacher. It was written after all of the teachers had conducted both the in-class interview, "What Teachers Need to Know about Navajo Kids" and individual out-of-class interviews, on "My Most Powerful Experience in School," and was meant to connect to themes of cultural conflict, choice, self-identity, and voice that not only run across *Dances with Wolves* and *Ceremony,* but also weave throughout the in-class and out-of-class interviews. Again, the point of printing the story here is not to generalize from its content—to argue that it stands in some way for other stories that the teachers told; it is to show how the processes of developing critical notions of schooling, power, and knowledge, of applying these notions to the understanding of informants' "most powerful school experiences," and of further analyzing the concepts in creating highly autobiographic fictional texts, have allowed the authors of *Stories of School* to reflect critically on their received circumstances and on ways for transforming them. As with the interview text, the story below is rendered in Navajo English. Conventions for transcribing Navajo are those of the author.

A Bag of Sugar

by Leo Platero

Between them stood a wooden counter, worn with scratches on the glass, made for the displaying of merchandise, figuring out credit, and lot of other useful things.[6] Neezbah stood on the wooden floor waiting for the old trader with a big mustache to figure out the price he was willing to pay for her small Yei bi Chai [Navajo deities] rug. As he held up the rug to inspect for flaws the Yei figure was looking at her.

Yei bi Chai figures to the Navajos traditionally represented a form of communication. Yeis are Holy People that lived in the rocks. In the beginning the Holy People taught many different individuals the way to live and how to do things. This is what the Navajo refer to as the Hozhonii Way. To live in harmony with all living things and to respect Mother Earth and Father Sky.

An old Navajo man behind the counter was noisily putting up can goods as she stood there in a hot July afternoon with the wind howling loudly outside the small window. She had already taken enough time looking and had decided on the merchandise.

Old Mustache, that's the name the Navajo gave him as he traded with the Navajos that live close to Lukachukai Mountains, took out his worn yardstick to measure the corners. He squinted and made a sound in his throat before he said, "Shi deez'i." He called her his sister to respect the younger Navajo girls. "Ten dollars biigha'!" Ten dollars for your rag, the trader declared and he cough a little. "The edge is a little crooked."

There was an awkward silence. Finally, Neezbah said silently, "Ha'-gooshii" OK. She didn't want to barter with him now. Most Navajos didn't barter and usually accepted the going price. She knew the edges weren't crooked. She heard Ganado Trading Post gave almost twice as much for rugs. Today might have been time to ask for more money from Old Mustache. But the sun was already past midday.

She already decided to buy some peaches this time. She pointed to the twenty-five-pound Blue Bird flour sack, a can of lard, a ten-pound number two sack of potatoes and a small can of Folgers coffee. Then she looked for the peaches.

Old Mustache was straining with the sack of flour as all the merchandise were behind the counter. He already knew what the Navajos usually bought, flour, lard, baking powder, coffee, potatoes, and sugar. Earlier this morning Neezbah's husband had to drink coffee without sugar but he didn't usually complain.

As Neezbah looked for the sugar it wasn't anywhere in the store. She

---

[6]At his request, this is the author's real name.

looked for the Navajo worker but he was gone. She knew the old Navajo knew a little English and he could interpret for her.

"Ashii l'kani lah nisin." To Old Mustache the words flowed so fast he couldn't understand.

"Ha'atiish, shi deez'i?" What is it, my sister? His hearing wasn't any good anyway. He bent over and cocked his head sideways to hear better.

"Ashii l'kani," she repeated this time a little louder. Please get the sugar because I need to hurry home. I have to ride fifteen miles.

"Chii lani?" He knew chii means red and lani was many. I wonder if she needs wool dye. He smiled and reached under the glass counter and pulled out an envelope of red dye. Neezbah shook her head. Again there was a long silence.

Old Mustache was about sixty-year-old German. His sister married an Indian trader. About ten years ago he died in a freak accident while hauling freight from Gallup. The Old German stayed among the Navajos and had been trying to learn their language. He has never been back to Pennsylvania. He knew enough Navajo to trade with them. He knew that if they were younger he knew to call the women shideez'i which means younger sister and if they were older sha'di' or shima'. Shima' means my mother.

Finally after a long silence Neezbah said "Nilee di'do'." That one also as she pointed to the row of peaches. The children will like that she thought as she pulled her green pendleton blanket tightly around her. She watched as Old Mustache pull on his suspenders and walked to the middle of the skinny hall and stepped up on a small wooden box.

"Di kwee?" How many he asked in his broken Navajo.

"Dii'go," she said in a quiet voice and to make sure she held up four fingers. Finally he pulled out a cardboard box and stacked the merchandise in the box. She waited patiently even though she was in a hurry to get back. He took out his round spectacles and began to write on a tablet.

"Taa' beeso left." Three dollars left he said as he didn't remember how to say three dollars and thirty-seven cents left.

"Ashii l'kani la nisin." I want sugar.

Old Mustache shrugged his shoulder and said hopelessly, "I guess I don't have it!"

Neezbah just nodded and began to pick up the box. But the trader's hairy hand reached out and gently held the box.

"Shi deez'i." He cleared his throat. "I need a big rug. This big," he said as he stretch his arm out. "Put some more Yeis on it."

Neezbah kept her eyes on the box and didn't see his outstretched hand. "I wonder what he wants?" she thought to herself. "I think what you're trying to tell me is Big Yeis has done something crazy again." Big Ye'ii is a nickname of the trader's son. He speaks Navajo better than Old Mustache.

He wasn't sure if he explained correctly so he walked back into another room and brought out her rug. "Dii nitsaa'go!" I need it this big.

She nodded her head and tighten her scarf. Before he could tell her he needed the rug in two weeks she walked out the door with her box in one hand and carrying the flour in the other. She knew she has to repack everything into the gunny sack in the hot windstorm before riding home.

That day she didn't buy the five pound bag of sugar.

Analysis

In this section, I describe what the interview and the story texts mean and how the processes that the Red Gap teachers followed in producing and publishing them have enabled critical pedagogy and curriculum development to ensue. But first I must disclaim. The critical appraisal of these particular texts, and others similar to them in *Stories of School,* has only begun. The difficult task of figuring out what the narratives imply insofar as schooling for students at Red Gap is concerned represents a logic to be developed and refined for many years, not simply completed over the course of a graduate seminar or two (see McLaughlin 1992, for an analysis of the long-term social-engineering efforts necessary for the development and acceptance of critical schooling for Navajos in a very different reservation setting). Likewise, the actual implementation of retooled teaching and program development practice is in its infancy.

All the same, I want to summarize initial analyses that Red Gap seminar participants have created thus far, and offer several specific interpretations of my own to indicate the utility of these personal narratives as tools for transforming normative teaching practice. In so doing, I do not mean to privilege my interpretations of the texts or those of anyone else, but to describe starting points for ongoing dialogue between the Red Gap project participants, individuals whose voices the teachers have captured, critical theorists who have devised important theoretical constructs for thinking about the narratives in terms of cultural politics, and myself.

At first glance, the interview and story texts may appear somewhat different from one another. The interview describes in the first person singular one individual's experiences growing up in schools and communities for the most part off of the Navajo reservation; the story describes in third-person point of view an encounter between a Navajo weaver and an Anglo trader on the reservation. The former tells of an odyssey of separation, perseverance, and hope; the latter speaks about miscommunication, misunderstanding, and missed opportunity.

Both are very much alike, though, in describing in minute, painful detail how Navajos are silenced not only in schools but also across Anglo-Navajo cross-cultural contexts. Throughout her dealings in Anglo-American schools, from her earliest experiences onward, the young learner in the interview is taken from, imposed upon, restricted, and denied. School and church authorities assume that they know what is best for her, as must her parents, who decide to "give their daughter up for herself" only because they believe—if they want to provide opportunities for her—that they have no other choice. Rarely is this person consulted about what she thinks, feels, believes, or desires. The very same might be said about the Navajo weaver in "A Bag of Sugar."

The trader at the reservation store takes from, imposes upon, and denies, perhaps less unsympathetically than the interviewee's dorm aides, for instance, but with quite similar results: in the end, as with the Navajo student, the weaver is left an object of forces bigger than she; her most viable option is to resist by giving in; she must return home without all that she had left for.

On two levels, the similarities of the interview and story texts point toward a cultural politics of life in reservation contexts that is not only woven across *Dances with Wolves* and *Ceremony* but also vital to an understanding of work in contemporary Navajo school settings. On one level, different Anglo-American and American Indian interactional systems, each with its own distinct rules, norms, values, beliefs, and preferences for believing, thinking, saying, and doing, can be seen to organize central tensions across Anglo-Indian dyads in the teachers' texts as well as the movie and the book. The Indians in these texts prize cooperation and individuals' autonomy; they value considerable decision-making distance from one another; their societies are egalitarian; they tend not to boss each other around. Anglos, on the other hand, prize competition; they value assertiveness; their society tends to be hierarchical, to have myriad roles stratified according to access to and accumulation of economic, cultural, and political capital; they are not afraid to tell others what to do.

On a second, wider, social-structural level, these differences can be seen to play out in institutional contexts, surrounded and supported by ideological systems grounded in the core principles of each culture, repeatedly with devastating consequences for American Indians (Scollon & Scollon 1981). In terms of American Indian ideology, as a function of consensus and respect for individual autonomy, Indians adapt to and resist Anglo encroachment stoically. In *Dances with Wolves*, they vacate their home territory. In *Ceremony*, the protagonist makes things right by means of a ceremony. The young Navajo student in "Important School Experiences" comes home, and the weaver leaves the trading post without the bag of sugar. In terms of Anglo-American ideology, as a function of competition, capitalism, imperialism, manifest destiny, war, and religious proselytization, when they are not killed outright, Indians are thwarted, lied to, stolen from, dictated to, incarcerated, removed, and "educated," all because others know what is best for them (Matthiessen 1984).

By analyzing "Important School Experiences," "A Bag of Sugar," and other personal narratives like them, Red Gap teachers have begun seeing how the organization of cultural beliefs and social structures that generalize across the interviews and stories filter into the content and process of schooling in present-day Navajo settings. They have begun to ask: Are my assumptions about teaching, learning, and curriculum contributing to the domination and subordination of the students and their local communities? Even against my best intentions, am I replicating the impositions of the interviewee's dorm aides, teachers, foster parents, or the simple misunderstandings and injustices of the Anglo trader?

Project participants' answers to these difficult, complex questions are beginning to emerge; again, of necessity, they will be developing in an ongoing fashion for some time. Some of the teachers have taken meaningful steps toward the development of instructional practices that work from critical notions of knowledge, culture, power, and voice. Some have employed the methods used to produce the interviews and stories of *Stories of School* to have their students produce personal histories and critically oriented fictional and nonfictional texts. Several have begun outlining a comprehensive K–6 language-arts program that builds onto, rather than "fixes," the native language- and Indian English-speaking abilities of the Navajo children and that proceeds from a sociolinguistic analysis of the forms and functions for speaking, reading, and writing in the community. Others have completely revised normative skills-oriented, basal-bound teaching approaches to weave storytelling, interviewing, story writing, and publishing across integrated portions of the K-6 curriculum. Spin-off projects have also occurred with other groups of Navajo teachers from across the Navajo reservation, who have read selections from *Stories of School,* analyzed the instructional methods used to produce the personal narratives, and begun to create alternate curriculum and teaching materials in the Navajo language for their own K–12 Navajo learners.

Conclusion

In this chapter, I have described how a group of teachers of Navajo students has produced personal narratives for developing critical perspectives of their teaching situations and of themselves. With these narratives, the teachers have begun analyzing their received circumstances and started charting courses for personal and educational program development. Interview and story texts have grounded critical theory in concrete instructional practice, and helped orient the teachers not to recreate existing inequities but instead to examine a host of contradictions, struggles, and injustices inherent to formal schooling for Navajo learners. In calling attention to several texts that the teachers produced, I have attempted to pinpoint the efficacy of a critical sociology of educational and school knowledge. I have recognized important starting points of this paradigm, and used dialectical notions of power as a justification for instructional strategies that use the production of personal narratives as a way of developing teachers' and students' voice.

Often, the calls of critical theorists amount to obfuscating rhetoric which, in theorizing what is wrong with mainstream school practices without identifying what teachers and school administrators of subordinated groups can actually do, simply add to the problem. One important way to move beyond critique is for teachers and their students to produce school knowledge, to have them tell their own stories—to create school and personal histories that will be valued by others at the level of school and community. Such narratives need to be more than simply taped and transcribed, however; they must be collected, produced, and measured against themes generic to critical studies of schooling: culture, race, class, gender, power, and voice. They must also be measured in ways that make sense to those with most to win and lose from their production—so that we weave the texts into what the children already know and need to understand; so that schooling enables teachers and their students to contest and transform, rather than serve and perpetuate, systems of silencing, exploitation, and harm.

References

Apple, Michael 1982. *Education and Power*. Boston: Routledge and Kegan Paul.

———. 1987. *Ideology and Curriculum*. Boston: Routledge and Kegan Paul.

———. 1990. *Teachers and Texts*. New York: Routledge.

Benally, Herbert. 1988. "Diné Philosophy of Learning." In *Journal of Navajo Education* 6, no. 1: 10–13.

Bernstein, Basil. 1982. "On Pedagogic Discourse." In *Handbook of Theory and Research for the Sociology of Education* edited by J. G. Richardson. New York: Greenwood.

Bourdieu, Pierre, & Passeron, J. 1977. *Reproduction in Education, Society, and Culture*. Beverly Hills, Calif.: Sage Publishers.

Bowles, Samuel, & Gintis, Herbert. 1976. *Schooling in Capitalist America*. New York: Basic Books.

Crow Dog, Mary. 1991. *Lakota Woman*. New York: Harper Perennial.

Dewey, John. [1938]. 1963. *Experience and Education*. New York: Collier Books.

Deyhle, Donna. 1991. "Empowerment and Cultural Conflict: Navajo Parents and the Schooling of their Children." In *Journal of Qualitative Studies in Education* 4, no. 4: 277–97.

Dorris, Michael. 1989. *The Broken Cord*. New York: Harper & Row.

Egan, Kieran. 1986. *Teaching as Story Telling*. Chicago: IL: University of Chicago Press.

Erdrich, Louise. 1984. *Love Medicine*. New York: Holt, Rinehart, and Winston.

Foucault, Michel. 1980. *Power/Knowledge: Selected Interviews and Other Writings*. New York: Pantheon.

Giroux, Henry. 1981. *Ideology, Culture, and the Process of Schooling*. Philadelphia: Temple University Press.

———. 1988. *Teachers as Intellectuals: Toward a Critical Pedagogy of Learning*. New York: Bergin & Garvey.

Giroux, Henry, & McLaren, Peter. 1986. "Teacher Education and the Politics of Engagement: The Case for Democratic Schooling." In *Harvard Educational Review* 56, no. 3: 213–238.

Grant, Carl, & Sleeter, Christine. 1986. *After the School Bell Rings*. Philadelphia: Falmer Press.

Graves, Donald. 1988a. *Investigative Non-Fiction*. Portsmouth, N.H.: Heinemann Educational Books.

———. 1988b. *Experiment with Fiction*. Portsmouth, N.H.: Heinemann Educational Books.

Harris, Stephen. 1990. *Aboriginal Schooling*. Canberra, Australia: Council for Aboriginal Education.

Harste, Jerome, Short, Kathy, & Burke, Carolyn. 1988. *Creating Classrooms for Authors: The Reading and Writing Connection*. Portsmouth, N.H.: Heinemann Educational Books.

Lamphere, Louise. 1977. *To Run After Them*. Tucson, Ariz.: University of Arizona Press.

Leap, William. 1993. *American Indian English*. Salt Lake City, UT: University of Utah Press.

Leap, William, & McLaughlin, Daniel. 1991. "What Navajo Students Know about Written English." Paper presented at the annual conference of the American Educational Research Association, Chicago, Ill.

McLaughlin, Daniel. 1989. "Power and the Politics of Knowledge: Transformative

Leadership and Curriculum Development for Minority Language Learners." In *Peabody Journal of Education* 66, no 3: 41–60.

———. 1992. *When Literacy Empowers: Navajo Language in Print*. Albuquerque, N.M.: University of New Mexico Press.

Scollon, Ron, & Scollon, Suzanne. 1981. *Narrative, Literacy, and Face in Interethnic Communication*. Norwood, N.J.: Ablex Press.

Silko, Leslie Marmon. 1977. *Ceremony*. New York: Signet.

Wigginton, Eliot. 1986. *Sometimes a Shining Moment*. Garden City, N.Y.: Anchor/ Doubleday.

———. 1989. "Foxfire Grows Up." In *Harvard Educational Review* 59, no 1: 24–49.

Wilcox, Karen. 1982. "Differential Socialization in the Classroom: Implications for Equal Opportunity." In *Doing the Ethnography of Schooling*, edited by George Spindler. New York: Holt, Rinehart, and Winston.

Willis, Paul. 1977. *Learning to Labor*. Westmead, U.K.: Saxon House.

Witherspoon, Gary. 1977. *Language and Art in the Navajo Universe*. Ann Arbor, Mich.: University of Michigan Press.

6

Self and Identity in a Postmodern World:
A Life Story

William G. Tierney

This chapter pertains to the life story of a faculty member who died of
AIDS in 1991. Robert Sunchild (a pseudonym) was a forty-year-old Native
American who had a promising career as a teacher and researcher. Over a
nine-month period Robert and I held a series of structured and semistruc-
tured interviews about his life. When he died we had completed thirty hours
of taped interviews. I also have a series of notes that I took from our unstructured interviews. Finally, Robert gave me his journal which covers
twenty years of his life. I will call upon all of this data in the development
of the text. Following Titon (1980), I have chosen to call this a life story in
the sense that the text was dialogically created, rather than a history that
was discovered and transcribed.

The objectives of this article are twofold. First, Robert's life is remark-
able for the inner conflicts and intersections that were posed by his background. "I've been thinking about my life in preparation for our talks," he
began in our first interview, "and you'll see that three—no four—things
emerge: being Indian, growing up poor, being gay, and now having AIDS.
These are the challenges of my life, how I have learned to define who I
am." As we will see, throughout his life the conflicts posed by, and the ability to synthesize, his ethnicity, class background, and sexual orientation demanded that he develop several different narrative voices.

One central challenge that AIDS presented to Robert was to integrate
these different conflicts so that people might see him as he saw himself,
rather than as one group or another wanted to define him. Indeed, for
Robert the purpose of our working on his life story was to highlight how
the demands of his life had forced a segregation of his manifold identities.

119

The intent here, then, is to offer Robert's narrative as a scaffolding for a critique of how we conceptualize the self. In so doing, I will pose what I call a postmodern alternative to how we traditionally think of self and identity.

Second, I will frame from a critical perspective the interactions between myself and Robert with regard to how his life story was constructed. The role of the author in educational research in general, and life history research in particular, demands more analysis than those of us involved in educational research have given it. Following a self-reflective vein in anthropology (Crapanzano 1980; Rabinow 1977), I will argue that in coming to terms with our subject's reality, we in turn help define our own. Thus, I will extend the first point by suggesting that how the author defines the self represents a dialectical process between author and subject to the extent that both interviewer and interviewee shape and are shaped by one another. In the final analysis, "narrative product" is thus mutually defined and shared.

My intent is to develop a text that enables the reader to reflect about his or her own life. I neither want to objectify Robert's life nor to reify the methods we used to develop this text; rather, my hope is that by coming to terms with the challenges one individual faced in a time of tremendous personal crisis we might be better able to reflect on our own lives and, in turn, we might enable the narrative voices both of our own selves and of those whom we teach to be heard. Critical theory and postmodernism have been rightfully accused of being far too abstract and disengaged from everyday life. Accordingly, my goal in this article is to show how one might define a critical engagement amongst individuals who routinely get defined as researchers, human subjects, colleagues, and ultimately, friends.

Defining Self

When we reflect on an individual's life history we often think of the major events in the person's life, rather than the more mundane, microscopic activities that take up most of our lives. When we examine the life of Martin Luther King, Jr., for example, we think of his marches and his speeches. When we read the life histories of less famous individuals such as Fools Crow (Mouffe 1990) or Rigoberta Menchu (1984) what we remember are the heroic stands that these individuals took. Even Shostak's *Nisa* (1983) concentrates on central events in the character's life. In reading about such actions, presumably, the reader not only learns about someone else's life, but also is supposed to learn the meaning of words such as courage or truth.

Yet Robert Sunchild never saw his life as a series of major actions, or of much importance to anyone other than those people connected to his life. In 1987 he wrote in his journal, "I look back through these pages and wonder what would they reveal to an outside reader? Arrogant of me to think (or have thought) I was living a life so unique that one would find it worth the chronicle." Robert thought his life was similar to countless others. Although some would argue that his life was quite different from the "norm" since he was a well-educated, gay Native American, it is easy to understand how Robert came to believe that his life was not "unique." As he continued in his journal: "I'm not extraordinary, merely a person searching for meaning in life. I look back on this journal and read about the seemingly major eras in my life—except in retrospect, they don't seem so major, just points that got me to where I am now."

Although there may not have been "major eras" in Robert's life, through-out his journal and the interview process Robert stressed specific topics that I raise here because they provide insight into how Robert came to define himself. I offer three themes that continuously resonate in Robert's stories—that of being an American Indian, that of being raised poor, and that of being gay. In some instances these themes intersect with one another, and at other times they conflict with one another. Often, these themes get enacted on the terrain of educational institutions.

The data that follows is not meant to summarize Robert's life in a nut-shell, for as with any life, Robert's cannot be neatly defined and summa-rized in a few pages. Yet when Robert reflected on his life he offered glimpses into his own self-definitions as he began to interpret his life as a person living with AIDS. Robert narrated these vignettes most often as they appear here—not in chronological fashion, but rather as a way to discuss a larger point. Thus, what follows is a retelling of different narratives that Robert told during the life story process.

Robert recalled:

On Being Native American

I've always lived among Indian people, even when we didn't live on the res. I didn't live on the reservation for most of my life, none of my child-hood. But Indians are a close-knit community. There are always people from my reservation somewhere. It's amazing, because I've lived in lots of places and sooner or later I'll run into someone from home.

Every summer we went home, back to the reservation. My family has al-ways been most important to me. My mom. I've never wanted her to worry and I've avoided telling her things sometimes, but she's always accepted everything about me.

When I went to college I became active in the Indian movement. I started affiliating with other Indians. We fancied ourselves as revolutionaries. I be-came involved in the political life in part because of my older brother. I felt obliged to go to Wounded Knee and Alcatraz and the air base [a site of a confrontation]. I forget how, but somehow I ended up with a gun at Wounded Knee! I was just shaking in my boots! Me, with a gun! I did those things out of a sense of obligation for my people. I have never been a leader. I'm very reserved, almost shy. My brother was a real leader in these movements. I thought all of these activities were at great risk to my future, but I thought they were obligatory.

When I went to Buffalo to get my master's degree I got involved in another kind of cultural life. I was much more comfortable learning about the cultures of different Indian tribes than being involved in political movements. We went to campuses and community groups and spoke. We formed a nucleus in Native American Studies and I really felt I had a learning experience.

At that time my younger brother died in an accident. He was going home to the reservation to the Sun Dance and the car he was in went off the road and he got thrown out and hit a brick wall. My uncle said one of Danny's brothers would have to fulfill his vow and dance the Sun Dance for five years. As a consequence I got involved as a participant in the Sun Dance. I haven't failed to dance since then. It is very important to me. It's a strong ritual. We often say that we shouldn't talk about such things. That's because it's very religious and you don't talk about it. For me it's a renewal of life with the tribe. It's an opportunity—not to atone for sins because we don't believe that—but to suffer for blessings. It's a way to give back, to pray for my family. I pray to the elders, we offer materials to the spirits, and I often ask to be a better person.

When I finished my master's I decided it was time to go home and work. I worked in the state at different colleges and schools. I have always been concerned with helping my people. At times I felt terribly exploited because I might be the only Indian working at a college and they'd give me a terrible salary, but they knew I was sincere in my commitment. My people have appreciated my work, and I feel sincere in my efforts.

On Being Poor

I was brought up in poverty. Being poor is being Indian, I guess. I remember poverty caused me a great deal of stress. I can remember wishing I was white, middle class. One of the saddest memories I have is being ashamed of my mother because she didn't dress and act like the other mothers at my school. I remember wanting her and my dad to go to a play that I was in once, I'd had some small part. I begged them to go, but they just didn't want to.

In the eighth grade I won the spelling bee for the school and my parents didn't want to go to the city championships, either. We know now that that's important for a kid, but my mom didn't know any better. I don't blame her. I had to catch a ride home with one of the other kid's moms and she couldn't believe my parents weren't there. It was a terrifically painful experience. As I progressed in school and people said I was a good student I remember my mom saying "If I have to scrub floors on my hands and knees for you to go to college I will." She really tried.

My earliest memories are running around the projects. We were the original latch-key children, me and my brothers and sisters. We'd just wander the streets at will. I also have memories of drinking. I remember going into a house once and seeing people passed out and vomit everywhere. People were dead drunk. I was exposed to alcohol very young; maybe it contributed to my own drinking and alcohol abuse. My mother, however, was never an alcoholic and never on welfare. She always worked and she always provided for us to the best of her ability.

But we were so poor. On holidays we expected presents and I remember getting a little clay set once, multicolored with a stick, and that was it for Christmas. It probably cost twenty-nine cents, but I was happy.

My mother also used to give my older sister a little money so she could buy a small bag of Fritos. My sister would give us kids one Frito at a time and we treasured it, eating a little nibble and then another. Can you imagine! One Frito! But that was my life.

When I entered the fourth grade I took some tests and they said I was smart and should take a special program, so I had to go to school across town away from my brothers and sisters. There was one other minority, a Hispanic kid, in the class and the rest were all white middle-class kids. They had material amenities and I didn't. I felt ashamed.

Often, we didn't have anything to eat for lunch. I'd go to school with a mayonnaise sandwich—just mayo and Wonder bread! It's funny to remember that now, but back then these other kids would arrive with colored lunch pails and it was just a luxury I couldn't imagine. And then they had Saran wrap for their sandwiches. They could buy milk. On the opposite side was me. We'd cut a large garbage bag, one of the brown bags you'd buy at the grocery store and make it into a small bag for my lunch so I could carry it to school. And we'd reuse it. I wrapped my sandwich in used tin foil, which was really out of it. I remember going to school and opening up my sandwich inside the bag so the other kids wouldn't see that I had this old tin foil.

When I got to high school I fell in with the in-crowd. But the in-crowd was real poor kids like myself. My best friend, Amey, was a prostitute. Everybody thought we were a couple, but we weren't. We'd sneak out at night and go to some bar and dance all night long; she'd also meet some pickup to take home. That's how we got money to dance. I've always identified with street people, the common man. I've met all of my lovers in the bar, and they were dive bars, too, not yuppie places at all. They were all common guys. I can talk with different people and be comfortable in lots of different crowds, but I've always been at home in common hang-outs.

On being gay

I believe I was born gay. I can remember being fascinated by men and their sexual organs at a very early age. I had my first sexual experience in eighth grade with an older man. I had a couple of other sexual experiences in high school and they were all with older men or with older school friends. I was always passive and they were never anything like a relationship.

I acted on my sexual preference with shame and guilt. Your mind is not ready to handle this when you're young and it is overwhelming. I could not accept being gay and I could not tell anyone. You act out these things in isolation and you feel so alone. You're totally unexposed to what's out there. You think that you are the only one. I was fascinated to learn that there were others like me. I had no gay friends. I use to pray to God when I was a child, "please make me straight."

But I began to realize the experience of being gay built my character. After a certain time, I accepted myself as gay, but I still was afraid, guilty, because I told no one. I decided in high school that I wanted to go to college in San Francisco so I could explore more easily being gay, but I didn't know what that meant, really. Because of the crowd I hung out with and because I'm Indian, my guidance counselor never thought I'd get to college. She told me to go to a community college. I got the largest scholarship in the school and my counselor couldn't believe it. I went off to the University of San Francisco.

I was asexual my first year. I was cognizant of my sexuality and I wanted it, I wanted it bad. But I was afraid and I had no idea what it meant to be gay. What did you do? Finally, I decided to go to a gay bar. I drove over there and parked way far away from the bar. I was scared shitless. I walked down the street and almost jumped into the place—the Rendezvous. I was really paranoid about being observed. I had never seen guys dancing together. I was inexperienced at natural, acceptable talk, romantic sex. I had never had romantic encounters. This guy asked me to dance; he put his hands on me in a real normal way, around my shoulder. I was terrified!

I have always been quiet about being gay. I have kept a strict split between my Indian friends and my gay friends. When I went to San Francisco I practically cut myself off from my family, I didn't see them for a couple of years. Finally my older brother came out to see me and I remember being paranoid about telling him. I practiced what I was going to say and when I finally told him, he said, "So what." He told my mom and then the rest of the family found out and nobody caused any problems, but I've always been reticent to discuss my sexuality with people. I don't let many people know me; my posture is very reserved.

I have never thought of discussing my sexuality in the context of being an Indian. I would care what people think, especially the Indian people. It's interesting isn't it? I wouldn't say in one of my classes that I'm gay, although

I realize that gay students need role models, that straight students need to have stereotypes changed. But I'm not the one to do it. What people think is still a matter of concern for me.

The Challenges of AIDS

I'm not bitter about having AIDS, even suffering to the extent that I do. Having AIDS has brought a lot of realizations and blessings in my life. It's brought out in a lot of people a lot of love, care, and compassion—with my friends, my family, and in the gay community.

I believe I'll go to heaven. We don't call it that. I definitely believe there's another world and in the other world life is beautiful. I look forward to seeing my brother who died thirteen years ago, my relatives, my Aunt Sally who just passed away, my gramma and grampa.

We don't believe in hell. Living on earth is punishment enough. I learned about dying by listening and learning and going to funerals. Old people will show you what to believe. Listening at the Sun Dance when those old people get up and speak. I burn sweetgrass and think, more than pray. I ask God to have pity on me. Indian people humble themselves. They believe they should humble themselves to a greater power. So I ask for pity because I am pitiful.

I've learned to accept my fate. I've learned what life is for. We develop as human beings as much as we can and then we move into the next world. I'm not bitter about my situation, but I'm afraid at times. Up until recently I had an illusion that I'd be back to normal someday, but that's an illusion now. I see the end.

AIDS is an expansion of my life. I mean, I view my life as I see my struggle with AIDS—one long challenge. I've been given the weapons to fight a long life battle. I see myself as a warrior, just as a warrior would be in the old days, but it's taken a different form, although in my own way I still have to struggle with the white man. I've had to fight the white man's way, his system, and hold onto my identity as an Indian. I try to live as an Indian would, in spite of all these forces that would have made me a middle-class white man. I don't live in a log cabin, but I still in my heart am an Indian. I believe in Indian ways, religion, and try to live in the world by Indian beliefs. I believe in Indian ceremonies and values.

Interpreting Self

What can we learn from Robert Sunchild's narrative? And how might we interpret these stories in terms of self and identity? Robert's life offers insight into the multiple voices an individual employs in the course of daily interactions. As a Native American he was proud of his heritage and used it in the struggle against AIDS. His beliefs about life derived from those native ways he had learned either from tribal elders or from religious ceremonies such as the Sun Dance.

Robert also used the poverty of his youth as a means to identify with the "common man." He noted how he was more comfortable with working-class people, and that he admired them. Further, he also defined being Native American with being poor. In this light the intersection of class and race was most significant, and his identity was shaped and synthesized by these factors.

The greatest divergence occurred with regard to Robert's sexual orientation. As a gay child, at first he found it difficult to accept his sexuality. Even later it was not something he was proud of or wanted to share with other individuals. When one looked at Robert one knew he was an American Indian; however, no one ever knew he was gay. Given the choice, Robert hid his sexuality.

In Robert's eyes, his class roots and sexual orientation fit together since he liked "dive bars." Robert also said that all of his lovers were "common guys." Presumably, his class roots and sexual orientation would not have been a problem if he had come from the middle class. Yet Robert explicitly tried to keep these parts of his identity separate; that is, he kept his sexual orientation segregated from his Native American self. Because he had no choice, when Robert was "gay" he also was Native American.

We gain a sense of how one individual navigated the difficult turf of self and identity. As always, a variety of interpretations exist about how Robert dealt with that terrain. I now turn to one possible interpretation—that based on postmodernism and critical theory. In what follows I first offer a sketch of what I mean by modernism, and then I discuss postmodernism and critical theory; in doing so I consider the concepts of *difference* and *empowerment*. My purpose is to highlight the multiple narrative voices that Robert employed in his life history. I will argue that a postmodern definition of self and identity works from a desire to provoke difference rather than unity; a critical notion underscores the need for self-empowerment and the development of voice.

Modernism

Modernist interpretations of Robert's life would strip it of the cultural and social contexts in which he resided. A modernist assumes that a life history can accurately describe an individual's identity based on common criteria of what counts as objective knowledge. Faith in reason allows the modernist to believe that empirical investigations create singular, accurate versions of a "true" self. "The modernist self," comments Kenneth Gergen, "is knowable, present in the here and now, just slightly below the surface of his actions" (1991, 47). Many modernists would argue that the advent of psychology helped us understand the motivations of the human psyche and self.

From this perspective we interpret Robert's life story as a singular narrative measured against other individuals' life stories. A unitary version of identity and self are employed. Again, as Gergen comments, "Problems such as phobias, homosexuality, depression, and the like [are] equivalent to malfunctions" (1991, 42). From a unitary understanding of the self, Robert's life would be judged against norms such as how well he adapted or assimilated in terms of race, class, and sexual orientation. This view, commonly known as "functionalist" or "positivist" or the term employed in this chapter, "modernist," assumes that law-like generalizations of the world and the self exist and that our investigations enable us to determine how one might better be able to conform to common standards.

The assumption, of course, is that a "true" interpretation exists about the individual and the world, and that the power of the interpreter is in the ability to define fully an individual's identity. Indeed, tremendous power is given to the researcher, as Rorty notes: "the modernist thinks that there is a connection between redescription and power, and that the right description can make us free" (1990, 90). Hence, the search for ideals such as "truth" by the researcher has the possibility of creating ideal communities. The researcher conducts a life history, because objective facts are to be revealed rather than a life story where the text is intersubjectively and dialogically created. The researcher's role is to describe fully the individual's life history in order to shed light on universals such as truth; the relationship between the researcher and the researched is relatively unimportant as long as the researcher subscribes to generally accepted rules about how to study objective reality.

Postmodernism

The postmodernist works from a completely different set of assumptions. Postmodernists reject the idea that humanity perfects itself through the power of rational thought. Universals such as "truth" do not exist. Communities cannot be organized around single ideas of the "common good" because there will always be groups and individuals who have been silenced because of their differences from the norm. In this light, the individual is not an autonomous agent who operates independently of social constraints. Individuals are no longer the fundamental units of society. The individual is decentered from a singular notion of the universe so that identity may no longer be defined in terms of universal concepts of the self (Cooper & Burrell 1988).

In essence, the postmodernist abandonment of objective truth forces a redefinition of what we mean by self and identity. Gergen explains, "The argument is not that our descriptions of the self are objectively shaky, but that the very attempt to render accurate understanding is itself bankrupt" (1991, 82). This notion has significant implications for how we conduct research and how we conceive of authority. The modernist believes that we study specific topics and gain knowledge in a cumulative fashion. The more one studies, the greater potential the individual has for becoming an authority on a specialized topic. Indeed, the specialization of knowledge into disciplines and subfields helps create figures of authority who have gained much knowledge about a specific narrowly defined concept. The researcher's task is to accumulate knowledge about a topic and the relationship with the researched is relatively unimportant except in terms of how the researched provide the researcher with valid, reliable data.

Postmodernists reject this assertion. Authority is discounted, and dialogue becomes essential. Rather than researcher-researched relationships where one individual is powerful because of the knowledge he/she holds and the other is powerless because of a lack thereof, individuals become engaged in modes of dialogue where all individuals are collaborators and participants.

When we reject the idea that experts control interpretation, we also discount the idea that a singular version of truth can exist. In doing so, we must accept that conflict and competing interpretations of situations are inevitable. Mouffe is helpful here by pointing out that postmodernism

> acknowledges the impossibility of a fully realized democracy and the total elimination of antagonisms. It views all forms of agreement as partial and provisional and as products of a given hegemony. Its objective is the creation of a chain of equivalence among the democratic demands found in a variety of movements—women, blacks, workers, gays and lesbians, or environmentalists—around a radical democratic interpretation of the political principles of the liberal democratic regime. Such an interpretation emphasizes the numerous social relations where subordination exists and must be challenged if the principles of equality and liberty are to apply. (1990, 63)

Thus, conflict is not only inevitable, it is desirable because it points out that competing interpretations of reality are being voiced and debated. The postmodernist struggle, then, is to generate oppositional realities and deconstruct singular interpretations of truth. In large part, how one breaks these singular notions of truth is by investigating how issues and problems have been initially structured. Foucault's work, for example, deals with this concern in one way or another (Foucault 1973; 1979) insofar as he highlights how different social problems—madness, sexuality, medicine, knowledge—came to be defined in different epochs. With each of his analyses Foucault redescribes how we have defined the individual in society; rather than assume that the idea of the individual is static and unchanging, Foucault points out how societies have shaped notions of self and identity over and against institutional and ideological mechanisms of power.

Robert Sunchild's life, then, needs to be seen neither in terms of a singular notion of self, nor in terms of words decontextualized from the situations in which he spoke. Robert spoke of multiple selves. The struggle in the text is to enable these different—and often conflicting—selves to be heard. Further, Robert reflected on his life when he had AIDS; his version of his life came at a particular moment in time. We must interpret his words not as if a concrete reality existed irrespective of the individual, but cognizant that his reality was socially constructed and constantly undergoing reinterpretation. Moreover, the relationship between Robert and myself was fundamentally different from that of a modernist conception of the researcher and the researched, but I will hold off on elaborating this point until we consider critical theory.

Critical Theory

To be sure, there are many versions of critical theory, some of which fit closely with modernism. Indeed, one of the chief architects of critical theory, Jurgen Habermas, is centrally situated in the modernist camp. I use critical theory here, however, to extend postmodernist assumptions rather than refute them. Along with Giroux (1988a, 1988b, 1990), I want to infuse a critical notion of society with postmodernism in order to define our research activities in terms of empowerment (Tierney 1991).

By utilizing critical theory I work from the assumption that individuals have a significant part in the creation of the reality that surrounds them, but they do not have a linearly deterministic role. That is, the social, cultural, and historical contexts in which individuals are embedded play an important role in the creation and substantiation of what individuals come to define as reality. This assumption has far-reaching implications for how we construct our institutions, how we construct knowledge, and ultimately, how we relate with one another. Indeed, a critical perspective argues that one of the central roles of research and institutions such as schools and colleges is to enable people to come to terms with their own historical circumstances.

Individual identity exists in social contexts that have unique ideological constraints. The assumption here is that the force of society as exhibited by our institutions is not toward human freedom and liberation; rather, ideologies tend to silence those individuals who do not fit within the norms of our culture. Ideology silences and disempowers individuals so that the powerful may govern. In this light, Robert's life story needs to be interpreted not in reference to norms governing self and identity, but in relation to how his multiple selves were defined and silenced. Robert's story of his childhood and an educational environment where he was made to feel ashamed of his parents and his poverty, as well as his belief that he needed to hide his sexual orientation, all point to how ideological parameters shaped and marginalized his identities.

The critical theorist struggles to uncover ideological constraints and overthrow them. Rejecting a singular version of truth where all must conform to particular attitudes, a critical analysis argues that human solidarity must be based on the concept of difference. At first, such an assumption appears contradictory. How can we create solidarity within community if we are all different? What, then, is it that ties all of us together? Unity comes from the acceptance of difference and the willingness to engage one another in dialogue about it. It also comes from communities' willingness to come to terms with the lives of those who have been silenced. Rather than make minority individuals conform to the established norms, we bring into question those norms and see how they might be reinterpreted given the needs of particular groups.

In this light, the purpose of community is to develop the conditions for empowerment where individuals may accept and honor one another's differences, rather than merely tolerate them or assume that those individuals who are "different" ought in some way to conform to the norm. The implications here stand in direct opposition to many of the assumptions of the modernist tradition. To highlight these differences it will be helpful to discuss the relationship between Robert Sunchild and myself.

Writing Stories of Self

A story is always told to someone. The postmodernist assumption is that the telling of that story in part depends on the storyteller's audience. Robert and I had been friends for about a year prior to our decision to embark on his life history.

Intellectually, we had common interests in Native American Studies. We were also similar in our sexual orientation; indeed, we found out that we were both gay when we happened upon one another in a gay bar. Both of these points are pertinent to Robert's story. For he was able to use shorthand about life on the reservation—"the res"—with me because he knew I had prior knowledge about American Indian lives. Perhaps more importantly, because I am gay Robert had no hesitation about talking about that side of his life.

At one point, for example, during the start of our interviews he commented, "I'm sure you'll want to know about the gay stuff, all the gory details, and I'll tell you. I'm not ashamed of any of it. But then, if you weren't gay, I don't know if I would ever bring it up or want to talk about it."

As noted earlier, Robert and I agreed to undertake this study when he had AIDS. In fact, the first time we discussed engaging in the life history was during his second hospitalization. The first time Robert went into the hospital was a minor turning point. "They told me when I was diagnosed with AIDS," he remembered during one interview, "I had a good possibility of staying well, of not getting infections. So when I went in the first time, I realized it wasn't true; I wasn't going to stay well. I don't cry very much, but I cried then." Yet Robert was soon released from the hospital and his life returned to normal. "When they put me in the second time, when we talked about doing this history," he recalled, "I knew that things would never be normal again. Like you said that morning, I'd have ups and downs. I'd be in and out of the hospital."

I originally approached this life story as a way for Robert and I to engage in a task that would be useful to him. I was more concerned about the process than the end result. I wanted to afford Robert the time and space to reflect on his life. I also knew that as he grew increasingly ill that this would be a task he could continue wherever he was—at the office, in the hospital, or at home. As Robert became more sick we continued our interviews even though other activities in his life fell by the wayside. He said one day, "I can't concentrate as much on office work anymore, on details, but I seem to want to turn more to our study. I was thinking about my childhood some more. Let me tell you." And he began another story of his youth.

Krall has written that good research "should bring deeper meaning into our daily lives without controlling the lives of others. It should not reduce the complexities of human interaction and learning to simple formulas but rather should elaborate and accentuate their richness" (1988, 474). I know from my work with Robert that I have changed, and my attitude toward research has changed. Surely anyone who watches a friend or family member die is changed, but I am stressing here that my sense of how we conduct research also was altered through my work with Robert. I do not want to reduce what I have learned into "simple formulas," but I do offer three lessons.

1. *Multiple Selves* To have studied Robert's life and concentrated on one aspect would have missed the manifold narrative voices that account for Robert. I am not suggesting that only a gay man can embark on a life history of a gay man, or that only women can study women, or that only white upper-class men can study their counterparts. At the same time in our research endeavors we need to be more concerned with difference than we have been. What postmodernism has taught us in theory, Robert taught me concretely. "People want to define me," he said, "I'm me, all of me, and most people don't want to see that."

2. *Research Goals* Again, I do not wish to be doctrinaire, but I am concerned about our overreliance on standardized goals that overlook the processes we take to reach those goals and that, in doing so, deny voice to those individuals involved in our research. Researchers need to become more fully engaged with those whom we wish to interview. Indeed, I would prefer that more of my own research studies followed the path I have attempted here; Robert set the agenda, and our final product became less important than the process in which we were engaged.

3. *Praxis* Words such as "empowerment" and "liberation" have be-

come so popularized in educational jargon that they have lost much of their meaning. This is unfortunate because ultimately structures and oppression change not because of anything I *write*, but because of what I *do*. As I saw my friend become more ill I felt it incumbent to learn more about AIDS, and to take a more active role in my university with regard to human rights issues. Many intellectuals of my generation have been too removed from the democratic sphere. The constraints of the academic system have placed us in structures where we have learned the discourse of the academy, and in doing so, we have privatized our language and lost considerable hope of fomenting change. Robert's life story teaches us to do the opposite: learn the discourse of the voiceless, create communities of dialogue based on difference, and work constantly toward the active creation of change.

Conclusion

Robert's life story presents a challenge for those of us who want to develop conditions that enable individuals to grasp hold of their identities and accept the various voices with which an individual speaks. Yet saying that we want to enable individuals to gain voice is not doing it; indeed, some might say that the very discourse itself creates a situation where those in power are once again trying to give something to the powerless, and at the same time they have not reconfigured overarching systems of power in which we reside.

To offer such a comment may seem paralyzing in the sense that to "reconfigure systems of power" implies a herculean effort that only saints or revolutionaries should be assigned. Robert's life story, however, is an example of what I am suggesting we should attempt. To be sure, most of us will not face a crisis of the magnitude of AIDS, yet we most likely have parts of our identity that either remain obscured or hidden. As educators, we also have students and colleagues who undoubtedly face struggles similar to those which Robert faced. The challenge for us is to create those conditions so that our friends, colleagues, students, and research "subjects" are enabled to deal with us on an equal footing.

By "equal footing" I mean to suggest that traditional mechanisms of power need to be challenged. Robert, for example, was clearly more than simply a research "subject" in this undertaking; indeed, he was co-producer in the development of it. My role as researcher went far beyond simply recording someone's life history and analyzing it. Many of these "unstructured interviews" took place en route to one store or another to fill a prescription or see a doctor. As I noted above, the primary purpose of the life story itself was not to produce articles of the sort that exist here, but rather to enable Robert to reflect on his life during a moment of intense crisis.

Self-reflexively, I conclude by pointing out that Robert's stories forced me to reconsider my own actions and my own life. I learned from Robert the intense dilemmas that individuals face in coming to accept those parts of themselves that society most vociferously aims to deny. Such lessons have helped me to reconsider how I teach, how I relate to colleagues and friends, and how I define myself. I struggle to develop pedagogies that enable students to develop their own voice rather than speak with one voice. I am trying to develop the notion of communities of difference in my own community so that the voices of others are not subsumed by me or the powerful. And I am trying to come to terms with my own subjugated histories and unearth them, so that as with Robert, not only will I learn, but so will others. It is in the revelation of the histories of our selves and our identities that we discover solidarity and liberation.

References

Cooper, R., & Burrell, G. 1988. Modernism, postmodernism, and organizational analysis: An introduction. *Organization Studies 9*, no. 1: 91–112.

Crapanzano, V. 1980. *Tuhami, portrait of a Moroccan.* Chicago: University of Chicago Press.

Foucault, M. 1973. *The order of things.* Translated by E. Gallimard. New York: Vintage Books.

———. 1979. *Discipline and punish.* Translated by A. Sheridan. New York: Vintage Books.

Gergen, K. J. 1991. *The saturated self: Dilemmas of identity in contemporary life.* New York: Basic Books.

Giroux, H. A. 1988a. Border pedagogy in the age of postmodernism. *Journal of Education 170*, no 3: 162–81.

———. 1988b. Postmodernism and the discourse of educational criticism. *Journal of Education 170*, no 3: 5–30.

———. 1990. The politics of postmodernism. *Journal of Urban and Cultural Studies 1*, no. 1: 5–38.

Krall, F. R. 1988. From the inside out—personal history as educational research. *Educational Theory 38*, no. 4: 467–79.

Mails, T. E. 1990. *Fools Crow.* Lincoln, Neb.: University of Nebraska Press.

Menchu, R. 1984. *I, Rigoberta Menchu* Edited by E. Burgos-Debray, translated by A. Wright. London: Verso.

Mouffe, C. 1990. Radical democracy or liberal democracy? *Socialist Review* 2: 57–66.

Rabinow, P. 1977. *Reflections on fieldwork in Morocco.* Berkeley: University of California Press.

Rorty, R. 1990. *Contingency, irony, and solidarity.* Cambridge: Cambridge University Press.

Shostak, M. 1983. *Nisa, the life and words of a ¡Kung woman.* New York: Vintage Books.

Tierney, W. G. ed. 1991. *Culture and ideology in higher education.* New York: Praeger.

Titon, J. T. 1980. The life story. *Journal of American Folklore* 93, no. 369: 276–92.

7

Fired Faculty:
Reflections on Marginalization
and Academic Identity

Patricia J. Gumport

Job loss can be one of life's most painful individual events. It can also be an opportunity to clarify identity, especially a sense of self in relation to work. Such personal stories abound of finding opportunity in devastation, acquiring wisdom through pain, recognizing gain in loss (Hyatt & Gottlieb 1987). While I draw on personal narratives in this chapter, my interest is not to search for, or to impose, a positive gloss on individual accounts of job loss. Nor do I intend to romanticize the suffering of individuals by casting them as tragic heroes done a grave injustice. Instead, I focus on narratives of three fired faculty to illuminate the social contexts in which academic identities are forged in higher education organizations.

Fired faculty convey that job loss can be a particularly painful and poignant occasion to reflect on academic identity, especially for full-time tenure-track faculty: painful because academics are unprepared, having been socialized in meritocratic ideals where careers are insulated from economic turmoil; and poignant because academia is characterized as "a good deal," with "good socioeconomic fortune and political freedom of expression" (Rosovsky 1990, 183; Hollander 1991, 163).

By the early 1990s, however, budget cuts of a sufficient magnitude to warrant elimination of academic positions have awakened a sense of vulnerability among faculty. While the uneasiness is tied to contemporary

This chapter benefitted from comments by Clifton Conrad, Elliot Eisner, Paula Fleisher, Gary Rhoades, Ann Swidler, and Bill Tierney. Carol Colbeck, Paula Fleisher, Chris Golde, and John Jennings provided valuable research assistance.

135

economic constraints, it is linked as well to underlying power relations that have become more evident in these times of pronounced economic strain. Higher education scholars have already begun to document some indicators that support this proposition, for example, in disputes over intellectual property rights and over retrenchment practices (Rhoades & Slaughter 1991; Slaughter, forthcoming). In one study of budget cuts, faculty saw their campuses as contested terrains where they clashed with administrators in attempts to clarify who runs the institution and what are their respective domains of expertise; faculty became more conscious of being measured in the differential valuing of academic units ostensibly based on cost-effectiveness standards and judgments of quality or centrality to mission (Gumport, forthcoming).

The explicitly contested quality of academic life points to some of the contemporary ways academic organizations sustain and reconstitute academic borders. A singular economic logic serves as the rationale for retrenchment practices. Euphemistically termed "downsizing" and "trimming the fat," a social-engineering approach to budget cuts is advanced as a transcendent economic necessity, one that calls upon utilitarian individuals to deliberate over anticipated gains and losses. Literature on the management of decline is dominated by procedural rationality and technical prescriptions for expenditure reduction by rectifying the inefficient use of resources across academic units (e.g., Mortimer & Tierney 1979; Cameron 1983; Altar & Shapiro 1990). Human costs, if acknowledged at all, are tallied as unfortunate consequences of mandatory structural adjustments.

Such approaches to higher education administration unduly emphasize depersonalized practices at the neglect of social relations. Beyond identifying this as a humanistic shortcoming, I offer a deeper conceptual criticism about the inattention to politics of academic identity, especially for faculty targeted as marginal and hence dispensable in a budget crisis. In times of abundance, academic identity issues are submerged in an ethos of pluralism. Faculty who advocate integrating personal, political, and professional commitments articulate struggles for legitimacy, yet they still find a location within a higher education system that mandates silence of the self (e.g., Gumport 1991, Krieger 1991; Tierney, forthcoming). Similarly, faculty who envision themselves as change agents altering purposes and practices of their campuses and fields characterize themselves as on the edge, in a location marginal and even oppositional to administrative priorities and conceptual establishments; a self-appointed exile to critique from the margin may be "a site one chooses to stay in, clings to even." (hooks 1990, 149-50)

Yet in conditions of economic scarcity with mandates for academic program reduction, issues of identity are more salient. The work of those located on the edge is most visibly threatened as it is redefined by the organization when the edge itself is moved to exclude them. Job loss is an externally imposed dismissal, quite literally the loss of a place for one's voice in the organization. Academic identity shifts are expected due to loss of personal investment in an academic territory. Yet this loss tends to be framed as a personal issue to be handled privately—what Mills (1959) calls a "personal trouble"—rather than as a public issue with explicit social and political as well as the commonly acknowledged cognitive and affective dimensions.

This chapter elevates the "personal troubles" of fired faculty to a public arena. Drawing from a multicase study of universities coping with state-mandated budget cuts in 1990, I focus on State University, a pseudonym.[1] The campus has been hit hard with a succession of cuts in legislative appropriations in the 10-15 percent range following a decade of reductions. According to an executive-level administrator, "The state higher education system has been under-resourced to begin with, and we've wanted to protect quality while eliminating the excesses of program duplication, especially in the service areas. . . . [We] took a three-pronged strategy: to cut enrollment by 10 percent, raise tuition by 40 percent, and do program reduction." For the latter, he continued, "we've leaned more heavily on centrality [to mission] than quality. Everything that was cut—all the affected departments—were top-ranked nationally." While hundreds of students were directly affected, roughly sixty tenure-track positions were eliminated. Administrators referred to the one-third who were non-tenured as "displaced faculty in disestablished positions."

Some School of Education faculty agreed to my request for interviews about a month after hearing they were cut. Although my initial intention was to examine how the budget cuts were determined, my interest broadened. The in-depth unstructured interviews became an opportunity for faculty to reflect with me on the meaning of what had happened for themselves, their colleagues, and the university. For this analysis, I spotlight three nontenured education faculty to show a range of perceptions and responses to having been cut. Jonathan is a White male with expertise in curriculum theory. Emily is a White female who studied creativity and learning processes. Will is a Native American male who worked on multiculturalism in education.

I select portions of their narratives, not to view the individual as the unit of analysis, but to see individuals as mediators of wider social conditions who can provide insight into some ways in which wider dynamics get played out locally. My main analytical purpose is to interpret the narratives for their social and moral significance. That is, *beyond* a psychological aim concerned with individual well-being or a liberal project "to consign the struggle of subordinate groups to master narratives," I invite critical engagement about prevailing forms of social relations in higher education: to con-

---

[1] It is ironic to use pseudonyms in a chapter that seeks to name silenced lives. For an analysis, see Gumport (in preparation).

sider how organizations shape identity via constructing "borders that define one's existence and place in the world" (Giroux 1990, 9, 14).

Jonathan

The rain and late afternoon hour made it damp and gray outside as I approached the Education building on the periphery of the campus. Jonathan's office was downstairs in a quiet back corner of a hallway of muted brown furniture, stark eggshell-colored walls, and clean, closed doors to faculty offices with no sign of life other than a small white card on each door stating office hours. Jonathan preferred the soft light from a small lamp on the rear corner of his mahogany desk, rather than the intrusive overhead fluorescent lights. A few neat piles of paper were stacked next to the State University blotter. Facing me, he gently rocked back and forth in his desk chair, glancing at the floor-to-ceiling wall of books and journals on the philosophy of education and curriculum theory. In the low light, the office felt like a warm private space, insulated from the cold outside.

"The worst part was that it came out of the blue. I had no idea. I learned about it from a student who called me and said, 'Guess what? Our program's been cut,'" said Jonathan with disdain when he described how the budget cuts were communicated. In his fifth year as an assistant professor, Jonathan felt personally "disappointed I could mean so little. . . . Being a graduate of [an elite university], my ego is large. . . . To the university it doesn't matter . . . even though I have done very well. I have co-authored several books, published things, you know. I am respected by people in the field. But the university couldn't care less. None of those things are worth anything."

As a professional educator, Jonathan considered the elimination of teacher education a mistake: "That makes a statement about teacher education and its value . . . within the culture at large . . . Something larger was lost in terms of any kind of respect or prestige for the School of Education. . . . There are kind of two dimensions to how I think about it. There is the decision to cut the program, which from my perspective was a mistake, a poor decision by almost any criteria. And then there is how it was implemented. . . . I think it is fair to say that the decision was a mistake, but bureaucrats make mistakes, so it is almost forgivable. How it was carried out is kind of adding insult to injury. It is what I will remember more ten years from now in terms of what has made it a nightmarish experience."

Jonathan candidly apologized for the partiality of his own perspective: "I am sure part of your agenda is to find out just what did happen, and I have no idea. I could not begin to speculate on what really happened. All I am probably good for is to say how it affected me: In some ways I think it has shaken my faith in the structures of higher education and my ability to work through them. In a sense I am retreating. At a certain point I decided that I want out and I want out now, rather than waiting for the end of the year. There were sacrifices involved in that, financial sacrifices. My wife and I had just bought a house. . . . That's just how I felt: the need to get out, feeling there is nothing I could do to make a difference here."

Jonathan said that the crisis caused him to "re-think where I want to be regarding style of scholarship that is valued, what I want personally, who I am professionally." The product of a prestigious doctoral program, Jonathan, in a little more than a whisper, confessed that he has fared well in this crisis: "I feel like a rat abandoning a sinking ship. I'm the first one to get out. . . . Escaping, getting away is my primary strategy." He secured a job as a tenured associate professor at "one of the best small private liberal arts colleges—which is really known as a university. They hired me to do teacher education, and that is the very reason I am losing my job here."

Jonathan explained that his choice for a new job resulted from self-searching and careful deliberation about what organizational context was most aligned with his expertise: "I've been groomed [for research], and I've always found myself at a large institution, a research institution. . . . So I always pictured myself in that kind of [setting]." Over time, he has become "disillusioned" with the "kind of crude accounting in which you bring in grant money for research that puts you in favor in the university. . . . " He quickly offered reassurance: "I am a big fan of higher education, you know, choosing it as a career. I've always been. Will be. It's the best our society has to offer. I've always negotiated it fine. But this experience has brought out the worst dimensions of the bureaucratic structure. . . . Very technocratic orientations. Usually you can hide from that. I had to ask myself: 'If the best thing I can say about a bureaucratic structure of the type I am used to is that it often leaves me alone, it doesn't recommend it very highly.' So I thought: 'I don't want to be at a small private institution.' And then I kind of re-thought: 'Wait. Maybe I DO want [that].' It was a definite realignment of my thinking. Who knows how much of it may be rationalization? I think I was as objective as I can be."

A major attraction of the new position for Jonathan is size, which he links to the potential for him to be a more central actor: "When I interviewed there I met everyone." In contrast, when he came to State University, he did not meet anyone "at the central administrative level," not even the dean of the School of Education. Jonathan believes the new organizational setting will be more conducive to deliberation with administrators about organizational purposes, as compared to the "lack of strong leadership" at State University: "The technocrats run this university. . . . There is absolutely no vision of what makes a good university, that whole dimension of the dialogue is missing and has been for some time. The mission is assumed. And they say 'we're going to protect our core people, we're going to protect our core programs;' and the only way we know what those core programs are is by the ones that aren't cut. . . . There is a set of values at work, but it's all implicit. It's not part of the discussion. It does something to the intellectual life. . . ."

Jonathan expressed a sense of powerlessness when it came to his doctoral students, who were few in number: "Two years ago I served as acting chair of the Graduate Studies Committee, and the deal I made was I will serve as chair but I won't take students. . . . [T]hat leaves me with many fewer students than other faculty, which is good because I am the first one out, so I haven't hurt anyone, but I won't be able to finish them all. . . . I'll be able to finish up four and the other four will have to find other faculty. . . . The policy is to find a new home for them. But in these circumstances the policy doesn't make sense. . . . I feel bad 'cause the students suffer. . . . It puts us in a situation where there is no way we can act in an efficient manner. There is nothing I can do about it. . . . Can I serve in an official capacity on someone's committee even though I am not employed by the university? . . . Somebody knows the answer somewhere, but I haven't been able to connect up with the right person. . . . I might be able to free up the time to come back, and I might be willing to do that, but who would be willing to pay for that? The university would never."

Since the budget cuts were announced, Jonathan said interactions with "unaffected" colleagues were "awkward," as if individuals were unsure what was proper conduct, and suggesting this was a matter of protocol: "I don't know if people are just worried about their own futures. My impression is now they don't know how to interact with you. It's like having a death in the family. People don't know how to act, what to say, whether to console you or whether to just ignore it and act as usual."

Emily

Emily's office was located further toward the periphery of the campus than Jonathan's. I sat on the well-worn olive green sofa. She sat on an old schoolteacher's chair with wheels that squeaked as she rolled toward the tape recorder, which quickly became less visible as she drew me into her narrative of grief and personal loss: "This was my fifth year. I was in the tenure review process when I was cut. A few months ago something came out saying we would not be threatened. So I didn't worry about it and, uh, I was absolutely flabbergasted. Completely shocked. . . . " Like Jonathan, Emily was dismayed at the lack of communication; yet while he was upset over hearing the news from a student, she expressed her anger in terms of moral injustice: "It was so horrendous that our dean and our associate dean never heard about the cuts until the morning we were told. I mean to have been told an hour before they had to come in and talk to us. It's just *unconscionable* to me that decisions can be made like that. . . ."

Emily spoke of her files in the "box," a strong visual image of the work she produced being passed around for review. Her "box" symbolized the bounded package within which lay her individual identity. In the pretenure review, her "box" was harshly criticized, which she attributed to an all-male committee: "In that review, . . . in my box I put the things that I was working on, thinking that certainly they'd want to see where I would be two years from now. . . . The feedback was that it looked like I was padding my file. . . . And I felt for sure that had women been on the committee they would have seen it. I hadn't been a feminist before this experience. By God, I'm becoming one. . . . " Upon hearing she was to be cut during her tenure review, Emily suggested that the dean "simply refuse to take the boxes back."

Emily's narrative conveyed injustice was done to her as an individual, as a professional teacher educator, and as a woman: "To make cuts like this is just unconscionable. . . . To eliminate the program is a slap to teachers as professionals. . . . It's the profession that is de-legitimized. It's the devaluing of education and children and women. It's not only here but in other universities in this state . . . and they've left administration, again you know white male and, gee whiz, it makes me angry."

In contrast to Jonathan, Emily's path through higher education was not the result of rational planning. Her narrative has a storybook quality. She was "a little poor kid from Pennsylvania" who "fell into" a scholarship arrangement to work with "a wonderful Renaissance man;" "urbanization was the key issue that was burning for me at that time. . . . I wanted to be Oscar Lewis Two." Emily came to education in an intuitive leap: "When I spent time in schools it hit me that there was a *calling* for me in the schools. They were so terrible; I was appalled. . . . I liked . . . young children, so I chose elementary. You know how your life takes different turns. . . . We got cutting-edge stuff and I was right on the edge. It served me well for many years."

In the context of this budget crisis, however, being on the edge did not serve Emily as well. Her response to the cuts was anger tempered with reason: "I must say that my first response was to try to have people see reason. It seemed to me that in a university that bases its life on rational thought, it seemed to me that if people here understood this program, they couldn't eliminate it." To no avail. She became "politicized;" in her words: "I did a couple of things. I became very active in organizing letters, talking to legislators, to state superintendents, just trying to get the word out. . . . I became political in a way that I had never been before. . . . Even lobbied in the state capitol."

For Emily the job loss also brought enormous grief: "This was a life-threatening thing and I was really feeling my whole life was threatened. I, I love this place. I was given the award last year for distinguished teaching. And at the ceremony I said that I was the most blessed of individuals here. I was doing exactly what I wanted to be doing in a job that was the perfect job for me. I, I love this job. I have had no ambition to do anything else besides what I'm doing. And I'm getting paid to do just what I want to do. . . . I love working with the students. I love the research. I've had such freedom to do what I want to do, to offer the kind of courses I want to teach, . . . to help my students find wings, to meet fascinating people. . . ."

A sincerity of commitment is prominent throughout Emily's narrative, exemplified by her account of two additional reasons for not wanting to move to another institution. The first is that she has established roots here, symbolized quite literally by a place—a farm that she bought a few years earlier with the stipend that came with the distinguished teaching award. "This is our retreat. It is the place that I refurbished myself. I always dreamed of having a place where colleagues, friends, students could come and work. And there is a little cottage. . . . It's a magical place. . . ." The grief in losing her position is matched in intensity by the imminent loss of this place: "It's a dream shattered for me. It's more than just losing a job. It's been a dream, this place. . . . It's very hard because I've invested so much of my soul here. And I really have felt that this is where I want my bones to rest, you know, this is where I want to be. It's devastating." The despair in this loss is accentuated by other circumstances in her life and in the United States which was at war in the Gulf: "It was just a tremendous sense of loss all the way through, you know, the death of my father, the war and then this, the most threatening things that could happen in my life all were happening at once."

Another reason for not wanting to move is her students. When Emily did receive a job offer from a comparable university, she declined: "I decided not to go. I on a gut level knew it wasn't for me. I don't—I can't even give you all the reasons, but I was feeling too squeezed . . . with a commitment to my students." She was supervising ten doctoral students to whom she felt deeply committed, given her own personal experience of being in their shoes two decades ago: "I went through cuts like this when I was a graduate student. . . . They cut 60 percent of the ed faculty. If my advisor hadn't continued to work with me, I don't know if I would have gotten my doctorate. . . . [S]he continued in spite of the tremendous cost to her. And I will bless her for it forever, because it was her caring and her kindness that carried me through." In the current situation, Emily sees her commitment as a matter of personal integrity: "I don't want to be a martyr. If something came along that was wonderful and felt right, I would probably feel like I had to take it. But a condition I [give is] that I feel I need to finish with my students. . . . I come with baggage right now. People have to understand that baggage and accept me the way I am. . . . It's the way I am."

Emily's conception of interactions with colleagues suggests the same passion and authenticity conveyed in her relationships with students. For faculty with whom she shares a perspective, she is devoted, even driven, to connect in order to work on improving how schools can cultivate human potential: "I have a constructivist way of looking, to focus on the child as the real center of the learning process. I [look] for strengths, interests, and abilities in all people. It's a much better way than what we typically do in school which is look for what kids can't do."

In the course of her narrative, Emily refers to her efforts to bring colleagues together beyond the School. For example, given an enduring interest in creativity, she started a faculty interest group in her first year at State: "The vision was to take people from various departments who focus on a particular aspect of the creative process. Like people who explore metaphor from dance, from the arts, from literature, from education . . . and put them off in a retreat setting. . . . It was really met with excitement. We don't do enough of that in universities and, for me, I'm so interested in how other people think. . . ."

The interview ended with Emily reflecting: "I keep feeling like I am being pushed into certain kinds of molds and I keep saying 'I want to do what's true to me.' I am interested in many things. . . . I don't do linear research. I do have one longitudinal study I have been working on. I have a crude draft [on it]. Now where. . . ." She searches through a carton on the floor: "This is my own version of my box. I try to keep something of everything." The interview ended with a question to me, reaching out in affinity with the academic struggle of arranging one's private possessions to present one's self for review: "So are you already putting your box together?" After chatting a moment, I walked out of her office, still looking back. She stood in the doorway in a cloud of anguish; her words hung in the air like an outstretched hand to me: "I still feel this place'll realize they need me. They can't let me go."

Will

Back in the main Education building, I climbed the stairs to meet Will in the sunny third-floor conference room frequently used by groups of teacher education faculty and students. Will greeted me in the lobby, where I had waited briefly watching students and secretaries animated in conversation and taking photographs of overflowing bulletin boards and doors to faculty offices. Among the cartoons and slogans was a photograph of a popular faculty member who, posed in a James Dean defiance, stating "Rebel without a job! " a sign stating "The beatings will continue until morale improves" and a list of "de-hired euphemisms," including "workforce adjustment," "redundancy elimination," and "coerced transition."

Will and I sat side-by-side at the long conference table. As I placed the tape recorder on the table, Will mentioned that he often used tapes to recapture dialogue from group meetings. The beginning of the interview was a little bumpy, as I sought an appropriate lead-in: "What I have been doing with people is trying to get a sense of their perceptions of how the decisions were made, what criteria were used, and how people reacted. . . ."Will reflected: "Hmmm. . . . That's almost the wrong question for me to respond to. So I'm going to have to reframe the question and then you can take it where you want." "Okay, talk to me about what you want. . . ." I said. He interrupted with "No. I see that as too linear for me. From my perspective it's far more complicated. . . . Maybe I should give you some background. . . ."

He began with an account of "a very intense ideological struggle" that "emerged" on campus *within* the School of Education. Will spoke in metaphors of dysfunctional family and political exile, as he matter-of-factly presented an array of observations about his division, teacher education: "We had signs for the past three years of being the least priority in the School. We have been stepchildren, bad children, the scapegoats ever since I came here six years ago. . . . We've been lied to, excluded, used, abused, and I hope this language is strong enough because that's exactly what happened. . . . We received less travel money. We were not put on key committees. We were not part of the final process of curriculum decisions. We were belittled for not bringing in a lot of grants, although we were building new programs without reduced work loads. We were the last to get computers, the last to get salary raises and equity pay. . . . We as a faculty were heavily beaten, psychologically and professionally beaten, for daring to put our dreams out on paper. . . . We did not behave in the behaviorist model which they knew was better for us. We were not treated as adults. . . ."

Will and other colleagues who were new to the campus about five years ago began working on a project of multicultural education. The growing affinity among them compensated for the difficult elements of struggle with others in the School: "Although we had different political or ideological perspectives, they were all people who had struggled and thought that out, professionals who made some decisions around where their work would be. . . . We merged. We coalesced into a very strong block." The significance of their coming together was far-reaching, not only in becoming a political group in the School, but in creating a vision: "Beyond that, a dialogue began between us for a whole year. We thought this is not the way we want to spend the rest of our lives if we are going to commit to an institution. We spent a year . . . just talking about what we could change. We met every Friday afternoon off-campus at one of our homes. . . . And there were some really intense exchanges and foundations built that first year. We set out to establish a working relationship and out of that grew a dream for a teacher education program, and a look at what public schools could be and how we could function as part of that connected community. It was a really powerful time."

Will described the momentum: "Some exciting things began to emerge two or three months into that. We found ourselves inviting each other to classes. 'Come on in and do this,' or 'would you do this article with me,' so collaborative work began. Physically we saw changes in our environment. . . . People emerged from doors and a dynamic grew that pulled all of us in, much like what should happen in schools and places where you see a community developing. . . . That second year we met not only every Friday but hundreds of hours in small and large groups, beyond our normal faculty load by the way. Four of the faculty were untenured."

According to Will, "the college wasn't used to that kind of intensity or . . . the political aspect where we won't just talk about a decontextualized educational process. . . . We're scholars and a good number of us have come to education from other arenas. . . ." As these relationships developed, "it upset the dynamics in the rest of the School." He and several colleagues "began raising hell at faculty meetings, asking 'What about this?' 'Well, why do this this way?' 'Why not do this?' 'Why not have seminars?' 'If we have a crisis why hide it?' 'Let's TALK about it.' 'Let's change the rules. It's our community.'"

Reflecting back on the difficulties that he and his colleagues have encountered, Will recalled a punitive stance by the administration: "At one point I was stripped of all my committee memberships in the college. I didn't have a voice anywhere. I was silenced. So I talked through my courses. . . . They punished my graduate students, including minority and women students. . . . Some of them lost their funding. They were attacked in class for their ideological stances, for writing outside of the model, for daring to do narratives, for daring to put their hearts into it, for daring to think they have a voice at age forty or fifty or sixty, for thinking their own experiences were valid. . . ."

An anecdote provides yet another insight into the divergence of this group from School norms. The graduate student assistants did not have office space, Will recalled, "so they put them out in a Quonset hut on the other side of campus. A number of us (three or four faculty) shared our offices with them, and it totally blew everyone out professionally: 'You don't do that with a graduate student.' But we did. It was that kind of thing that broke down barriers. . . . The grad students sat in on every part of the five-year process. The staff also has been part of discussions. . . ."

Will interpreted being cut as "the culmination of a very intense, long-standing ideological struggle." "You could feel the political climate, and I felt we were the target," which stands in contrast to Emily's and Jonathan's shock. Reflecting on being Native American, Will explained that "I wasn't as surprised as the others; that's what happens politically. We have a long history of broken treaties. And I see this as a broken treaty. I see the administration of the university and at the School level as having broken trust with people who have served them well."

"The worst part," Will stated strongly, "has been to see our dream handed over." Having rebuilt the program over the past six years, Will clearly had made an investment with his colleagues to design a collaborative, multicultural program whose values directly conflicted with the behaviorists who dominated the School as well as with the university's profit orientation in sponsored research and "big science." He spoke consistently in the first-person plural about how the collective dream was "disowned," rather than a personal dream shattered. He reflected angrily: "We gave our hearts for years. We had a heart here and they ripped it out. . . . I've faced that before. I've had to define my own life, to stand up and be bad children in order to have a perspective, and then have it discarded. It's still really hard."

In recalling the morning they were called together as a faculty to hear the news that their program and positions were eliminated, Will said the response of his colleagues was "physical and emotional shock . . . that was just devastating." For Will there were clues that something was up; he noticed they had never had a faculty meeting across campus; nor had they ever been served coffee or tea. "We walked in and there was a long table with all kinds of food—fruit, vegetables, donuts, croissants, coffee—and I said to my colleague, 'something bad is coming down.' I just felt it right there because they've not cared about us. . . ." On a profound level, Will was both spectator and participant: "It was that moment of truth for a lot of people, and a lot of white males in particular, or women who have followed a white male model and have felt safe in them. I am not sure if they felt safe as people, but they felt safe in those roles in the profession. As a person, that was a powerful moment to watch. I got to see that, and I am still dealing with that. I haven't put it in any place yet. . . . The only other place I have seen that kind of intensity was when I worked in the refugee camps in Southeast Asia with people who had lost everything. And I sense, for a number of people here, their careers have become the most important things in their lives . . . and everything else is secondary. That happens a lot in academia. And I saw what happened—it was like ripping their hearts out too."

Unlike Jonathan, whose strategy was to quickly secure an academic position at another institution, Will spoke with pride of his "way of surviving through community ties, professional ties across the country and a campus-wide network of support. . . ." Although he felt "personally, totally disacknowledged," and neither he nor any of his close colleagues had definite plans for subsequent academic positions, Will was confident that they will carry their dream onward into other organizational arenas: "The good part is we've all survived. With colleagues and graduate students and community members, we will take this out to share with other people. There are strengths to this, despite our differences, an enormous amount of integrity of what collegiality can do when it is really working. . . . There is tremendous empathy for people, even those people who wouldn't normally be the best of friends. There is a caring. There really is a caring."

At the close of our meeting, Will confessed that he had been reluctant to meet. "I didn't want to talk to you today, by the way. I was hesitant yesterday; you might have felt it. I was brushing you off. I need to tell you that now as a human being. I was reluctant even at lunch today and I said [to my colleagues] 'I am not ready. I am too raw.' So I appreciate your gentleness with this, 'cause we are trying to work it out as well. It's still *really* hard. . . . I'm sure we will cross paths again?"

Discussion

Narratives of fired faculty raise complex issues for people in higher education organizations to consider. I distill the issues into four major points that reflect an intermingling of organizational, ethical, political, and methodological concerns.

First, higher-education literature on retrenchment tends to distance the organization from its participants. Euphemisms like "downsizing," "trimming the fat" and "re-structuring" bolster a language that essentially obliterates human experience. In this light, the narratives aim to restore to consciousness some human dimensions of retrenchment decisions: For Jonathan, who was "disappointed I could mean so little," "the worst part was that it came out of the blue;" for Emily, who had "life-threatening" grief over a dream shattered," her experience was "outrage" over moral injustice done to her by the organization in which she "invested" her "soul;" while for Will it was "a broken treaty" where "we gave our hearts for years, . . . and they ripped it out." Clearly, consideration of human experience is appropriate not only for those fired but for the many levels of staff who, as Sutton (1988, 395) notes for managers, also experience distress. Perhaps, in this light, creative collective deliberation on revenue-generating activities becomes a more attractive response than drastic cuts.

Second, the narratives are expressions of a "common though individuated struggle" of identity work within higher-education organizations, when we view universities as sites in which a "central activity is the work of becoming somebody" (Wexler 1988, 308-10).[2] In examining identity work, organiza-

---

[2]For Wexler (1988) identity work occurs in vertically arrayed class institutional sites. I extend his concept to universities. Since identity is collectively produced but individually appropriated, it is a political issue: identity values are socially produced and contextually negotiated within historical possibilities. Given limited space, I apply these ideas within one site by seeing narratives as postmodernist expressions of heterogeneous subject positions, in which individuals are not bounded entities (rational or moral agents) but are fluid and socially contingent (Giroux 1990 and Aronowitz 1992). I use Gergen (1991) to distinguish among multiple discourses of modernism, romanticism, and postmodernism for the narratives of Jonathan, Emily, and Will, respectively. For other attempts to restore the micro-macro link via contextual meanings, see Collins (1981), Alexander et al. (1987), Scheff (1990), and Huber (1991).

tions are seen not simply as intellectual or emotional environments; instead they are seen as interactional fields where identity is a production of collective social labor, even though it is often assumed by individuals and attributed as an individual property. While the narratives in this chapter are limited to faculty at one site, they generate an interesting proposition—that different orientations to identity work may have been a factor in the inability of fired faculty to mobilize as a collective voice in response to being cut. The basis of this proposition is grounded in the two types of identity work most prominent: an orientation to "boundary work" as illustrated by Jonathan and to "community work" as reflected by Emily and Will, respectively

For Jonathan, becoming somebody was synonymous with academic achievement, where identity is the sum of accumulated merits. The irony, of course, is that Jonathan's faith was shaken after years of being a loyal supporter; he was rejected by the organization when it devalued his accomplishments. Boundary work enables him to sustain his academic identity. He differentiates himself from the university (the bureaucratic organizational "other" from which he hides out), himself from the students (whom he wants to "finish up" efficiently yet believes "there is nothing I can do about it"), himself from his colleagues who were not cut "they don't know how to interact with you," and himself from his fired peers (who are left to drown on the sinking ship while he, self-identifying as a rat, escapes). He sees the elimination of his program as a mistake that is "almost forgivable," while he keeps a faith in the potential for universities to pursue shared objectives. In isolated introspection, Jonathan withdraws his commitment to the university but not to the profession.

In contrast, Emily and Will each recognize that the locale of their identity work exists outside formal structures and requires creative invention. As community work, they engage in daily practices in their own small space to affirm their value.

Emily's narrative clarifies her efforts to develop an alternative economy outside the university's push for unlimited commodity production: she nurtures the potential for people to connect in spite of formal structures that isolate individuals into roles and programs. Emily's narrative expresses a devotion if not an urgent drive to bridge chasms between separate selves, wherein the greatest loss is being rendered silent, defeated, unheard, displaced from, in her words, the place "where I want my bones to rest." It is significant that she actually has two versions of her "box," one with polished publications that was submitted for review in conjunction with organizational demands in the commodification of knowledge, and one in her office that includes "crude" drafts to share with close colleagues. Emily's narrative is about creativity as a research interest and as a practice of initiating informal networks. Although she lost her position, she was transformed into expressing an intellectual and political identity that extends beyond the organization.

For Will, identity work was community work that was fought for daily, since he assumed that the administration did not value his work. Whether it be for stubbornness, idealism, or an explicitly transformative agenda, Will's orientation would be seen as dysfunctional by the administration for it undermines standard top-down governance practices and stirs up trouble by accentuating differences. From Will's perspective, disagreement is unavoidable; it is the concealment of conflict—not conflict itself—that is undesirable. Will's repeated call for direct interchange based on trust highlights that his starting point and ending point is interdependence through building foundations that are alternative to the hierarchical university organization, e.g., in his efforts to remove barriers between those in academia and those outside as well as among faculty, students, and staff. Although their project was "disowned," Will knew the ripples would extend outside the organization that excluded them. Consistent in his orientation to community work, Will agreed to do this interview, perhaps more ("I'm sure we will cross paths again?").

Distinguishing among types of identity work has significance for developing ethically informed organizational arrangements that take into account multiple subject positions, using Giroux's (1990) term. If becoming somebody is a central organizational activity, how we cope with our immediate interdependence given scarce resources may not lie in clarifying decision-making criteria, measures for quality, or incentives for faculty productivity. Nor is it satisfactory to stress the potential for economic scarcity to spur innovations (Whetten 1981). We may need to wrestle with bold questions beyond a corporate mindset of "downsizing" in order to resist having the economic order determine the identity values in the social and moral order. As a starting point, it is inappropriate to presume intersubjective agreement, since dissonance persists even in a context of interdependence; nor is it sufficient to apply an ethic of caring with an individualistic premise in which organizations in the aggregate cannot be considered ethical (Noddings 1984, 177). Rather, it may be crucial to consider the social forces constructing subjectivity and ask what social practices foster dialogue, vision, and compassion in academic communities, a challenge Giroux (1990, 25) has posed for the postmodern era.

A third and related point about the desirability of prevailing organizational arrangements is to consider politics, specifically marginalization in higher education. The three faculty in this chapter all experienced being devalued as professional educators. Yet the way they perceived this varied: Jonathan was personally disappointed for education to lose "respect and prestige" and perceived a blow to his self-esteem; for Emily it was unconscionable on moral grounds for the university to devalue teachers and children, while simultaneously it made her angry to be eliminated not just by bureaucrats but by men; and for Will being cut was "the culmination of a very intense, longstanding ideological struggle," that included the administration's harsh disapproval of his pedagogical practices that validated experience and voice. It is even more illuminating that Will would not speak specifically about "affected faculty" as a subpopulation in the School of Education since everyone was affected. A colleague of his concurred, noting the crisis brought about a sense, among those fired and those spared, of vulnerability he called "our own mortality. People are crankier, more contentious than ever. There is a chill rippling through this place. . . . If this can happen here, it can happen anywhere."

That they are all located in a School of Education makes a formidable statement about the importance of organizational contexts in shaping academic identities, especially in terms of what and who is perceived as dispensable in a budget crisis. Not only was the School located on the geographical periphery of the campus, but it housed programs that were deemed on the edge of the university's mission—even though several people in eliminated programs did "cutting-edge" research, teaching, and service. Moreover, the narratives make apparent some systemic features that sustain the marginalization of professional educators: the emphasis on sponsored research grants as more valuable than the service of educating teachers, the alignment of behaviorist approaches with "big science," and the vulnerability of units comprised largely of untenured faculty, especially with a disproportionate percentage of women. It is noteworthy that, of the three fired faculty, the identity of only one, Emily, was significantly transformed as she gained an awareness of some of these structural constraints that determine her marginalization. In contrast, Jonathan sustained his sense of self-worth in an intact academic identity; whereas Will's already politicized identity was reproduced and affirmed in his persistent refusal to separate intellectual and organizational issues from the wider political and moral contexts in which they reside.

Using the narratives to invite critical conversation (Fine 1991), we can consider not only who makes the decisions about academic program reduction and based on what criteria, but how it is that some people and programs are perceived as dispensable regardless of stated criteria? What is the nature and direction of the unchecked drift that sweeps across campus in the frenzy of fiscal urgency, rendering fired faculty institutionally silent and some surviving faculty in marginal units lying low in fear that they will be next? These are questions that point to a need for analysis beyond the level of individual adjustment to job loss (Ragland-Sullivan & Barglow 1981). Further analysis needs to situate these questions more broadly to clarify how universities are social arenas that display divergences in professional power and in the political economy of academic fields. We can begin by examining how particular values get played out in organizations, how those values are passed on across professional generations through the intimate lineage of faculty mentors, and whether those values can be renegotiated across campuses. More specifically, we can ask: How is faculty authority as a whole compromised when, behind closed doors, administrators deem particular kinds of academic work and workers more valuable than others? And what is the desirability of a technical tightening of organizational arrangements without rethinking the relations between centers and margins of power? Can "borders of meaning, maps of knowledge, social relations, and values" be not only crossed but renegotiated? (Giroux 1990, 27)

The fourth and final point concerns the nature of field research that gives primacy to individuals' accounts in order to convey a range of human experience. Whether viewed as stories or as partial narratives, two layers are especially noteworthy: the narrators want to show that they interpreted a new situation appropriately and acted accordingly; and the narrators imply a moral evaluation rather than a modal point of view (McCall 1990). The relational nature of the interview makes explicit that narrators "decide what to tell about what happened" and that researchers become necessarily implicated in that which is selectively shared (McCall 1990, 147; Connelly & Clandinin, 1990). From the perspective of traditional social science, these subjective dimensions are major methodological limitations to making reliable and valid conclusions. Yet, the inherently relational nature of interviewing may be precisely that avenue into experience that illuminates understanding, a power of connection that enables us to imagine and to envision "the familiar hearts of strangers" (Ozick 1986, 68).

The social relations in the conduct of this research illustrate that identity can be viewed as a continuing social quest. The interview situation itself became an opportunity for faculty to re-present themselves, this time not only as educators whose positions had been eliminated but as narrators telling the story of how they adapted to losing their jobs. The interview became a new forum for them to create the kind of self/other social relations they had sought to have valued in their work setting: for Jonathan it was an opportunity to call into question the assumed mission of the university and the frustration of ineffective bureaucratic practices; for Emily it was therapeutic to share her enormous grief and anger as well as validating to see that another colleague from outside the university was eager to hear about her academic interests and her transformed political identity; for Will it was an occasion for dialogue, a matter of re-creating community in his daily practices and perhaps connecting with a kindred soul who shared a vision for change if not precisely the same spirited commitment to improve schools by changing the way we prepare teachers.[3] Of the three narrators, both Jonathan and Will conveyed an awareness of being in a role of narrator, the former apologizing for the partiality of his view and the latter noting with humility the limits of language for communicating about his experience in order to facilitate my understanding.

A puzzle remains about how to be with one another—whether in interview situations or beyond. This is more than a methodological issue of appropriate fieldwork practices for emotionally hot topics, as noted by Sutton & Schurman (1988), and more than an epistemological issue of the validity of retrospective interview data. Instead, it is a question of how we conceptualize ourselves as researchers and how we conceptualize the research process in which we engage one another. In this light, the puzzle is an ontological set of questions infused with ethical and political implications.

---

[3]Conveying that the interviews functioned in this way is limited by the medium of written discourse. Moving from initial face-to-face exchanges to tapes to transcripts to selected passages without creating stick figures is exceedingly difficult. What is lost is analogous to using a campus map to portray a campus visit or sight-reading a stark melody off a black-and white page instead of hearing the fully textured music.

References

Alexander, J., Giesen, B., Munch, R. and Smelser, N. 1987. *The micro-macro link*. Berkeley: University of California Press.

Altar, H., & Shapiro, J. 1990. Are retrenchment decisions rational? *Journal of Higher Education* 61, no 2: 121–41.

Aronowitz, S. 1992. *The politics of identity*. New York: Routledge.

Cameron, K. 1981. On the microfoundation of macrosociology. *American Journal of Sociology* 86: 984–1014.

Connelly, F., & Clandinin, D. 1990. Stories of experience and narrative inquiry. *Educational Researcher* 19, no 4: 2–14.

Fine, M. 1991. *Framing dropouts*. Albany: SUNY Press.

Gergen, K. 1991. *The saturated self*. Basic Books.

Giroux, H. 1990. The politics of postmodernism. *Journal of Urban & Cultural Studies* 1: 5–37.

Gumport, P. 1991. *E pluribus unum? Review of Higher Education* 15, no 1: 9–29.

———. Forthcoming. The contested terrain of academic program reduction. *Journal of Higher Education*.

———. In preparation. *The social production of anonymity*.

Hollander, P. 1991. *The survival of adversary culture*. London: Transaction Publishers.

Hooks, b. 1990. *Yearning*. Boston: South End Press.

Huber, J. (ed.) 1991. *Macro-micro linkages in sociology*. Newbury Park: Sage.

Hyatt, C., & Gottlieb, L. 1987. *When smart people fail*. New York: Penguin.

Krieger, S. 1991. *Social science and the self*. New Brunswick: Rutgers University Press.

McCall, M. 1990. The significance of storytelling. *Studies in Symbolic Interaction* 11: 145–61.

Mills, C. 1959. *The sociological imagination*. New York: Oxford.

Mortimer, K., & Tierney, M. 1979. *The three "R's" of the eighties*. AAHE-ERIC Report No. 4. Washington: AAHE.

Noddings, N. 1984. *Caring*. Berkeley: University of California Press.

Ozick, C. 1986. The moral necessity of metaphor. *Harper's*, May, 62–68.

Ragland-Sullivan, E., & Barglow, P. 1981. Job loss. *Journal of Higher Education* 52, no 1: 45–66.

Rhoades, G., & Slaughter, S. 1991. Professors, administrators, and patents. *Sociology of Education* 64: 65–77.

Rosovsky, J. 1990. *The university*. New York: W. W. Norton.

Scheff, T. 1990. *Microsociology*. Chicago: University of Chicago Press.

Slaughter, S. Forthcoming. The political economy of restructuring postsecondary education. *Journal of Higher Education*.

Sutton, R. 1988. Managing organizational death. In *Readings in organizational decline*, edited by K. Cameron, R. Sutton, & D. Whetten, 381–96. Cambridge: Ballinger.

Sutton, R., & Schurman, S. 1988. On studying emotionally hot topics. In *The self in social inquiry*, edited by D. Berg & K. Smith, 333–49. Newbury Park: Sage.

Tierney, W. Forthcoming. On method and hope. In *Power and method*, edited by A. Gitlin. New York: Routledge.

Wexler, P. 1988. Symbolic economy of identity and denial of labor. In *Class, race, & gender in American education*, edited by L. Weis, 302–16. Albany: SUNY Press.

Whetten, D. 1981. Organizational responses to scarcity. *Educational Administration Quarterly* 17, no 3: 80–97.

8

Self-Portraits of Black Teachers:
Narratives of Individual and
Collective Struggle against Racism

Michèle Foster

Introduction

Growing up in an extended family, I heard many stories of my grand-father's grandmother's, and mother's experiences. Though many of these stories were of the routine and mundane activities associated with their jobs, a significant number of them had a decidedly political orientation. My grandfather had, for instance, been a charter member of the Brotherhood of Sleeping Car Porters, one of the first all-Black unions, which sought to se-cure protection and labor rights for its all-Black membership. For a brief time, my grandmother worked as a showgirl in the all-Black Broadway musicals in the 1920s, and my mother studied to be a nurse at the Harlem School of Nursing when most predominantly White schools maintained closed-door policies to Black women seeking to study nursing. At the time, I was unaware of the significance of these stories. Only much later, during graduate school, did I realize that they were examples of Blacks who had confronted racism, resisted it despite its attempts to limit their achievements and make them feel less than men and women, and overcome it. In so doing, they had managed to create a space for themselves in a world struc-tured to oppress them.

I acknowledge funding for this work from the University of Pennsylvania Research Foundation and the Spencer Small Grant Program. A Spencer Postdoctoral Fellowship from the Natinal Academy of Education, a Carolina Minority Postdoctoral Fellowship and a Smithsonian Fac-ulty Fellowship enabled me to work full-time on this study. I am grateful to Jeanne Newman for her careful transcription of the interviews.

In 1988, when I began interviewing Black teachers, the stories from my childhood influenced the course of my research. The life histories which form the basis of this chapter were undertaken to enable Black teachers to speak for themselves, to call forth their own stories of resistance and survival, and to recognize their perseverance and unacknowledged victories. Though many of the teachers interviewed were not consciously aware of the overarching political nature of their struggles, they were pleased that their experiences were sought, and insisted that their stories be preserved and passed on to younger generations in order that we might not only remember our past, but be able to profit from its lessons as well. Along with the teachers, it is my hope that this chapter will become part of a collective memory of the Black community's struggle against oppression.

Silenced Voices

For the first six decades of this century, teaching was one of the few occupations open to Black college graduates, a condition reflected in the oft-heard phrase, "the only thing a college-educated Negro can do is teach or preach." Despite this fact, the experiences of ordinary Black teachers have not been well documented. Though some biographies of famous Black educators who have made significant contributions to education do exist, these accounts do not encompass the experiences of thousands of Black teachers who, though not historically significant, nonetheless played a critical role in the education of Black children (Collier-Thomas 1982; Committee on Policy for Racial Justice 1989). The voices of Black teachers are not adequately heard in first-person narrative accounts. Of sixty-five first-person teachers' narratives written in English in this century that I have reviewed, for instance, only five were written by Black American teachers. Also, though the anthropological and sociological literature is somewhat more inclusive, with Black teachers appearing more frequently in this genre, except for a few balanced portrayals (Lightfoot 1978; Lerner 1972; Sterling 1972), the typical representation of Black teachers is unequivocally unflattering (Rist 1970; Conroy 1972; Spencer 1986).

One characteristic of the educational literature written about Black teachers between the mid-1960s and the present is its almost singular focus on describing how these individuals worked to maintain the larger social order. Rarely do any of the accounts describe how Black teachers actively resisted the status quo. This chapter seeks to address this omission. It focuses on the various individual and collective means through which Black teachers have resisted racism and consequently challenged the status quo. In so doing, it gives voice to nineteen Black teachers, who though not historically significant are nonetheless considered exemplary by the Black communities that they have served.

A total of nineteen teachers were interviewed for this study. Each has worked between twenty-four and sixty-six years in different regions of the United States in both urban and rural settings. Fifteen were female, and four were male. At the time they were interviewed, seven were elementary school teachers, five taught high school, and one taught junior high school. Four were retired. The remaining two were school administrators though they had previously been teachers. All of the males taught high school or junior high school. The women teachers were almost evenly divided between elementary and high school levels; four were high school teachers and five were elementary school teachers. The teachers were raised in twelve states within five regions: the Northeast, Middle Atlantic, South Atlantic, West North Central, and West South Central. The regions were derived using the 1989 109th Statistical Abstract.

All of the interviewees were chosen by community nomination, a term coined and a method of selection that I developed specifically for this study. That is, teachers were chosen by direct contact with African-American communities. Periodicals, community organizations and individuals provided the names of the teachers. Informants were questioned about their family, childhood and community life: their elementary, high school, college and teacher-training experiences; their decisions to become teachers; the various positions they have held; the changes they have observed during their lives and careers; and their philosophies and pedagogies of education. The interviews ranged from two to four hours in length. Where required, follow-up interviews that build on previous sessions were conducted.

Twelve of the nineteen teachers spent their childhood years in communities where schools were segregated by law. Six grew up in communities where no laws required segregated schools, but where de facto segregation meant that schools were racially isolated, nonetheless. The remaining teacher spent half of her childhood in a segregated community before moving north with her family. Three-fourths of the teachers attended historically Black colleges, including three raised in the North who attended majority White elementary and secondary schools. All who attended predominantly White colleges, except one however, spent their precollege years in segregated schools.

Whether raised in the North or South, all of the teachers began their professional careers during the era when separate but equal was the law of the land (Tyack 1984; Franklin 1979; Curry 1981; Anderson 1989; Ethridge 1979; Dilworth 1984). Five of the teachers reared in the South began teaching in segregated southern schools, two of them in schools where they had once been students. Though two later relocated to the North and began teaching, three remained in the same school districts through the desegregation and post-desegregation years. Four of the teachers began their careers in schools where White students made up the majority, with the remaining ten having begun their careers in school systems which, though not legally segregated, nonetheless maintained racially imbalanced schools. Eight of the teachers worked in the same district for two decades and continue to teach a second generation of learners.

This chapter explores institutional racism as practiced in northern and southern school systems. It compares and contrasts racism in northern and southern school systems, and highlights the intersection of geography and racist conditions and practices. It also illustrates how the teachers in the various sites both understood and responded to the racism that they encountered. It deals with the various means, both individual and collective, by which these nineteen teachers have opposed discriminatory practices. The chapter concludes with a discussion about the potential utility of such narratives both as cultural memory and praxis.

Racist Practices: North vs. South

Despite the fact that the teaching profession was open to Blacks, historians have amply documented that the careers of Black teachers have, nonetheless, been sharply circumscribed by racism. For years Black teachers were paid less than White teachers, rarely hired except to instruct Black pupils, discriminated against by largely White unions, dismissed in large numbers following the *Brown* vs. *Board of Education* decision, and denied access to teaching positions by legal and extralegal means. Though the peculiarities of racism varied according to region, the material conditions under which Black teachers have labored have been unique. In communities where laws mandated it, there was a clear and unambiguous pattern of segregation in schools. Teachers who began their careers in legally segregated communities were concentrated in separate schools; however, within these confines the range of teaching and administrative opportunities was open to them. Northern communities, where de jure segregation was absent, employed unofficial and more subtle practices to concentrate African-American teachers in certain schools and restrict them from certain grade levels. The result was that northern and southern Black teachers resorted to different pattern of resistance, a fact borne out in these interviews.

Resisting Racism: Southern Style

This section considers some of the day-to-day manifestations of racism encountered by southern Black teachers. It examines the inequitable school expenditures that resulted in dilapidated buildings, damaged textbooks, and the differential salaries. Then it concludes with a discussion of the individual and collective actions and struggles waged by Black teachers over local control and quality schooling for Black children.

One of many inequities in dual school systems was the discrepancy in per-pupil expenditures in White and Black public schools. Included in these expenditures were textbooks, teaching supplies, school library books, and other instructional supplies and salaries. In North Carolina, considered one of the most progressive southern states with respect to Black education, the per-pupil expenditures for Black students in 1939–40 were 72.6 percent of those for White students. Fourteen years later, the gap narrowed considerably; the per-pupil expenditure for Black students reached 94.3 percent of the expenditure for White pupils (U.S. Department of Health, Education and Welfare 1954).

These discrepancies were evident in differential salaries paid to Black and White teachers. The salaries for White rural and urban North Carolina elementary school teachers in the 1928–29 school year were $724 and $1,181, respectively. Black elementary teachers who worked in rural areas, on the other hand, earned 57 percent of the salary of their White counterparts while Black elementary teachers who worked in urban areas obtained 61 percent of the salary of urban White elementary school teachers. At the secondary level, the discrepancies were slightly less; Black high school teachers earned 72 percent of the salary received by White teachers. In North Carolina in 1933 Black teachers were required by law to meet the same qualifications as Whites for comparable certification. Yet, this same law specified that Whites possessing the same qualifications as Blacks were to receive 30 percent higher salaries. Salary differentials such as those in North Carolina were commonplace throughout the south. In cooperation with the NAACP, Black teachers, through their National American Teachers Associations (founded in 1902 as the National Association of Teachers in Colored Schools, an organization of teachers from the twenty states which had separate schools for Blacks, and a counterpart to the all-White segregated National Education Association) fought to eliminate these salary discrepancies. In 1933, 2,500 Black teachers met in Raleigh to listen to speakers and to voice their protest against the inequities in school funding, including teachers' salaries (Streator [1933] 1990).

Though the outcome of this demonstration is unclear, a decade later, Black and White teachers' salaries were still unequal. Everett Dawkins,[1] who began teaching in Chatham County, a rural county less than fifty miles from Raleigh, recalls how he and his colleagues in the North Carolina Black Teachers Association fought for salary equalization:

> When I started to work in 1943, two things that I look back on now bother me quite a bit. Number one, teachers, period didn't make anything. I mean money, financially. It was like ninety dollars month. A month. In addition to that Black teachers were not paid on the same rate as Whites in North

---

[1] All informants' names are pseudonyms. The place names remain unchanged.

Carolina. So where we were getting like $90, *they* were probably getting like $120 a month. But through the leadership of the North Carolina Teachers Association, we were able to bring enough pressure to get the salaries at least equalized. The North Carolina Teachers Association was the Black teachers of North Carolina band[ed] together in an association. We had our own association called the North Carolina Teachers Association. They [the salaries] weren't very high, but at least they were equal. Everybody was making the same thing with the same certification. So that is one thing that has bothered me all these years. I feel like somewhere down the line somebody owes me some money.

• Do you remember when you got your salaries equal?

It had to be about 1945 or '46, somewhere in that general area I can't pin it down as to date, but I do know that it was in the 40s. I'll put it that way. Somewhere between '43 and '50. You know I just feel like we got ch—well, I know the Black teachers got cheated in that respect. I don't have any real animosity with anybody, but it's just the fact that it seems to me that they were given a little more consideration, too, the fact that we were not paid on an equal basis.

Salary differentials were not the only inequality in supposedly separate but equal school systems. Teachers, especially those from rural counties, recalled that their schools had inferior physical plants and fewer supplies and materials than White schools. Lacking gymnasiums, students could only have physical education outside when the weather permitted. Black teachers in segregated southern schools never received teachers' manuals or other equipment and were responsible for purchasing their own school materials. Discarded from White schools and sent to Black schools, the textbooks were often so badly worn that they were unusable.

Ella Jane, who began teaching in East Texas in 1955, spoke about the conditions she taught under for nine years before she was transferred to the previously all-White school after desegregation:

In the Black schools, we only got—the textbooks that we got were the books that didn't have a space to write our names. They were torn out and the books came from the White schools after they were ready to put them in the trash. We didn't have teachers' editions. And in the year that our school burned down, I didn't even have textbooks. Not any kind. Our school, my high school burned down. Where I went to school, where I was working in '61 or '62 something like that, the school burned down. But the remainder of the school year I didn't have any textbooks. We didn't even get any more. We taught in the church. But the school did not furnish anything. You just managed on what you could find. You cut out stuff, you bought stuff. You bought your own construction paper, you bought your own glue, you bought your own Kleenex. You bought everything that you used. Maybe you would get a record player. For your class. But you'd have to get your own records. You just didn't have anything. You didn't have anything to work with. It was real hard. We didn't even have a gym. If we played ball, you had to play when the weather was good, and you had to play outside.

Echoing these sentiments, Bernadette Mosely described the conditions in one of the two segregated schools in Hampton, Virginia in which she taught:

Underwood was a very old school. Whenever the temperature dropped below 30 or 32 degrees, we were cold. And there were times when the principal had to double up classes, it was so cold. Now how can you teach in a doubled up situation? It was just not ideal at all. I can remember one time the books were so worn out, I remember a first grade teacher in the faculty meeting at the end of school said, "Mr. Holmes, I want to talk about these books that we have given these children." She said, "I don't even want to touch them myself. They're old and the state adoption has been passed." And everybody was talking out. He (the principal) said, "I'll tell you what you do." And at that school they had a coal furnace. And he said, "You go through them and all the old books that you think are not usable just stack them outside your room and I'll have the janitor bring them down here by the furnace room." You know, two or three days after we got those books down there, the superintendent came in the school and made him take every one of those books back up into the classroom. "What's wrong with this? You can still read it."

Given these conditions, it may seem impossible that Black teachers would have been able to expose Black students to a rigorous curriculum or to educate them effectively. Though there are some documented exceptions (Jones 1981; Sowell 1974, 1976), the inferiority of segregated Black schools is a widely assumed and accepted fact. Detailed descriptions of Black schools in segregated southern school systems and comparisons of the material conditions of Black and White schools establish this point (Kluger 1979). Unarguably, segregated schools were severely underfunded and lacking supplies and equipment. Though lacking materially, it cannot be assumed that the students who were enrolled in segregated schools were automatically deprived of challenging coursework.

In *Simple Justice,* the seminal history of the *Brown* decision, Kluger informs his readers that at two of the four Black schools in Topeka "more of the teachers held master's degrees than at any of the White grade schools and their devotion to their work was exemplary." In a profile of Mamie Williams, who by community-wide agreement was Topeka's best black teacher, Kluger describes her as "a master teacher" despite the fact that she taught in all-Black schools (Kluger 1979).

Thousands of Black teachers such as Mamie Williams were able to challenge their students and educate them effectively despite the material constraints imposed by segregation. Everett Dawkins, a retired teacher whose earlier narrative mentioned the struggle waged by members of the North Carolina Teachers Association for equal salaries, is an example. Dawkins, who taught in a rural North Carolina school district for forty-one years, twenty-seven in segregated and fourteen in desegregated schools, agreed that segregation had a deleterious effect on the amount and quality of materials available to his county's Black public schools. Nonetheless, he was the first math teacher in his county to offer an advanced math course to students in his all-Black segregated high school:

> Everyone today says that Black kids can't do math, but in my little segregated school I had lots of kids who loved math and were good in it, too. Even though I had to teach a whole lot of subjects—because in all Black schools you had to be able to teach what they needed—math was my major and my favorite subject. So I decided that a lot of my students were ready for advanced math and I just started teaching it. It was the first advanced math class ever taught in the county. And, I taught it to Black kids for about two years, before the school board found out and made me stop until the White high school could get the course going in their building. You know they couldn't stand that Black kids were gettin something their kids weren't gettin.

Though forced to comply with the school board's decision, Dawkins recognized the implementation and subsequent cancellation of the course as a political struggle over who was to control the content of Black education.

Controlling the education of Black children is a theme that surfaced repeatedly in the life histories of teachers who began teaching in legally segregated schools. Remembering the fight waged by the teachers and parents when Georgetown County tried to close a local Episcopal parochial school known for its quality courses and instruction, Miss Ruthie, an eighty-year-old South Carolina teacher who has taught at the school since 1938, described how Black parents and teachers actively resisted the county's efforts to exercise control over their children's education:

> The county had just built a new school and they wanted all of us to go together to the new school. So we told them no. So they said that they were gonna see that this school closed down. My husband told them, "We'll see that it stays open." So that was the argument between the superintendent and us. So they stirred the people up telling them how they felt. They said if the children came here to school that when they finished here they couldn't go into public school for a higher education. And that's when the parents started to roll and we started keeping Columbia [the state capital] hopping. We got the Department of Education hopping. To answer the questions that they were putting out. We kept on going, but some of the parents, you know how they can frighten some off. The next year, the dio-

cese said they couldn't support the school, but if we wanted to keep it open we could do it. They did everything they could to make us close the school. And we didn't. So then the diocese said if we wanted to keep it and the community wanted it we could do it without support and that's what we've been doing ever since.

Though Black teachers are often portrayed as middle-class individuals who invariably uphold the status quo (Rist 1970, 1973; Conroy 1972; Spencer 1986), there is evidence in these interviews that within segregated school systems, despite threats of retaliation, censure and personal risks to themselves, Black teachers actively resisted racism. Sometimes individually and sometimes collectively with other teachers and parents, they challenged an inequitable system by fighting for equal wages and more control over the education of Black children.

Everett Dawkins refused a lucrative position with the federal government that involved computers because of a promise made to his mother that he would serve his community as a teacher. Likewise, Miss Ruthie attended Avery Institute, a school with a reputation for elitism. Despite this privileged background, she began teaching in "the rurals," living with the "little people" and has consistently stood with Black parents against the South Carolina Department of Education as it has tried to dismantle the local independent school, which since 1903 has provided an alternative to the substandard education previously offered in segregated schools and the discriminatory one now offered in the desegregated schools in the South Carolina coastal areas (Drago 1990).

Resisting Racism: Northern Style

Northern Black teachers were not immune to racism. Like southern Black teachers, they also confronted racist hiring practices. Often when they tried to integrate previously all-White schools, they encountered explicit as well as implicit racism. Northern Black teachers usually responded with individual challenges to the status quo. Though some decided to integrate the teaching ranks of all-White schools, many chose not to desegregate the suburbs, but to remain in inner-city schools where they were most needed. These obstacles and the strategies that northern Black teachers used to counter them are addressed next.

Irrespective of region, Black teachers have been victimized, in particular, by racist hiring practices. Three Black teachers in this study who taught in New England told of the subtle and not-so-subtle means by which northern school districts discriminated against them. Two teachers who relocated from the south in the 1950s recalled how central-office placement practices insured that Black teachers were to be assigned to some schools and not others.

After having taught for several years in Jacksonville, Florida, a certified high school English teacher was denied a position as a high school teacher in Hartford because of an unwritten policy that banned teachers from working at the secondary level in all but a few racially isolated schools. Not until she became certified at the elementary level was this teacher able to secure a permanent position in the public schools. Another teacher who moved to Hartford from West Virginia told of similar difficulties that she encountered securing a teaching position:

> Then I came to Hartford. Did not get a job immediately. I applied. This was in '53. I applied each year that I went back to West Virginia, but they didn't have any openings, or they never called me. . . . I subbed at the Noah Webster School which was in the Northwest section of the city which was predominantly White—it was White. I was a long-term sub for two months because the teacher there was on maternity leave. At the end of June the principal asked me what was I gonna do next year. I said I didn't know. She said, "Well, why don't you put your application in." I told her it had been in. So she called downtown and she said, "I want Bobbie here." They say, "We don't have an application." Course, I know where the application went. When I applied, it went in the wastebasket. Because of the color of my skin. This was in 1953. I don't know how many Black teachers it might have been, maybe six or seven in the city. I'm not sure of how many at the time, but there weren't that many Black teachers.

In Boston, prior to the 1974 desegregation order, Black teachers were severely underrepresented among the teaching force. As in Hartford, those Black teachers who did manage to secure positions were isolated in specific schools. Jane Vanderall, who began teaching in Boston in the 1950s, explained what it was like for Black teachers in those years:

> At the time I started teaching, Black teachers were assigned to just that strip going from the South End into Roxbury, between, let me see, Tremont Street and Washington. You didn't get any choice. That's where you were sent and most of the Black teachers had a very hard time out of town [the area where Black teachers were assigned].

During the school desegregation suit in the mid-1970s, the Boston Teachers' Union went to court to try to preserve the privileged status of its largely White membership. Shrouding the issues in the cloak of seniority, they attempted to restrict further the number of Blacks entering their ranks.

Though local Black teachers' organizations existed in some large northern urban centers, there is little evidence in the interviews here to suggest that these Black northern teachers worked collectively with other Black teachers within their schools systems to challenge racism. In general, their challenges to the status quo seem to have been individual ones. Given the choice, some northern Black teachers, believing that taking positions in all-White schools was not in the best interests of their Black students, staunchly opposed being transferred to predominantly White schools. Others recognized that their success might force White parents and students to confront their own feelings of superiority. When given the opportunity, they chose to desegregate all-White schools.

Two teachers explain below their reasons for choosing to stay in urban Black schools. Both came of age during the 1960s. Pamela Owens, a high school English teacher, the 1981 California Teacher of the Year and the first Black to be so honored, spent three years on the state commission on the teaching profession and two years on the credentialing commission. Ten years later, still in great demand as a speaker to various civic, business, and professional groups, she has been besieged with invitations to transfer to several of the more affluent White schools in the district. But Pam has remained at the same school. She tells people that she will "do what I want to do," that she is "going to be where I *need* to be and where I can be of some good."

In the following passage, Cheryl Thigpen, who began teaching in 1969, elaborated this view more fully. She began by describing the financial incentives that encouraged teachers to enter urban schools without first assuring that they were actually committed to working with urban students.

> You know, in the beginning with the urban ed crisis, I've seen two things. One, I saw a lot of teachers who came into urban ed because of the fact that that was the time that the government was offering education loans, and you did not have to pay the loan back if you went into what they called a validated school. And a validated school was a school in which the children, a certain segment of the children, are below the poverty level. So, a lot of teachers came into the urban schools because of that. They did not have to pay their student loans back. That was thing number one that I saw.

She gave her own reasons for staying in urban schools, which differed from the reasons that she criticized earlier. While articulating why she elected to continue in her present position, she conceded another view that acknowledged that White as well as Black children benefit by the presence of Black teachers:

> But I always knew that I was there because that's where I wanted to be, because I felt that with the knowledge that I have, why am I going to pass it out to little White kids? Because they're going to make it in this world, and all the White folks out there, if they don't learn how to read or write, the White folks are still going to give those White kids jobs. So, I felt that I was too talented and I had too much to give to White children. I've always felt that way, whereas I have a friend who's in a White school, and she feels just the opposite of me. She feels that if Black teachers don't go into White schools, these White kids won't know about Black people, and that Black people are capable of doing things such as teaching, which I agree with.

When Black teachers did press to be allowed to teach in desegregated settings, they sometimes met with organized resistance from the White community. Evelyn Taylor, who spent half of her childhood in a segregated southern school before moving north to complete her elementary and secondary education, spoke of hostility, resistance, and unexpected sources of support that she encountered, when in 1960 she became the first Black teacher assigned to teach in a California Bay-area community:

> All right, so I got the job. But after I got the job, I was assigned to a school on this side of town and it was just horrible. I had been away that summer and when I came back I didn't know that all this stuff had gone on. They had called my house, "Nigger, nigger, nigger." They had held a what do you call it, a community meeting in the church and had all the people there. The principal came over to my house. It was hard for either of them [her husband or the principal] to tell me. There was even a dispute about the man who led this movement wearing his scouting uniform at that time. There was an article in the paper because you're not supposed to wear your uniform when you do—it was a mess. One of them told the principal that if I were permitted to teach here—and this is a shackey place over here—that I may want to live here. And at that time, there were no Blacks on this side of town. I knew that the whole community didn't want me. But I decided that OK, I'm going to get through those gates that morning. I'm a teacher like everybody else. I'm trained and by golly, that's just the way it's going to be. But it was real good that the teachers at the school supported me.

In some cities, inter-district programs have been used to achieve desegregation. Boston and St. Louis provide two such examples. Believing that such programs benefit suburban districts at the expense of city districts, Marcia Gray, who works in a city which participates in urban-suburban desegregation, commented that the programs in their communities subtly devalue and discriminate against Black teachers. The 1974 Missouri Biology Teacher of the Year, she recalled how she and another Black science teacher were recruited to work in two suburbs participating in desegregation:

> Not too long after they started the cross-district busing, I was recruited to take a job out in one of the suburban schools. Just like they try to skim off the so-called cream of the students, I guess they thought since I'd won the teacher of the year award, they'd be getting the cream of the teachers as well. That doesn't surprise me. In the south during desegregation, school systems were known for stealing the best Black teachers from Black schools and putting them in the White schools. But there was a twist here; they were going to put all the Black kids in a class together and they wanted me to teach them and my other assignment was going to be dealing with all of the White kids that no one else wanted to be bothered with. I guess that tells you what they think of Black folks—pupils and teachers.

After learning of the school system's proposal, she declined. The other teacher, unaware of her teaching assignment, transferred to the suburbs only to find that all of the Black students were placed in one of her five classes. In keeping with the custom set during desegregation, these desegregated school districts continue, with slight alteration, siphoning off the most competent Black teachers from all-Black schools to desegregate all-White faculties, and enlisting them to teach undesirable suburban students (Monti 1985).

North Goes South

Because of dual school systems Black teachers were better represented among the teaching force in southern than in northern states. Desegregation, however, had a deep and lasting effect on the careers of many Black teachers. It is estimated that between 1954 and 1979 in the seventeen southern and border states, approximately 32,000 Black teachers were forced from their jobs (Ethridge 1979). The number of Black teachers in Kentucky declined by 41 percent during 1955–65, even though an additional 401 would have been needed merely to keep pace with the increasing student population. Moreover, a study of 467 school districts revealed that 127 of them had dismissed 462 Black teachers, so that by 1970, the Black student/teacher ratio in the south was over twice that of the White student/teacher ratio (Stewart, Meier & England 1989). Demotions, negative and unfair evaluations, outright dismissals, and reassignment of the most competent Black teachers to White schools were some of the mechanisms employed by school districts to rid themselves of Black teachers.

Concealed by these statistics are the stories of thousands of Black teachers who were forced into stereotyped roles and whose careers were thwarted by desegregation. In the following interview, a math teacher from North Carolina recalled how he and another Black male teacher, neither of whom had ever played any kind of college athletics, were appointed coach and assistant coach of the football, basketball, and baseball teams in a newly integrated high school:

> When I went to the White school after desegregation, they appointed me and one other Black teacher to be coach and assistant coach of the football, basketball, and baseball teams. Now mind you, I'd never played sports in college, hadn't been a coach at the all-Black school, and neither had the other guy. But that didn't seem to matter to the White folks in charge. They just assumed that Black men were supposed to be good at sports.

Internal segregation was another problem, as was described by Lamar Lancaster, a Chicago urban high school English teacher whose two sisters have taught in Alabama for more than twenty-five years. He observed that though schools in the south appear to have been more easily desegregated, the irony is that the schools are internally segregated. Speaking of the staffing patterns in his small hometown in Alabama, he remarked:

> Black teachers, if they are in the school at all are teaching for the most part remedial courses that are all Black. Very few Blacks are teaching courses that you would value, literature, history or social studies. They are teaching remedial reading for Blacks or home ec. Schools are all segregated within. In the one high school that has all the wealthy kids—the so-called city high school as such—they've got one Black teacher. She teaches home ec or gym or something like that. The one gym teacher—you know, a Black guy teaches there, assistant coach. They don't want you to be coaches either down there, because sports is a big thing, you know, foot-ball. You can be assistant coach, but very seldom do you see a White one there. That's the sort of thing I am talking about. They will push him out or find a reason to push him out or something. Well, initially especially, they didn't want any Black principals down there and they trumped up charges against a lot of them and that sort of thing. And then the coaches. And it's not so subtle either.

Finally, the enduring racism experienced by Black teachers who teach in desegregated schools is captured in the narrative of Ella Jane, a teacher from a small East Texas town. After graduating from Prairie View A & M, she began teaching in 1955, first in a consolidated all-Black school. In 1964, sum-moned from her classroom to the superintendent's office, she was informed that she was to be one of only four Black teachers from a staff of twelve to be placed in the newly desegregated school. She remembered that day:

> I got in the car, left the school which was about eight miles out, and came over to the administration building. I was sandwiched between a high school principal on one side and on the other a secretary to the superin-tendent. And they carried me through the wringer. That's how I got here. The questions they asked were ridiculous. They said, "Ella Jane, did you know that we have to have some Black teachers?" And I said, "Yes." And he said, "Did you know that you are going to be very fortunate because you are going to be one of the Black teachers that we're going to hire?" And he said, "You're the best teacher I have in the system, Black or White. I did not have to tell you that and if you tell anyone I said that, I'm gonna tell 'em you lied." He says, "Do you get my meaning?" And he said, "It should make you feel very proud whether you do or not that you're going to be one of the ones who are retained." That's how that happened.

Ella Jane explained how she and her cousin, even though both possessed master's degrees, reported to school each day but neither of them was given a class. Instead, they sat in a classroom for half of the school year without teaching a single student because the White parents did not want them to teach their children. Finally, in response to White teachers' protests, Ella Jane and her cousin were assigned to teach remedial reading classes for

Black and poor children. For three years, they continued teaching these classes. During this period, the other teachers showed their contempt for them and the Black students. Ella Jane described their treatment:

> We were just glorified students. Incidentally, I couldn't use the bathroom with the teachers and everything. I would use the bathroom with the students. I didn't eat with them [the other teachers] You know, they just kind of treated me like dirt. We brought our Black students. The teachers, the White teachers, would put the Black kids, this is the truth, on one side and White ones on the other so they wouldn't touch, and so they wouldn't mingle and that's the truth. This was starting in '64. This went on for a long time.

As one of only two Black teachers now remaining in the small rural school district that has been desegregated for 26 years, Ella Jane has had to stand virtually alone against institutional racism. She has resisted the school system's effort to push her out of the district and confronted the individual racism of White colleagues and parents.

Bernadette Mosely also recalled the hostility that she and other Black teachers and the children encountered from the principal and his faculty upon transferring to an all-White school. Sometimes she had to intervene in order to protect Black students from excessively harsh treatment by White teachers, many of whom quit rather than teach Black students. In addition to being ignored by White teachers, Black teachers in this school were systematically harassed by the principal. In the following excerpt, she describes how Black teachers banded together to support each other:

> The principal was pretty nasty. The very first day of teaching, he or somebody had hired a Black teacher at the last minute. The day before the teachers were to go. And she didn't know where the school was. He had given her some directions. And of course she got lost looking for the school. She got there and we were sitting in a meeting. And she came in quietly and he looked up and saw her and said, "I told you that you were supposed to be here by nine o'clock," in front of everybody. "If this is going to be your habit, maybe we ought to discuss your employment." It was terrible. . . .
>
> We had another teacher who retired from NASA [the National Aeronautics and Space Administration], a Black teacher who was teaching in another Black school that they were ready to get rid of and they had to place her, and they placed her at my school in the sixth grade. And so I don't know why he didn't like her. He was just on her all the time. I remember one afternoon after school I was trying to show her some methods I used. He had observed her social studies and he didn't like what she was doing. He had written up all this stuff on her and gave a copy of it on things that she could have been doing. And I said, "Yeah, there were a lot of things that you could do, but you were doing some things that I considered

right." And then one day, he had antagonized this Black teacher so much that he had started sending for all the different supervisors to observe her. One of the elementary supervisors went in and she was Black and she didn't see anything wrong. So he was going over her head. He sent for another supervisor. But my point is that he made it so hard for that Black teacher that she didn't even wait 'til the end of year, she just walked out.

That Black teachers encountered such unqualified racism in desegregated schools should not be surprising; historians have amply documented how Black teachers have rarely fared well in unitary school systems (Tyack 1974).

Segregation, Desegregation, and Racism

Blacks have consistently fought to improve the schooling opportunities available to their communities. Though some of these efforts have included creating and maintaining private, independent schools, fighting for community control, and attempting to provide challenging academic programs within segregated schools, Blacks have spent much of their energy and placed most of the hopes for securing better schooling for their children by seeking desegregation through the courts.

According to a recent survey conducted by a leading Black periodical, however, many Blacks now question the wisdom of desegregation. More than half felt that the quality of public school education for Black children had decreased in the past decade; less than one-fourth responded that the quality of public-school education for Black children had improved or remained the same. The respondents' rating of the quality of public school for White children was significantly different. Asked whether the quality of public-school education for White students had improved, worsened, or remained the same, about one-third felt the quality had increased, less than 20 percent felt it had decreased, and almost one-fourth felt there had been no change. Asked to assess whether the education of Black children had improved in the thirty-five years since schools were desegregated by court order, more than half felt that the education was the same or worse; almost 50 percent answered that the education that Black children were receiving was worse; less than 15 percent felt there had been no change. Finally, asked whether public school teachers had neglected the education of Black and White students in their particular communities and in the nation, the respondents were two and one-half times more likely to state that this was the case for Black students more so than for White students (Black Enterprise 1990b).

Conversations with Blacks who attended segregated schools reveal that they consider integration to have been a mixed blessing. While they acknowledge the improved material conditions that have resulted from desegregation, many Black teachers complain that the gains in material resources have not compensated for a loss of sense of community, the feeling of alienation, and a loss of pride that too many Black children now experience in White schools (Blauner 1989; Cohen 1991).

Some Black legal and political analysts contend that the benefits that have accrued to Black children from desegregation have not offset the terrible toll resulting from it. Not only has the Black community suffered from the loss of Black professionals, but it has also suffered the loss of their accumulated wisdom about how to educate Black children effectively. Cruse and Bell both correctly note that no one concerned with pushing *Brown* vs. *Board of Education* ever considered the pedagogical influence or the salutary effect of Black schoolteachers (Bell 1987; Cruse 1987).

Conclusion

As these interviews have shown, in their own ways all of the teachers with whom I spoke have actively resisted racism. Because their battles have been waged on different terrains, their tactics have necessarily varied. Nonetheless, these teachers have struggled to develop in Black children the individual and collective resources needed for self-fulfillment and group advancement in an unjust and racist society. In these interviews is evidence that the teachers made conscious efforts to socialize Black children toward a "double consciousness" by cultivating in them the individual resolution, mettle, moral strength, and clarity of purpose while simultaneously developing strong racial consciousness and pride, a task that they claim is now made more difficult for African-Americans living in a racist society masked by a rhetoric of equal opportunity. Because in-depth analyses of these teachers' political awareness, teaching philosophy, and teaching practices appear elsewhere, such analyses are not undertaken here (Foster 1990, 1991a, 1991b, 1992a, 1992b). But, it is worth mentioning that these teachers all share the view that the Black community will only achieve advancement if Black students develop political awareness along with keen intellectual skills, insist on self-determination, and engage in collective struggle against racism.

The point I want to emphasize here is that, in contrast to depictions of Black teachers which portray them as individuals who invariably uphold only the status quo, these teachers not only are aware of institutional racism of American society, but throughout their careers have acted in ways that have challenged the existing social order. Scholars of decidedly different philosophical and theoretical orientations have called for communities to reclaim their histories through stories, oral histories, and narratives (Giroux 1988; Lightfoot 1988). By failing to tell our own stories, we in the Black community have abetted White scholars who, in much the same way that they have promoted the myth of the culturally disadvantaged Black child, have by omission, distortion, and misinterpretation created the myth of the inadequate Black teacher. Not only are Black teachers more often characterized unfavorably than are White teachers, and as lacking the political awareness and resolve to challenge racism, but these negative characterizations diverge from the portrayals of Black teachers found in the essays, sociological studies, and autobiographies and narratives written *by Blacks themselves*. Though not scholarly analyses, these accounts portray Black teachers as individuals who not only forged productive relationships with their Black students, but who in their own ways have challenged the status quo (Cohen 1991; Blauner 1989; Kluger 1975; Baker 1987; Clark 1962; Fields 1985; Monroe & Goldman 1988; Reed 1990).

Though the larger story of Black teachers remains untold, these narratives are a starting point. They demonstrate that a community's heroes can be found among ordinary people. By collecting stories such as those presented in this chapter, we recognize the perseverance and the often unacknowledged victories of the ordinary people who came before us. All the same, the process of reclaiming our stories is multilayered. Collecting narratives is but a first step. The next and most critical step is to use these narratives to initiate social change. Not only can these stories help us better understand our oppression, but they can be used to demonstrate that no matter how oppressive the circumstances, ordinary people have the power to act. Reclaiming our stories is necessary not only to pass them on to future generations, or to understand the resilience and strengths of Black communities, but to incorporate what was *best* about the past into our communities and schools.

References

Anderson, J. 1989. *The education of Black in the South, 1860–1935*. Chapel Hill: University of North Carolina Press.

Baker, H. 1987. What Charles knew. In *An apple for my teacher: 12 authors tell about teachers who made the difference*, edited by L. D. Rubin, Jr. Chapel Hill: Algonquin Books.

Bell, D. 1983. Time for the teachers: Putting educators back into the Brown remedy. *Journal of Negro Education* 52, no 3: 290–301.

———. 1987. *And we are not saved: The elusive quest for racial justice*. New York: Basic Books.

Black Enterprise. 1990a. Survey, a view of the past, plan for the future. *Black Enterprise* January: 69–75.

———. 1990b. Survey Results. *Black Enterprise* August: 85–94.

Blauner, B. 1989. *Black lives, White lives: Three decades of race relations in America.* Berkeley: University of California Press.

Clark, S. 1962. *Echo in my soul.* New York: E. P. Dutton.

Cohen, M. 1991. Growing up segregated. *Emphasis Chapel Hill Sunday Newspaper,* 24 February, C1–2.

Collier-Thomas, B. 1982. The impact of Black women in education: An historical overview. *Journal of Negro Education* 51, no 3 (Summer): 173.

Committee on Policy for Racial Justice. 1989. *Visions of a better way: A Black appraisal of public schooling.* Washington: Joint Center for Political Studies.

Conroy, P. 1972. *The water is wide.* Boston: Houghton-Mifflin.

Cruse, H. 1987. *Plural but equal: Blacks and minorities in America's plural society.* New York: William Morrow.

Curry, L. P. 1981. *The free Black in America 1800–1850.* Chicago: University of Chicago Press.

Dilworth, M. 1984. *Teachers' totter: A report on certification issues.* Washington: Institute for the Study of Educational Policy, Howard University.

Drago, E. 1990. *Initiative, paternalism & race relations: Charleston's Avery Normal Institute.* Athens, Georgia: University of Georgia Press.

Ethridge, S. 1979. Impact of the 1954 Brown v. Topeka Board of Education decision on Black educators. *Negro Educational Review* 30, nos. 3–4: 217–32.

Fields, M., with K. Fields. 1985. *Lemon swamp: A Carolina memoir.* New York: Free Press.

Foster, M. 1990. The politics of race: Through African-American teachers' eyes. *Journal of Education.* 172, 3.

———. 1991. Connectedness, constancy and constraints in the lives of African-American women teachers: Some things change, most stay the same. *NWSA Journal* 3, no. 2: 233–61.

———. 1991. "Just got to find a way": Case studies of the lives and practice of exemplary Black high school teachers. In *Readings in equal education volume 11: Qualitative investigations into schools and schooling,* edited by M. Foster, 276–309. New York: AMS Press.

———. 1992. African-American Teachers and the politics of race. In K. Weiler (ed.), *What Schools Can Do: Critical Pedagogy and Practice.* Buffalo, N.Y.: SUNY Press.

———. 1993. Educating for competence in community and culture: Exploring the views of exemplary African-American teachers. *Urban Education* 27, no. 4: 370–94.

Franklin, V. P. 1979. *the education of Black Philadelphia: The social and educational history of a minority community 1900–1950.* Philadelphia: University of Pennsylvania Press.

Giroux, H. 1988. *Schooling and the struggle for public life: Critical pedagogy in the modern age.* Minneapolis: University of Minnesota Press.

Hochschild, J. 1985. *Thirty years after Brown.* Washington: Joint Center for Political Studies.

Jones. F. 1981. *A traditional model of excellence: Dunbar High School of Little Rock, Arkansas.* Washington: Howard University Press.

Kluger, R. 1975. *Simple justice.* New York: Vintage Press.

Lerner, G. 1972. *Black women in White America: A documentary history.* New York: Vintage Press.

Lightfoot, S. 1978. *Worlds Apart: Relationships between families and schools.* New York: Basic Books.

———. 1988. *Balm in Gilead: Journal of a healer.* Reading, Mass.: Addison-Wesley.

Monroe, S., & P. Goldman. 1988. *Brothers: Black and poor—a true story of courage and survival.* New York: Ballantine Books.

Monti, D. 1985. *A semblance of justice: St. Louis school desegregation and order in urban America.* Columbia: University of Missouri Press.

Reed: I. 1990. Reading, writing and racism. *San Francisco Examiner Image* 19 August, 27–28.

Rist, R. 1970. Student social class and teacher expectations: The self-fulfilling prophecy in ghetto education. *Harvard Educational Review* 40: 411–51.

———. 1973. *The urban school: A factory for failure.* Cambridge: MIT Press.

Sowell, T. 1974. Black excellence—The case of Dunbar High School. *Public Interest* 35: 3–21.

———. 1976. Patterns of Black excellence. *Public Interest* 43: 26–58.

Spencer, D. 1986. *Contemporary women teachers: Balancing school and home.* New York: Longman.

Statistics of State School Systems, Organization, Staff, Pupils and Finances, 1953–1954. (Biennial Survey of Education in the United States, 1952–54, ch 2., p. 114, table 48.)

Sterling, P. 1972. *The real teachers: 30 inner-city schoolteachers talk honestly about who they are, how they teach and why.* New York: Random House.

Stewart, J. K. Meier & R. England. 1989. In quest of role models: Change in Black teacher representation in urban school districts 1968–86. *Journal of Negro Education* 58, no 2: 140–52.

Streator, G. W. [1933] 1990. The colored South speaks for itself. In *A documentary history of the Negro people in the United States, Volume 4: From the New Deal to the end of World War II,* edited by H. Aptheker. New York: Citadel Press.

Tyack, D. 1984. *the one best system: A history of American urban education.* Cambridge, Mass.: Harvard University Press.

9

"*I'm Me Own Boss!*"

Grace Mest Szepkouski

I first met Margaret in the summer of 1985. She was sixty-seven years old, about five feet tall, gray-haired, slightly overweight, and limped on her right foot. She had recently been released from a state institution for persons with mental retardation and was attending an adult day-care program where I was working part-time. Margaret worked in the "higher-functioning" group and I ran the activities for the "lower-functioning" clients, so our contact was limited. When I returned in January of 1986 to collect data for an ethnographic methods course, Margaret and I began a series of conversations that led to the decision to co-write her life history. I spent two years, 1986 and 1987, observing Margaret in her work and residential settings, and in the community. During that same period I also reviewed official institutional and current case notes associated with her, and interviewed her, her family, and caretakers. We have maintained a close friendship since the end of our "official" relationship in January of 1988; we talk on the phone about once a month and see each other for dinner every other month.

Margaret's life can be characterized by three distinctive phases: (i) life before institutionalization, thirty-one years in the community; (ii) institutionalization, thirty-five years in Valleyview Hospital and State School; and (iii) deinstitutionalization, her present life in the same community where she grew up. This chapter will explore how an individual, cut off from the traditional mode of education, became a learner by reflecting upon and using everyday life experiences as her curriculum. Theoretical perspectives on dehumanization within institutions and empowerment within the life-history process provide a framework for Margaret's story. The following section provides a brief overview of her life and significant events related to her exclusion from educational institutions. Subsequent to that, a theoretical groundwork will be laid providing a context for the details of Margaret's exclusion.

"Naming Margaret's Life"   (1918–present)

Margaret was born in February, 1918, in a large city on the East Coast. She is the youngest of four children (two sisters and a brother), and the daughter of a couple who owned a small business, a "taproom," below their home. Margaret's oldest sister, Regina, tells the following story about Margaret's birth, as told to her by Margaret's mother (Mrs. Drew): a midwife was hired for the birthing and when Margaret arrived the woman told Mrs. Drew that the baby was dead. As the midwife prepared the water to clean and remove the "dead" infant, Mrs. Drew said she heard a roll like thunder emerge from Margaret and all of a sudden she began to cry. The family sent for a doctor and after examining Margaret, he said she had infantile paralysis (interview, April 1988). This story of Margaret's birth seems representative of her life in general: she overcame the odds and remains an active participant in a life often manipulated and directed by others.

Regina, Margaret's sister, stated that "Margaret was a perfect baby until she was three years old," and that then she began to "take" seizures many times during the day and evening (interview, April 1988). Medical records from Margaret's later institutionalization note that "mental retardation was noticed at three years of age when convulsions are reported" (Valleyview discharge summary, 1985).

Scheerenberger (1983) notes that by 1900, special education was adopted by many urban school systems. In 1911, New Jersey passed the first law requiring mandatory special education for children with mental retardation, and Pennsylvania soon followed suit. However, the notable exception to the law was if a child was diagnosed as having both mental retardation and epilepsy, then he/she was not guaranteed a public education under the newly created laws. Since Margaret was labeled "mentally retarded" at about age three when she began to have seizures, the likelihood of her being accepted in a public school would have been minimal. A private facility might have been a viable alternative, but Margaret tells the following story regarding her educational options:

> And my sister just told me before l left there the last time . . . she said she had an argument with my father before he died that he could have sent me to a private school, you know, learn that way, but she said he wouldn't do it, you know. She said it was his fault that I didn't get that. It wasn't my fault, she said, it was his fault. (interview December, 1986)

Regina echoed this incident (interview, April 1988), explaining that their father feared the possibility of Margaret having a seizure on the playground or in the classroom and getting hurt. He was strongly opposed to her attending school because of her seizures and his desire to protect her from harm.

While Margaret's brother and sisters attended school, she helped her parents around the house and in their taproom. After her parents died, when Margaret was thirty years old, her sisters took turns caring for her in their homes. Both sisters were married and had small children, and as Regina describes it, Margaret's behavior toward their children was selfish and jealous. The decision to send Margaret to Valleyview State School and Hospital emerged as both a response to the problems the sisters had with her in their homes, plus a desire to give her some form of education which they believed might exist since the official title of the institution contained the words "state school" (interview April 1988).

Margaret's placement in an institution was not an abnormal occurrence for persons with her label. What was unusual was her age at the time of her placement—thirty-one years old. Census reports from the National Institute of Mental Health (#233, 1952) reporting the number of persons institutionalized in Margaret's home state in 1949 indicate that only five persons over the age of thirty were admitted while 391 persons under the age of twenty-nine entered institutions. She remained in the institution for thirty-five years, released at the age of sixty-eight.

According to Margaret's discharge summary from Valleyview, initially, when she was placed in the institution at age thirty-one she was enrolled in the facility's sewing program (case record, 1986). However, a case manager's report in July of 1975 stated that five years prior to the date listed, or July 1970, Margaret became involved in the sewing room. We find, then, that Margaret did not get involved in a program until twenty-one years after she had been admitted to Valleyview. Margaret's memory of that period is essentially nonexistent and the case notes I received from the institution offer nothing to help me prompt or jar her memory. When asked what happened when she first entered the institution, she acknowledged, only once, having to wait "some time" before beginning work in the woodshop, but does not recall the sewing program even when directly questioned about it (fieldnote September 1987). How much time she meant by "some time"' is unclear, but she never complained of a long period without work. This will be discussed further in the section about institutionalization. Margaret was transferred from the sewing room to a sheltered workshop in 1975. She remained in that program until her discharge in 1984.

As early as June of 1970, Margaret's case notes from Valleyview institution indicate that she was referred to the local county for potential community placement. A combination of factors worked against her release, as indicated in the case notes:

July 1975

When asked her feelings about leaving Valleyview, Margaret said she does not want to leave . . . however, she was interested in hearing just what a group home was, and I got the feeling that she was mouthing the opinion of her sibling who is very much against Margaret leaving Valleyview.

March 1982

Regina's (sister) preference is that Margaret remain at Valleyview. Margaret is not being considered for community placement as she chooses to remain here.

June, 1983

Addison (local community) will not be placing Margaret this year as they are staying away from clients who are over 65.

Margaret did not advocate her own release because she listened to her sister's arguments about the dangers of the community, had them verified on the nightly news, and was of an age not given top priority for immediate release. Fourteen years after the first reference about placing her in a community setting, Margaret was finally released (1984). It is significant to note that her release stemmed from a court order closing the entire institution rather than because an appropriate community placement was located.

Margaret's first community placement after leaving Valleyview was a large group home in the same city where she grew up. She shared the house with five roommates, all "low-grades" according to Margaret's self-measurement scale: low verbal skills and a wide range of required aid for daily living needs. She voiced anger and frustration with this placement when we first met (May 1985) until she was moved from it in the spring of 1988: ". . . I can't understand it. Maybe I'm wrong, but I figure that I should be with either, if they want me in a house, you know, with somebody, I should be with brighter people than the ones I'm with now" (interview, December 1986).

Several direct-care staff and administrators associated with Margaret discussed her misplacement in that first group home with me:

Fieldnote, June 1987: Conversation with Supervisor of Margaret's group home:

> I asked if Nancy thought Margaret belonged in this house and she said she (Nancy) thought Margaret was misplaced and she had tried to dig to the bottom of how it happened.

Fieldnote, June 1987: Conversation with the Agency Director of Housing:

> . . . she agreed with the group home supervisor and case manager that Margaret is misplaced . . . she thought Margaret's medical file makes her appear less intelligent/socially adept than she truly is.

Fieldnote, June 1987: Conversation with staff at Margaret's workshop:

> Dan said the thing that strikes him strongest about Margaret is her unhappiness about where she lives. That unhappiness seems to pervade everything else she does in her life.

Interview, March 1987: Director of the agency caring for Margaret

"I think it's pretty obvious that she doesn't belong in that house. She's higher functioning than the rest of them. . . . I think she would do much better in a smaller place. . . . One of the problems she has is that she doesn't perceive herself being like the other people (in her house) and she really should be with higher functioning people."

The director of the agency, and other administrators and direct-care staff associated with Margaret, admit she was misplaced when first moved to the community. The large flux of persons leaving Valleyview, entering the community where Margaret was placed, created a high demand for group homes. It is not impossible to imagine a number of persons like Margaret who might have had their physical needs met by their original placement, but not their social needs. Locating a more appropriate placement was recognized as a much-needed goal for Margaret, but the realities involved with the process took two-and-a-half years. As Margaret waited for a new placement, complaining about her isolation in her current position, the director of the agency noted one of Margaret's problems was her recognition of her higher-functioning status compared to her housemates. Why was this *Margaret's problem* if he and the other staff cited above also recognized and agreed with her assessment? Perhaps having a client complain about an issue such as this created an urgency or pressure to produce action not necessarily present when only staff and administrators recognize the problem.

In early 1988, two-and-a-half years after her placement in the first group home, Margaret was moved to a two-bedroom apartment with a peer from the other group home. The new living arrangement offered Margaret a more "normalized" physical environment, but the decision to bring a predominantly nonverbal peer from the previous setting did nothing to alleviate her social isolation. A year after this placement Margaret was moved to her own apartment in a rundown building and neighborhood (1990). Ironically, as her social needs were better met in this new apartment, due to community excursions with staff, her environmental conditions decreased. Margaret remained in that apartment for almost two years before the building was sold and slated for major renovations (1991); she was then moved to an apartment of her own in a housing complex in a safer section of the city.

Theoretical Background

As noted at the beginning of this chapter, Margaret lived with her family in the community for thirty-one years, was institutionalized in a state hospital for adults with retardation for thirty-five years, and has been living in the community for the past eight years (she is currently seventy-four years old). She never attended any type of school until she was in her late sixties and just reentering the community. Margaret cannot read, write, or understand basic numerical concepts. What she has managed to learn throughout her life has come from her immediate context. This section will focus on the generalized experiences of institutionalization and participation in a life-history work, to illustrate how these contexts might influence an individual's development. Margaret's specific responses to these experiences will appear in the next section.

Institutionalization   Erving Goffman's classic work on total institutions (1961) defined them as:

> [a] place of residence and work where a large number of like-situated individuals, cut off from the wider society for an appreciable period of time, together lead an enclosed, formally administered round of life (p. xiii).

He hypothesized that the central feature of any total institution, whether a jail or an institution for persons with mental illness, is the fact that the inhabitants' lives are controlled by others. One's sense of self fades away as he/she is assigned a number, forced to wear the same clothing as everyone else, lives collectively, and loses, "the privacy of one's life history and personal cleanliness habits (using toilets without doors, for example). The issue of control extends to the regimented schedules within institutions, from everyone getting up at the same time to receiving a predetermined number of toilet-paper sheets per person (MacAndrew and Edgerton 1964). Most importantly, Goffman (1961) notes, the self is constantly torn apart by the staff and their schedules in an effort to keep the inhabitants malleable and open to the workings of the institution.

Schur (1980) agrees with the mortification process described by Goffman, noting that when stigma is successfully imposed on individuals, as it would be through the institutionalization process, an "individual's confidence and self-esteem [can be lowered] (1980: 33). Foucault adds that total institutions are a symptom of our larger depersonalizing social system (1977). Wolfensberger specifically describes institutions for persons with retardation as "a deindividualizing residence . . . in which they are highly regimented; in which [the] physical or social environment aims at a low common denominator. . . ." (1971: 15). The resounding message from these theorists is the loss of one's sense of self-worth and uniqueness when institutionalized.

The staff and administration within institutions rationalize the dehumanizing system they practice as a necessary means to maintain control over a large number of patients (Goffman 1961). Ryan and Thomas (1980), having interviewed institutional staff, note that the staff often view their job as surveillance, thus equating patient care with patient control. The highly routinized schedules of the institution allow staff to meet the basic physical needs of their patients while also limiting their freedom of movement, in turn reinforcing staff control. Ryan and Thomas also observed staff emotionally distancing themselves from their patients in order to verify in their own minds, within such close proximity, the difference between themselves and those they care for: "Ordinary people can talk over their dinner . . . it does them [persons with mental retardation] good to be told to shut up now and again" (1980: 85).

Davis and Anderson (1983) note that the worst form of punishment in total institutions is the absence of meaningful work. Since our society highly values individual achievement and success in the marketplace, those placed into a context where the opportunity to produce is limited or nonexistent lose the power to show their worth as measured by the mainstream.

Sternlicht and Bialer's (1977) review of the effects of institutional life on persons with mental retardation begins with the caveat that institutions may not always be the worst place for this population. Specifically they reason that institutions provide a context where competition is not the main theme, and peers may be more tolerant of one another's behavior than those on the outside. Braginsky and Braginsky (1971) describe institutions as a haven for some persons with retardation against the stares and stigma of nonlabeled peers. The problem with these perspectives is that society's overachievers, intolerant of difference in the social and economic system, receive little or no responsibility for making the outside world such a difficult place for persons with retardation. By claiming that the institution provides a safe haven for the development of self against the negativism and harshness of society, the authors end up blaming the victim (Ryan 1976) instead of the creators of the segregationist system.

Life History Work and Empowerment As just indicated, placement into an institution threatens the maintenance and continued development of one's unique sense of self. Margaret's thirty-one years in the community prior to her institutionalization provided her with positive and supportive experiences, to be detailed later, which helped her develop a sense of self-worth and significance within her immediate surroundings. Her thirty-five years in Valleyview State School and Hospital, as suggested by Goffman (1961) and others, most likely weakened Margaret's belief in herself as a useful, productive member of society. This section will explore the issue of (re)discovering one's voice, sense of self, through the process of collaborating on one's life history. The specifics of how Margaret's participation in our life-history work came to represent another type of nontraditional learning in her life will follow later in the chapter.

Langness and Frank's text *Lives* (1981) traces the history of the appearance and growth of stories about the lives of single persons rather than those of groups or cultures. It also details the methods involved with individual in-depth research, such as intensive, long-term observation of a field setting, participant observation, in-depth interviews, review of official records associated with the person(s) and/or institution of interest, and perhaps most importantly, the establishment of rapport with the life-history participant. The value of this methodology is that it allows researchers to enter into the culture of others through the insider's viewpoint (Bogdan & Taylor 1982; Geertz 1973; Langness 1965; Langness & Frank 1981; Langness & Levine 1986). The emphasis on the emic perspective moves researchers away from the official explanation of persons and events, meaning how those outside of a particular label define and view those within the label.

Life histories with persons with retardation began with Robert Edgerton's work *The Cloak of Competence* (1967). His long-term observations and in-depth interviews with persons recently released from a state institution made a significant statement regarding the value of the thoughts and words of persons with retardation. Bogdan and Taylor (1976, 1982) and Langness and Levine (1986) support the methodology and its usefulness with this population, emphasizing the opportunity it affords to see persons with retardation as "enormously complex in their personalities, behavior, and abilities" as opposed to the stereotype of them as a ". . . single homogeneous group best characterized as an I.Q. range" (Langness and Levine 1986: xiv).

Langness and Levine describe life-history work with adults with retardation as an opportunity for them to "entertain, engage in, and identify with the process of making their own worthwhile contribution to a literature of direct bearing on their future" (1986: 14). This process allows individuals usually denied a voice regarding their care system a chance to critique and suggest alternative solutions. Langness and Frank add that "writing one's own life story is a way of creating coherence or meaning" (1981: 103). My experience with Margaret embodies these statements as well as adding an unexpected twist—the development, or, perhaps rediscovery, of her voice. Through the retelling of her story, Margaret's language changed and began to reflect an increased awareness of the validity of her own thoughts and opinions. She began to express a sense of control and power over her life circumstances that did not exist when we first met or throughout the first year of our work together.

Although not using the current term *empowerment*, Carl Rogers describes a process in person-centered therapy somewhat similar to what I suggest happened to Margaret. The seven stages of movement from "fixity to flowingness" (1961: 130) reflect a continuum of growing self-awareness and ability to experience the self rather than just talk about it or feel it as an object. The therapeutic relationship differs from the life-history relationship in that the former generally has a defined location and structure, while the latter can exist in multiple settings at varying times and is unstructured. However, the basic premise of Rogers's stages of movement from "a fixity in which the individual is very remote from his experiencing . . . to the self . . . much more frequently something confidently felt in process" appears to reflect a continuum Margaret traveled from the belief that others ruled her life (". . . I have a sister that's my boss . . ." [interview, February 1987]) to a sense of self-responsibility ("I'm me own boss and I can take care of meself [interview, November 1987]).

In the following sections detailing what Margaret learned despite her exclusion from schools and mainstream society for thirty-five years, connections between the theoretical issues discussed above will be made with her learning experiences.

Exclusion from Educational Institutions

Childhood and Young Adulthood

Margaret was denied access to the public school system in the early 1920s because of a state law prohibiting children with dual diagnoses of mental retardation and epilepsy from attending. Private school, a potential alternative for Margaret, was dismissed by her father who feared for her safety in case of a seizure while at school. Although excluded from a formalized education, Margaret learned many valuable functional and social skills in her childhood and early adulthood from her parents.

> Yeah, I used to help my mother during the day, you know. Cooking supper for her, she taught me how to cook, you know. Learned me how to cook, learned me how to run a house . . . like I'm doing now in my own room, you know. And, and she learned me how, you know, be kind to people if they give you anything. You know, if they give me anything I say thank you.
>
> Even, my father had a taproom one, one time before he died, and . . . I took care of the house and cooked, you know besides. And, and after she went to bed [mother] then, then me and my brother used to get ready and go down to help him at 3 o'clock the morning. (interview, April, 1986).

This informal education by Margaret's parents influenced her development in both concrete and abstract ways. On an obvious external level, the domestic skills taught by her mother prepared Margaret for some degree of self-sufficiency. She speaks with pride in her voice when she describes her ability to care for her room within the group home: "And last night I cleaned the carpet myself, you know. When I go back I'll wash my clothes myself . . . maybe Saturday I'll dust my own furniture . . . " (interview, April 1986). When asked by the director of the agency, "Who takes care of your room?" Margaret repeatedly told me that she said, "I take care of everything that's up here of my own personal things!" (fieldnote, February 1987). Margaret's mother provided her with functional skills and pride in self-responsibility. These two areas have helped her not only survive in the community since her deinstitutionalization, but have also allowed her to "work" the system more successfully than many of her peers.

Margaret's work in the family taproom offered her varied knowledge about domestic skills and afforded social contact with the neighbors. Her sister notes that Margaret was popular in the neighborhood and taproom; everyone knew her and interacted with her (interview, April 1988). The social exchanges observed and participated in by Margaret in this context, throughout the first third of her life, strongly influenced her understanding and use of etiquette. Margaret often criticizes her labeled peers and the staff associated with the agency for not following the social norms she learned as a child, particularly saying "thank you" or "excuse me" when appropriate.

> I was talking to Jeff, from upstairs, [another client] and that woman that brings the pills [staff person] came up and stuck her hand in. You know half the people who work here must not have been raised right. I was raised, me, my two sisters, and my brother in a taproom. If my father was talking to a customer we were supposed to wait if we had to go to the store for my mother [meaning to get money from him] and not interfere. *The ones that work here weren't raised right even with their education.* (interview, April 1986).

Margaret acquired another type of knowledge during those early years with her family, something more abstract and yet clearly evident in her current understanding of herself and others: the development of self-respect as someone who works. Bellah et al. state "however we define work, it is very close to our sense of self. What we 'do' often translates to what we 'are'" (1985: 66). Margaret described herself as a central figure in the inner workings of the family home and business, thus she perceived herself as an *essential* caretaker and aid to her parents. In her eyes, her lack of schooling was both understandable and acceptable because she thought of herself as fulfilling an invaluable role within the family.

Institutionalization

Margaret's institutionalization at age thirty-one must have been frightening for her: "they didn't ask any questions they just put you there . . . they don't give no satisfaction, they just put you there" (interview, February 1987). The direct positive feedback she had received for more than thirty years from her family and neighbors regarding her self-worth was gone, so she had to rely on what she had learned from those experiences: work hard and take care of yourself. However, as mentioned earlier, Margaret was not placed into any type of academic or vocational training during the first twenty-one years of her stay at Valleyview. Imagine viewing yourself as a person who works, who is important because you contribute something, and then being denied the opportunity to do that for twenty-one years.

Goffman (1961) describes the process of having one's sense of self gradually stripped away by centralized authorities in institutions as mortification. Margaret's loss of her self-valued role as a worker and her inability to produce a change in her status exemplify her mortification process. Recalling Davis and Anderson's (1983) comment that the worst form of punishment in total institutions is the absence of meaningful work, Margaret's twenty-one years of nonwork might have felt like an unexplained punishment. She has never provided any insight to her feelings about that period of time; most often she denies any lag time between her entry and immediately beginning work in the woodshop. When a peer of mine recently asked me if she describes *anything* from that period of time—a visit from a family member, the death of someone—I reviewed our interview transcripts and then met with Margaret (January, 1992) to see if her response had changed from the point of our last official interview in December 1987. In support of her previous statements, Margaret said, "I went to Valleyview and then they put me in the woodshop."

Just as I have forgotten or repressed painful moments in my life, Margaret has forgotten a period of time that represented the height of her loss of control over her recognized and valued self. The residual effects of that loss of control occasionally appeared in our conversations after she was discharged from Valleyview in the mid-1980s: "I thought, 'oh no, they're going to call the cops and take me back where I came from'" (interview, December 1986).

Margaret's case notes from the institution include comments like the following about her behavior: "she can also be verbally abusive. She tends to be bossy with other residents;" "Margaret presents a lethargic appearance," and "She can be sociable if prompted" (case notes, 1977, 1979, 1982). Linking the information about her extended period without work with the comments regarding her sometimes confrontational social interactions, it is not difficult to understand her boredom, frustration, and sense of loss regarding her "self."

Margaret did learn several things while in the institution which broadened the knowledge base begun during her years in the community. Perhaps the most significant lesson learned involves the existence of reference groups (Merton 1959). Her previous thirty-one years in the community were marked by a supportive and largely insulated family and neighborhood context. The positive words she used to describe that period in her life provide no indication that she perceived herself as different, in a negative or less worthwhile sense, from those around her. However, her language in the interviews changes dramatically when she describes entering the institution. Categories were formed that separated her from others within the same context.

> We didn't live with or see those people. Up there they have what they call
> cottages and the *low grades,* that's what I call them, lived in different cot-

tages than the *bright ones*. The bright boys and girls worked in the wood shops and never did nothing with the low grades. (February 1986)

And the lowest girls . . . they had a cottage of their own, but they *never went to work like we did.* (interview, April 1986)

Similar to nonlabeled persons' tendencies to separate and mark those who are perceived as different to verify their own "normalcy" (Goffman 1963; Hahn, 1988; Jones et al. 1984; Megill 1985; Schur 1971), Margaret created categories that separated her from those threatening her sense of "normalcy." She created an "other" to stabilize her sense of being part of the "same" she had known from her earlier life (Foucault 1967). The difficulty for Margaret, in terms of maintaining her previously formed sense of self, was that her new institutionalized reference group possessed a label that those in power applied to her as well. She developed her own "stigma-theory" (Goffman 1963), using her family and community standards, to explain and justify her self-perceived uniqueness from her reference group of commonly labeled peers. Her overt verbalization of distinctions between herself and peers she considered "low grades" allowed her to retain a sense of competency and self-sufficiency, two qualities valued in her prior experiences by her parents and nurtured by the responsibilities they gave her around the home and business.

Another type of information acquired by Margaret while in Valleyview was indirectly learned. She saw and heard others, most often those she calls "low grades," being abused by staff: "'The reason why they did it [close the institution] was 'cause they used to beat the low grades, you know. . . . And they used to put some of them in restraint jackets . . . and tie them in their room" (interview, February 1987). Recently Margaret recalled seeing institutional staff trying to "play house" [sexual contact] with the "low grades" (conversation, February 1991). Although she never directly experienced these types of beatings or abuse herself, Margaret left the institution with a strong sense of personal space that emerges when people, especially staff or her labeled peers, bump against her unexpectedly. She related a story about a visually impaired woman in her workshop who bumped into her the day before a visit in February 1991. I asked what happened and Margaret said she hit the woman and accidentally ripped her clothing. When I suggested that the visually impaired woman probably did not realize she was there, Margaret quickly defended her own actions saying that the woman should have known. Her excessive physical response may be connected to the assaults she saw during her institutionalization.

Deinstitutionalizaton Margaret left Valleyview in 1984 due to a court order concluding that the institution was incapable of providing the minimal requirement of habilitation, and the likelihood of improvement in the future was almost nonexistent because the very nature of an institution "does not provide an atmosphere conducive to normalization" (Ferleger &

Boyd 1980: 168). As noted earlier, Margaret was placed in a group home with five other women with limited or no verbal skills, from October 1984 until the spring of 1988. Her second placement, in a two-bedroom apartment with a peer from the first community residence, lasted about a year. Her third placement, a one-bedroom apartment with no roommate and full time staff, lasted for two-and-a-half years. In the fall of 1991 Margaret moved to her fourth placement in eight years, at the age of seventy-four.

Margaret had her first official school experience when she reentered the community at age sixty-seven. She attended night classes for adults with retardation at a local high school. The subjects were cooking, banking, and community awareness, like the ability to distinguish between a male and female bathroom symbol. Margaret received a certificate at the end of each class and she proudly displays them in her room. Although the classes provided her with an opportunity to socially interact with others, they did not teach her many skills beyond what she already knew from her early life experience. She often voiced an interest in learning how to write, particularly to sign her name, but classes or IHP (individualized habilitation program) goals for that type of learning were not specified.

Beyond the "education" offered Margaret at the local high school program, she was involved with a variety of programs at the adult day-care center. From her earliest days at the center, a distinction was made between incoming institutional clients who were verbal and higher-functioning versus those with limited verbal skills and in need of more direct care. The center's separation of the "bright ones" and the "low grades," (Margaret's terms) into prevocational training and self-maintenance skill groups, reaffirmed her perception of self as more "worthy" or significant than many of her lower-functioning peers: "I mean they don't act, you know, like human beings would. . . . I like to go with people that's got more sense, you know, gots a civilized mind" (interview, April 1986). Margaret's vocational training and work at the center included activities such as putting the clips on plastic skirt hangers and counting and bagging party items like hats and utensils.

I visited Margaret at her workshop, the same one being discussed, in August 1991, and noted that she was still counting the number eight by using a cue board; eight circles drawn on construction paper. After seven years of this type of work, she has not "learned" what the number eight represents and it is clear that she and her peers are not expected to understand it. As long as Margaret meets her quota of production for the day, her performance is praised. She deserves praise for her diligence and effort, however, it is unfortunate that teaching something like number concepts in conjunction with contract work is not being used within this setting. The lack of coordination between something like Margaret's night-school experience, which lasted for one year, with her work programs allows issues like her unaware-

ness of the most basic concepts of numbers to exist. Her care system provides Margaret with job training, a good intention, but it limits her development and encourages her continued reliance on the system by not providing her with the literacy skills to translate her experiences into higher cognitive functioning (Rothman, 1981; Vygotsky 1978).

Learning Through the Life History Process

I approached Margaret about the possibility of the two of us co-creating
her life history in October 1986. We were already familiar with each other
from my summer work at the adult day-care center in 1985, and from my
weekly visits to the center throughout 1986 doing observations and interviews for an ethnographic methods course. Our rapport was natural and re-
laxed by the time we decided to commit ourselves to the exploration of
Margaret's life history.

The observational and informal interview data collected during 1986
prior to the official start of the research provided a fairly thorough understanding of Margaret within her work environment. Thus the majority of
our work throughout the remainder of 1986 and throughout December of
1987 was spent in her group home and the community. Twenty-two interviews, averaging three to four hours in length, took place during late 1986
and in 1987, usually while we were traveling to a restaurant and then during our meal. Fieldnotes were written after every interaction, including detailed information that might have occurred when the tape recorder was
not in use. The interviews were a combination of structured and unstructured questions. I had a series of topics (example: childhood memories,
feelings about being institutionalized) I hoped to cover at each meeting, but
if some of them did not arise naturally, I put them away for a later interview (Spradley 1979; Taylor & Bogdan 1984). The ultimate goal was to
allow Margaret to reveal her life history as she recalled it, and to note how
the emphasis or memories changed through the process of our work (Bogdan & Taylor 1982; Langness & Frank 1981; Langness & Levine 1986;
Taylor & Bogdan 1984). During this same time frame, I continued to visit
the adult day-care center each week and spent approximately three to four
hours observing Margaret in her workplace, while talking with staff and
peers associated with her.

Several events which occurred throughout my relationship with Margaret
during the collection of data for her life history indicated to me that the
process of telling her story to another, someone not labeled, and hearing
positive feedback about herself and her skills, brought her a newfound sense
of self-worth and power. Nothing I had encountered in the life-history literature fully prepared me for the side effect of the process: potential empowerment of my informant. Perhaps the self-respect Margaret began to display

was not truly new, but was a resurgence and further development of the lessons learned in her earlier life with her family. The following incident lends insight into Margaret's developing voice.

In October of 1987 I received a phone call from the director of the agency Margaret was affiliated with, regarding what he termed her "belligerent" behavior. A series of phone calls, visits, and meetings with administrators associated with Margaret revealed that her perceived "belligerent" behavior was largely the result of a doctor prescribed overdose of her seizure medication. The side effects of mysoline—emotional swings and lack of appetite— were viewed as evidence of Margaret's "history of behavioral problems" (case manager interview, October 1987). No effort was made to view her behavior, whether biochemically influenced or not, within her current context of misplacement in a group home with no verbal peers. Margaret's actions were interpreted outside of her circumstances, an exceedingly frustrating situation for her and me since I had been told by the agency director, "I think it's pretty obvious that she doesn't belong in that house. She's higher-functioning than the rest of them. . . . I think she would do much better in a smaller place, even by herself or with one other individual that's higher-functioning than she" (interview, March 1987).

This series of events marked a significant point in my work with Margaret, because I was forced to examine the effects of our relationship upon her behavior. Was part of her interpreted "belligerence" a result of feeling empowered through the life-history process? I began to consider the ramifications for Margaret of someone listening to her, a nonlabeled person, and responding with interest to her memories and thoughts about life. No one had seriously listened to Margaret for years. The staff termed her comments "Margaret's line" because the socially agreed-upon definition of retardation generally does not include the idea that labeled persons can be trusted as accurate sources of information about their lives (Bogdan & Taylor 1976; Schalock 1990; Sigelman1980). After reexamining our interviews over the previous twenty months, I found shifts in her language which reflect a growing awareness of self and personal rights.

When Margaret and I first met and discussed her institutionalization, she used language which implied that others possessed power or control over the events in her life.

> After they [parents] died *I had to go to court* and then, and then I went to Valleyview for fifteen years. *They* always take you to court when you come, go to another place. (interview, April 1986).

> Yeah I had to go to court. And then they, *the court, the judge put me there.* . . . No he just put you there. *They didn't ask any questions* they just put you there. They don't give you no satisfaction, they just put you there. (interview, February 1987)

> *You can't trust,* you know you can't trust . . . I mean *they* [county offi-
> cials] *could send you another place,* you know. (interview, April 1987)

Within these examples, the state and county were perceived as having
ultimate power over what occurred in Margaret's life. She was a passive entity in these perceptions; a self she observed rather than experienced or controlled (Rogers 1961). About a year and a half after I began the project with
Margaret, in the spring of 1987, she began to express some awareness (although the degree of her conscious understanding of the change is not
known) that she had opinions and feelings about events that deserved to be
heard. Although the following examples still exemplify an external locus of
control, they also represent a gradual shift from powerlessness to large, impersonal factors to smaller, known entities. This signifies an overt awareness of individuals, persons she knows, having power along with faceless institutions such as the state.

> I said, "Well you're not my boss and I'm three times seven" I said, and
> "I'm twenty-one and I'm over twenty-one." "*You're not my boss. My sis-
> ter's my boss,*" and I said,"*Zena's* [staff person] *my boss, not you.*" (inter-
> view, February 1987)

> Just between you and me, this one and the sister that died, never bothered
> with me in Valleyview. *They put me in there* and they never bothered with
> me. I don't know why she wants to bother with me now so much. (inter-
> view, August 1987)

> I wanted to ask you about that some time when we were out, *am I my
> own boss?* (interview, September 1987)

> *I'm me own boss and I can take care of meself.* (interview. November 1987)

While these changes in Margaret's language were occurring, I did not
consciously recognize the process. It was not until I was forced to deal with
her new label of "belligerence" that I began to consider Margaret's movement toward empowerment. Our relationship, although not a formal or traditional mode of education, taught Margaret that her voice matters, that
people—myself and my family and friends—were interested in her thoughts.
Her newfound voice was not always welcomed by the administrators and
staff that dealt with her on a daily basis. Perhaps because an elderly woman
yelling, "Grace told me I have rights and I don't have to take a bath if I
don't want to" disrupts the traditional staff-client relationship by tipping
the scales of power toward a more level position. As I told the staff person
who angrily confronted me about this statement, I did tell Margaret she had
rights and should talk with staff when she felt upset about anything in the
group home, work, etc., but I did not specifically tell her she did not have
to take a bath. Margaret's movement through the process of experiencing

her self as an object, something manipulated and directed by others as she had been in the institution, toward a developing awareness of her self as an active, central participant in her life exacerbated situations like when to take a bath because they represented the struggle between the passive Margaret and the newly emerging "boss" (Goffman 1961; Rogers 1961).

Margaret recently applied her ever expanding voice to a situation at the agency regarding plans to move her to a new community residence. Administrators at the agency had been working, for several months, to find a new apartment for Margaret in order to move her out of what they described as a poorly constructed building and a potentially dangerous neighborhood, and to increase opportunities for her integration into a population of older adults, mostly nonlabeled. Margaret initially liked the new apartment, but soon began to raise concerns about staffing and access issues. She initially conveyed her concerns verbally and when she felt they were not taken seriously, she refused to take her medication, eat, or interact with administrators. The administration claims the staff biased her thinking in order to avoid shifts in their job location and schedules, while the staff say the administrators do not know Margaret the way they do and only they recognize how stressful the change would be for her. Aspects of both arguments are probably true, but Margaret's actions and her conversation with me about the incident reveal that she *consciously* chose her potentially dangerous behaviors to bring about what she wanted. She forced the administrators to put *their plans aside* and consider *what she really wanted*. A project director, only at the agency for three weeks, called me a week after Margaret's fast began and explained that the agency had given up their lease at Margaret's current residence and had already signed at the other, thus the move was inevitable. However, the administration was interested in Margaret's desires, independent of input from themselves or staff. He asked if I would consider speaking to her as an outside friend and advocate to get her opinion on the situation. I agreed to speak with her, especially after hearing she had not taken her medication, but stated that I would not tell her what to do. I would only listen and help her to sort out what she told me. By the time I was able to make the three-hour trip four days later, Margaret was eating again, taking her medication, and talking with administrators. No one, including Margaret, can explain what specifically produced the truce, but a visit to the new apartment, with staff persons Margaret trusts and promises that her requests regarding staff hours would be met, solved the immediate crisis.

When Margaret and I discussed the upcoming move and her feelings regarding the events leading to it, I voiced concern about her approach of not taking medication to get her point across. She acknowledged understanding the importance of taking it to help prevent seizures, but she also added with a smile and the closest thing I have ever seen her do to a wink, "I just wanted to see how far they would go" (conversation, August 1991). Margaret has learned to "work" the care system and to control events as much as possible within her present context. She did not have the power to stop the move from taking place, but she used the resources available to her, such as her medication and not eating, to make her own interests heard. Margaret has become a skilled negotiator using the tools she acquired during our life-history work: the (re)discovery of her voice and a sense of rightful power over events in her life. Some might argue that her methods of negotiation are "unfair," but I argue that she uses what is available to her. If Margaret yells and screams about something, her point may be heard or at least acknowledged by the administrators and staff, but more likely it will be overly interpreted like the "belligerence" situation cited earlier. By using her body to make her point regarding the seriousness of her interests in this move, Margaret gained a degree of attention that does not normally appear in response to her "line."

Learning Outside the Mainstream

Margaret is a *learner*. She does lack traditional academic knowledge; she cannot read, write, do basic math, or tell time. However, despite her exclusion from formal institutions of education, she has acquired knowledge from her personal and social world which has helped her not only survive, but also thrive.

When discussing the effects of institutionalization, the theorists cited earlier, such as Davis and Anderson (1983), Foucault (1977), Goffman (1961), Ryan and Thomas (1980) and Wolfensberger (1971), describe the loss of control and sense of self persons experience at the hands of rigid schedules, staff eager to maintain a distance between themselves and those they care for, and false perceptions of homogeneity. Education is not directly discussed in these works, although coping strategies like Goffman's colonization and conversion (1961) consist of learned behaviors patients adopt in order to survive in institutions.

Margaret's institutional experiences bring these theories to life by focusing the mortification process, the threat to self, on one person: (i) her involuntary commitment at age thirty-one by her siblings; (ii) the lack of meaningful work for twenty-one of her thirty-five years in Valleyview, and (iii) her exposure to a peer group perceived as "one" because of a common label, yet quite varied in Margaret's perception of self-care and responsibility. Valleyview State School and Hospital did not provide Margaret with the education its title suggests, although her age at entry may have made her an unlikely candidate for that type of programming. What she did learn at the institution was largely self-taught based on a need to develop coping mechanisms in her new environment. Margaret applied the knowledge she acquired

in her childhood and young adulthood about the value of work and self-responsibility to her new context. Thus, she dealt with her new reference
group by creating categories reflecting her previous experiences, those who
did not work or care for themselves became "low grades" while those who
did work became "bright boys and girls." When Margaret was not working
for those first twenty-one years in Valleyview she probably felt dangerously
close to the "low-grade" status and has chosen to deal with that experience
by not recalling its existence. Margaret survived her institutionalization better than many others who were sexually and physically abused; however, the
damage to her sense of self must have been harrowing and continued to influence her behavior for several years after she was released.

Margaret's participation in the telling of her life history yielded another
opportunity for learning. Beyond simply retelling stories about her past and
present to me, Margaret listened to her own words and began "creating coherence or meaning" out of a previously unanalyzed series of events. Slowly
over our two years of data collection, and throughout our continued informal relationship for the past four years, Margaret's language and behavior
changed to reflect a growing awareness of her significance and power over
events in her life. The life-history process allowed her to rediscover and en-
hance the self that had been psychologically threatened and abused in the
institution. Margaret no longer passively allows others to make decisions
about her life, believing her voice is meaningless; she speaks out, and if necessary uses the one tool that is totally her own—her body—to make others
listen. It is impossible to know if Margaret's current empowered stance in
the agency would have been the natural progression she followed after deinstitutionalization. Based on my in-depth work with her over the two years
immediately following her discharge from Valleyview, I suspect she would
have regained some of her voice over time. However, the life-history process
accelerated the recovery of her sense of self that had been so negatively constrained by thirty-five years of institutionalization.

Perhaps the greatest skills Margaret has acquired over the years relate to
her ability to survive. She has coped with exclusion from schools as a child,
the loss of her adulthood to an institution, and multiple moves and roommates in the latter part of her life. Margaret has learned how to live a life
largely controlled by others and within the past five years has begun to reclaim areas of that life for her own.

References

Bellah, R. N., Madsen, R., Sullivan, W. M., Swidler, A. & Tipton, S. M. 1985. *Habits of the heart: Individualism and commitment in American life.* New York: Harper & Row.

Bogdan, R. & Taylor, S. 1982. *Inside out: The social meaning of mental retardation.* Toronto: University of Toronto Press.

————. 1976. The judges not the judged. *American Psychology* 31, no 1: 44–52.

Braginsky, D. D., & Braginsky, B. M. 1971. *Hansels and Gretels: Studies of children in institutions for the mentally retarded.* New York: Holt, Rinehart, and Winston.

Davis, N. J. & Anderson B. 1983. *Social control: The production of deviance in the modern state.* New York: Irvington Publishers.

Edgerton, R. 1967. *The cloak of competence: Stigma in the lives of the mentally retarded.* Berkeley, Calif.: University of California Press.

Ferleger, D., & Boyd, P. A. 1980. Anti-institutionalization: The promise of the Pennhurst case. In *Normalization, social integration, and community services,* edited by R. J. Flynn and K. E. Nitsch, 141–66. Baltimore: University Park Press.

Foucault, M. 1967. *Madness and civilization: A history of madness in the age of reason.* London: Tavistock.

————. 1977. *Discipline and punishment.* New York: Pantheon.

Geertz, C. 1973. *The interpretation of cultures.* New York: Basic Books.

Goffman, E. 1961. *Asylums: Essays on the social situation of mental patients and other inmates.* New York: Anchor Books.

————. 1963. *Stigma: Notes on the management of a spoiled identity.* Englewood Cliffs, Prentice-Hall.

Hahn, H. 1988. The politics of physical differences: Disability and discrimination. *The Journal of Social Issues* 44, no 1: 39–48.

Jones, E., Farina, A., Hastrof, A., Markus, H., Miller, D., & Scott, R. 1984. *Social stigma: The psychology of marked relationships.* New York: W. H. Freeman.

Langness, L. L. 1965. *Life history in anthropological science.* New York: Holt, Rinehart, and Winston.

Langness, L. L. & Frank, G. 1981. *Lives: An anthropological approach to biography.* Novato, Calif.: Chandler & Sharp Publishers.

Langness, L. L. & Levine, H. G. Eds. 1986. *Culture and retardation: Life histories of mildly mentally retarded persons in American society.* Dordrecht, Holland: D. Reidel.

MacAndrew, C. & Edgerton, R. 1964. The everyday life of institutionalized idiots. *Human Organization* 23, no 4: 312–18.

Megill, A. 1985. *Prophets of extremity: Nietzsche, Heidegger, Foucault, Derrida.* Berkeley: University of California Press.

Merton, R. K. 1959. *Social theory and social structure.* Glencoe, Ill.: Free Press.

National Institute of Mental Health. 1952. *Patients in mental institutions: 1949.* U.S. Public Health Service # 233. Washington: U.S. Government Printing Office.

Rogers, C. R. 1961. *On becoming a person.* Boston: Houghton Mifflin.

Rothman, D. J. 1981. Afterword. In *Doing good: The limits of benevolence*, edited by W. Gaylin, I. Glasser, S. Marcus, & D. J. Rothman, 171–91. New York: Pantheon.

Ryan, J. & Thomas, F. 1980. *The politics of handicap.* New York: Penguin.

Ryan, W. 1976. *Blaming the victim.* New York: Vintage.

Schalock, R. L. Ed. 1990. *Quality of life: Perspectives and issues.* Washington: American Association on Mental Retardation Publications.

Scheerenberger, R. C. 1983. *A history of mental retardation.* Baltimore: Brookes.

Schur, E. M. 1971. *Labeling deviant behavior: Its sociological implications.* New York: Harper & Row.

————. 1980. *The politics of deviance: Stigma contests and the uses of power.* Englewood Cliffs, N. J.: Prentice-Hall.

Scott, R. 1969. *The making of blind men.* New York: Russell Sage Foundation.

Sigelman, C. K., Schoenrock, C. J., Spanhel, C. L., Gromas, S. G., Winer, J. L., Budd, E. C. & Martin, P. W. 1980. Surveying mentally retarded persons: Responsiveness and response validity in three samples. *American Journal of Mental Deficiency* 48, no. 5: 479–86.

Spradley, J. P. 1979. *The ethnographic interview.* New York: Holt, Rinehart and Winston.

Sternlicht, M., & Bialer, I. 1977. Psychological aspects of institutionalization in mental retardation. In *The psychology of mental retardation: issues and approaches*, edited by I. Bialer and M. Sternlicht, 603–44. New York: Psychological Dimension.

Taylor, S. J. & Bogdan, R. 1975. *Introduction to qualitative research methods: A phenomenological approach to the social sciences.* New York: Wiley-Interscience Publishing.

Vygotsky, L. S. 1978. *Mind in society.* Cambridge: Harvard University Press.

Wolfensberger, W. 1971. Will there always be an institution? 1: The impact of epidemiological trends. *Mental Retardation* 9, no 5: 14–20.

PART III

10

Border Disputes:
Multicultural Narrative, Identity Formation,
and Critical Pedagogy in Postmodern America

Peter McLaren

Grand Hotel Abyss

We live in dangerous times. The current generation is facing a world in which market forces are stronger now than they've ever been in American history. Not only are public schools under a massive and coordinated assault, but the very idea of public institutions is increasingly becoming threatened by the New Right's clarion call for privatization of the public sphere. It is an era of economic terror propped up by "enterprise culture" and the growing number of transnational corporations whose omnipotent sway in foreign policy brought us Grenada, Panama, and Desert Storm. International bankers have become the new "warrior-prophets" of postmodern culture; their synthetically manufactured political mythology has ushered in a new global agenda of takeovers and buy-outs. On the one hand, the world has been bequeathed, to borrow a description by Vincent Pecora (1991: 130), "one grandly obfuscating vision of global harmony and interdependence policed by Conan the American—the 'new world order,' a phrase whose historical resonance alone demands the keenest suspicion of all that it attempts to name." On the other hand, post-Fordist capitalism has effectively transformed the relationship between subjectivity and the structures through which experiences become constituted such that subjectivity is now experienced as decentered and radically discontinuous. Our identities have been respatialized and reinvested in new forms of desire. Our agency has been dispersed on the horizon of micropolitics with no common understanding of oppression or collective strategy to challenge it.

Historical reason mocks us as we allow it to linger in our educational thinking and policies; for one of the lessons of modernity has been that a teleological and totalizing view of scientific progress is antipathetic to liberation. Paradoxically, it has produced an intractable thralldom to the very logic of domination and malignant chaos which it has set out to both contain and contest and in doing so has reproduced part of the repression to which it so disdainfully pointed. The inevitability of alienation has been accepted and has fostered a growth in intellectual markets where fashion-prone theories of dissent and a voguish nihilism are being recuperated by academic establishments who have turned marginalization and alienation into a profitable business.

We have produced a culture modeled on a masculinist heroics, a reactive desire and a "manic compulsion to consume" (Mort and Green 1988: 30). As in the film by Wim Wenders, *Until the End of the World,* the flesh of our dreams has been soldered to the electronic circuitry of high-tech gadgets which reroute our desires in the service of profit and corporate advantage. What is significant about these "new times" is that we have become the wardens of our own souls through the global logic of "consumer sovereignty" and the thrilling self-indulgence that marks the ecocidal desire to endlessly consume. This new form of democracy asserts that consumers vote with their dollars in a free market where consumer demands determine the products, amount of goods produced, and the prices charged for these products. Of course, it doesn't matter that there exists only a select number of wealthy customers—a hypertrophic cult of the "rich and famous"—whose millions of dollars for luxury items considerably "outvote" masses of people who can barely afford to purchase food and shelter (McGovern 1981). Nevermind that consumer sovereignty allots votes according to income and permits one person to be worth a thousand votes while another—as long as he or she manages to survive—is worth only one. This is a time when the gap between the wealthy and the poor is widening vertiginously, a time ironically termed "the age of democratic capitalism" (McGovern 1981: 317), a time of corporate partisanship and the rationalized machinery of social power acting on behalf of the most privileged groups.

Felix Guattari and Toni Negri describe the structuring on a global scale of "capitalist voraciousness" as the production of poverty by exploitation, marginalization, and death. They write:

> To a certain extent, the poor find themselves produced twice by this system; by exploitation and by marginalization and death . . . there are only differences in degree between exploitation, destruction by industrial and urban pollution, welfare conceived as a separating out of zones of poverty, and the extermination of entire peoples, such as those which occur in the continents of Asia, Africa, and Latin America. . . . On all levels, on all scales, everything is permitted: speculation, extortion, provocations desta-

bilization, blackmail deportations, genocide. . . . In this virulent phase of decadence, the capitalist mode of production seems to rediscover, intact, the ferociousness of its origins. (1990: 59, 61)

These "new times" weigh heavily on the breast of history. The promotional dynamics and self-stagings of right-wing politicians, linked to the market imperative that drives our social universe, have instilled a vision of democracy in the American public that is a mixture of talk show mandarinism, game show enthusiasm, and the reckless effrontery of "new world order" jingoism: "We're number one!" In the distempered vision of moral apocalypse put forward by conservative political fundamentalists (as frighteningly portrayed in the 1992 Republican National Convention), the reality of "democracy" has become continuous with the totalitarianism it seeks to displace. The elaborately staged self-celebrations of national identity now revolve around Euro-American strategies of, to borrow a phrase from Gayatri Chakravorty Spivak (1990: 789), "[Making] the straight white Christian man of property the ethical universal."

These "new times" are also reflective of the narratives we live by. They mirror the stories we tell ourselves about ourselves, stories that shape both the ecstasy and the terror of our world, disease our values, misplace our absolutes, and yet strangely give us hope, inspiration, and framework for insights. We can't escape narratives but I believe we can resist and transform them.

Narratives form a cultural contract between individuals, groups, and our social universe. If narratives give our lives meaning we need to understand what those narratives are and how they have come to exert such an influence on us and our students. My position is that we need to be able to read critically the narratives *that are already reading us.* My general thesis is that all cultural identities presuppose a certain narrative intentionality and are informed by particular stories. Put another way, I want to argue that identities are partly the result of the narrativity of social life. Every claim to selfhood implies a narrative that recognizes temporal and ethical aspects of human knowing. It implies a politically, historically, and ethically meaningful succession of events. One issue, of course, is whether or not there can be a "true" speaker of narratives. Do narratives speak us or are we spoken through narratives? We use different kinds of narratives to tell different kinds of stories, but we also sanction certain narratives and discount others for ideological and political reasons. To a large extent, our narrative identities determine our social action as agents of history and the constraints we place on the identities of others.

In other words, narratives can become politically enabling of social transformation or can serve as strategies of containment that locate "difference" in closed epistemological discourses. Homi K. Bhabha notes that, with respect to the former function,

> Narrative and the *cultural* politics of difference become the closed circle of interpretation. The "Other" loses its power to signify, to negate, to initiate its "desire", to split its "sign" of identity, to establish its own institutional and oppositional discourse. However impeccably the content of another culture may be known, however anti-ethnocentrically it is represented, it is its *location* as the "closure" of grand theories, the demand that, in analytical terms, it be always the "good" object of knowledge, the docile body of difference, that reproduces a relation of domination and is the most serious indictment of the institutional powers of critical theory. (1988: 16).

This is not the time to present a full-dress account of narrative theory. Since I will frame my discussion of narrative quite specifically in the context of questions of domination and liberation, it is not my intention to discuss narrative in isolation from the material struggles over identity and dignity that are so integral a part of our increasingly terroristic social order. Consequently, I shall forgo a more semiotic and linguistic analysis of narrative; for instance, examining narrative as a scheme of predicates in a transformational-generative sense; nor is it my purpose to expand on the way, for example, linguistic narrative works—in either a protostructuralist (e.g., Frye, Propp) or poststructuralist (e.g. Derrida, Barthes) sense (see Coste 1989). This is not to denigrate the importance of narrative grammar which has, over recent years, become an increasingly important field. Rather than explore the work of notable figures such as Eco, Propp, Greimas, Lévi-Strauss, Culler, Bremond, and others, and the world of specialized grammatical forms, such as the production and interpretation of sign-functives, I wish merely to bring narratology into the provenance of historical and textual practices. This more modest approach to narrative is designed to concentrate on what Coste (1989: 15) calls narratology's "overtly incestuous relationship with theories of action" and how narratology "lives in the shade of the concepts of history that prevail in our cultures and . . . impinge[s] on the strategic programs and games of various socioeconomic groups." In other words, I am more interested in approaching "the formative or enslaving exchanges that obtain between 'history' and its subjects and objects" (Coste 1989: 15) outside of a purely linguistic or metahistorical approach to narrative. To a large extent I follow Paul Ricoeur's lead in establishing a relationship among narrative, identity, and ethics.

The organization of this paper is not governed by a need to follow a single narrative order but rather to offer a series of commentaries about narrative's intersection with subjectivity, agency, and identity and the way it structures our very theoretical approaches to these topics. My primary focus will be on narrative as the production of interested projects, as textual practices and social symbolic acts linked to the practice of theory and the theorizing of practice. I will be concentrating on what I call the "narrative economy of textual identities" and the development of "postcolonial" narratives that are able to unfix, unsettle, and subvert totalizing narratives of domination as well as engender an infinity of new contexts for destabilizing meaning. Further, I will draw attention to imperialist narrative as a form of epistemic violence, that is, as constituting dominative systems of knowledge and structures of intelligibility that construct forms of social life—textual practices that have distinct, though contradictory, social effects. Another purpose is to provisionally sketch out some new narrative practices in pedagogy—a new narrative economy of social texts of sorts. Such a pedagogy is grounded in what I call "critical narratology." Critical narratology means reading personal narrative (our own and those of our students) against society's treasured stock of imperial or magisterial narratives, since not all narratives share a similar status and there are those which exist, highly devalued, within society's rifts and margins.

While I am interested in examining narrativity in terms of teleological aspects of representational effects, I will not make fine-grained distinctions among narrative, plot, and story. Scholars who work in literary studies will possibly find my discussion of narrative much too general. In fact, I intend to employ a minimalist definition of narrative as a "discursive representation of a sequence of randomly connected events" (Rigney 1991: 591). Narratives, in other words, may be said to organize relationships of difference and such a process is socially determined and context specific. This general description of narrative and the more detailed accounts that follow are intended to serve as heuristic devices to enable teachers to grasp social life and the production of identity—and theorize about it—as various forms of story.

While I am interested in narratology as it has been employed in poetics, this present essay focuses on narrativity and narratological discussion primarily as it has been linked to historiographical debates. Narratological reflection in poetics deals mainly with fiction whereas history writing focuses on the representation of "real" occurrences. While my concerns are both historiographical and poetical, the former will figure more prominently. For instance, the ideological character of narrative (as a tension between desire and the law) has been stressed in Hayden White's *The Content of the Form: Narrative Discourse and Historical Representation* (1987) where narrative is defined as

> a particularly effective system of discursive meaning production by which individuals can be taught to live a distinctly "imaginary relation to their real conditions of existence," that is to say, an unreal but meaningful relation to the social formations in which they are indentured to live out their lives and realize their destinies as social subject. (cited in Rigney 1991: 597).

Following this perspective, narratives may be said to be invested with imaginary coherence through the form of content and rhetorical persuasiveness (White 1987; Rigney 1991). Of particular interest is narrative's socializing function and the way it constructs a specific moral realm—that is, on the way narratives introduce individuals or groups into a particular way of life through their authorial voice and legitimating functions. Theories, ideologies, and social and institutional practices—and our relationship to them—are all informed by narratives. What gives these narratives structural, rhetorical, and discursive solvency? What secures their anchorage in our histories? How do narratives enable us to see cross-dimensionally? To cast and recast our identities spatiotemporally? To construct the boundaries of the self through forms of imaginary coherence? What is the specific rhetorical appeal of certain forms of narrativized morality? How do narratives occult our identities in the name of objectivity and truth? How are narratives implicated in the distribution of privilege within the larger capitalist society and why do the identities of certain groups often share a common narrative finality based on relations of race, gender, class, and sexual orientation? This essay offers no definitive answers to these questions but rather attempts to pose them as challenges for educators and cultural workers who wish to explore their implications for critical research and teaching.

The Politics of Narrative

Narratives help us to represent the world. They also help us to remember and forget both its pleasures and its horror. Narratives structure our dreams, our myths, and our visions as much as they are dreamt, mythified and envisioned. They help shape our social reality as much by what they exclude as what they include. They provide the discursive vehicles for transforming the burden of knowing into the act of telling. Translating an experience into a story is perhaps the most fundamental act of human understanding. Terry Eagleton (1981: 72) notes that "we cannot think, act or desire except in narrative; it is by narrative that the subject forges that 'sutured' chain of signifiers that grants its real condition of division sufficient imaginary cohesion to enable it to act."

Narration provides us with a framework that helps us hold our gaze, that brings an economy of movement to the way we survey our surroundings and the way we suture disparate images and readings of the world into a coherent story, one that partakes of continuity, of a fiction of stasis in a world that is always in motion.

There exists to preontological or pretextual reality that prevents its refraction by rhetorical structures and tropes. That is, narrative neither precedes nor follows historical time because each presupposes the other. They are mutually constitutive, mutually informing, interanimated (Connerty 1990; Ricoeur 1974). Narrative is implicated not simply in our autobiographical accounts of ourselves and others, but because the basic formations of our thinking and theorizing are informed, in one way or another, by narratives and their constituent interests. The narratives we live by are not only evident in the way we reflect upon and analyze the past, present, and future, but are ingrained in the very theoretical formulations, paradigms, and principles that constitute the models for such reflection and analysis. Anthony Appiah (1991: 74) has presciently remarked that the relation between structural explanation and the logic of the subject (theories of agency and structure) is not one of competition over causal space but rather for *narrative space.*

Theories are not just about seeing the world in different ways, some truer than others, but rather theories are about *living in particular ways.* What Appiah is saying is that *all theories presuppose a narrative intentionality* as well as an empirical, social outcome. That is, all theories have a story to tell about social life and an attitude towards it; theories reflect the theorist's situatedness in a particular way of life.

Peter T. Kemp (1989) observes a number of features that may be attributed to narrative. Narrative transforms the paradigmatic order of daily action into the syntactic order of literature or history. Narrative action is always already articulated as the fundamental "cultural codes" (signs, rules, and norms) of the society. Daily praxis orders the world temporally. If life (Die Lebenswelt) were not structured as narrative we would have no experience of time. Narratives possess a dialectical quality—they are "told in being lived and lived in being told" (1989: 72). Personal identity is linked to the coherence of one's life story. To take on the burden of being the storyteller of one's own life (after Heidegger) is not only to give life coherence, but to preserve one's identity. Action itself prefigures the world of narrative composition and without such narratives there can exist no ethics; however, a narrative structure is a necessary but not sufficient condition to constitute an ethical vision. Grand narratives which transcend individual biographies must not be turned into law of the sort which represses members of the community; however, the fact that some grand narratives serve absolutist and authoritarian roles should not suggest that all historical narratives are of destructive import.

Richard Harvey Brown makes similar observations to those of Kemp, placing perhaps a stronger emphasis on the act of predicating or naming reality as a way of guiding perception and constructing public spheres. The textual or narrative grammar of individuals, notes Brown (1987: 130), "constitute them as a polity." Brown (p. 143) defines narrative as "an account of an agent whose character or destiny unfolds through events in time." Plot is an essential ingredient of narrative and is taken by Brown to describe "the means by which essential features of human existence are expressed through specific event." Defined as such, the very existence of narratives presupposes, for Brown, "a social order of meaning in which significant action by moral agents is possible" (p. 144). As an "emblem of a larger social text," a narrative "requires a political economy and collective psychology in which a sense of lived connection between personal character and public conduct prevails."

Brown describes the appearance of the postmodern text as having been ushered in by the disintegration of the human community which "bears witness to the problematic nature of contemporary meaning, identity, and experience" (p. 159). According to Brown, our lived experiences have become integrated with our moral existence through forms of technical rationality when what is really needed is a *public narrative discourse*. With the postmodern disintegration of community "has come a reintegration, not of community, but of the cybernetic state" (p. 160). Echoing Brown's insight, Felix Guattari and Toni Negri (1990: 58) write that at the heart of global capitalist integration "one finds the immense enterprise of the production of cybernetic subjectivity [*subjectivité informatisée*] which regulates the networks of dependence and the process of marginalization."

Brown goes on to defend three central assertions: "that narrative logic is universal and that hence other logics are derivative of it; that epistemological crises in the philosophical tradition of positivistic science are conflicts of narrative traditions; and that paradigm shifts in science itself are reformulations of cognitive traditions in terms of narrative logic" (p. 164). Brown's answer to the question of overcoming technical rationality and developing a narrative discourse of public life is to read social life from the perspective of a *dialectical ironist*—one who engages in a resistant social practice. His position very much resembles Adorno's concept of negative dialectics. Of course, I have no problem with teachers becoming ironists, even dialectical ones, as long as this does not mean that the master trope of political subversion for the decade ahead will be geared to turning out stand-up comedians or that revolutionary praxis will be reduced to academic forms of deconstructive playfulness which leads to a detachment that is disdainful of everyday life. After all, the world of electronically produced identity in the form of postmodern advertisements often flatters the ironist and strokes the skeptic as a marketing orientation. Irony can become a means of containing the political rather than challenging it.

Narrative and Oral Histories

Some very important observations of narrative based on the treatment of oral histories and life histories have been advanced by Allen Feldman in his brilliant ethnography of political terror in Northern Ireland, *Formations of Violence*. Feldman's insights are germane to the critical poststructuralist focus of this essay. According to Feldman, it is impossible for life histories to uncover that point where intention and discourse are essentially the same thing. Feldman correctly argues that subjective intention is not the archic site of truth since if "the self is the referential object of the life-history recitation, then it is interpellated by that discourse and cannot be prior to it" (p. 13). He understands that objects of discourse cannot exist outside of or prior to discursive formations. Here he follows Stuart Hall who similarly argues that "events, relations, structures do have conditions of existence and real effects, outside the sphere of the discursive; but that . . . only within the discursive, and subject to its specific conditions, limits and modalities, do they have or can they be constructed with meaning" (1988: 27). The conception of identity that follows from these observations is instructive:

> The self is always the artifact of prior received and newly constructed narratives. It is engendered through narration and fulfills a syntactical function in the life history. The rules of narration may perform a stabilizing role in the cultural construction of truth, but then both self and truth are subordinate to the transindividual closures of narrative (spoken or written). (Feldman, 1991: 13)

Following Lyotard's (1973) insight that the relations between events, agency, and narrative are not linear but rather *achronic*, and that altogether they form a *narrative bloc*. Feldman is able to describe the role of the self as someone who is both narrator and who has been narrated. He writes:

> In a political culture the self that narrates speaks from a position of having been narrated and edited by others—by political institutions, by concepts of historical causality, and possibly by violence. The narrator speaks because this agent is already the recipient of narratives in which he or she has been inerted as a political subject. The narrator writes himself into an oral history because the narrator has already been written and subjected to powerful inscriptions. (p. 13)

Oral histories *are narratives of other narratives* which, in Feldman's (p. 14) terms, "fabricate temporalities and causalities such as linear time." Following Ricoeur's (1984) notion of narration as emplotment, Feldman observes that "The event is not what happens. The event it that which can be narrated." Consequently, making history and narrating history are really two sides of the same process with agency occurring "at the moment of enactment" (p. 15). The performance of a narrative can thus "exceed the social conditions of its production and thus exceed any particular ideological closure associated with its site of emergence" (p. 15). One of Feldman's most important insights is that the oral history of domination cannot completely codify the body—they site of living flesh—through violence and so oral histories emerge as the only narrative forms that can contain lived experience and resistance. Here, narratives emerge in symbiosis with the body through embodiment (what I have elsewhere referred to as "enfleshment"). Narratives of domination that are produced in oral histories consequently serve to mediate "the dissonance between the instrumental imaginary of political rationality and the semantic excess of material violence" (p. 16). Narratives rooted in the body can accommodate semantic excess. They are the only narratives that can.

Towards a Postmodern Narrative Ethics

Both Kemp and Brown make use of the work of Alistair MacIntyre and in doing so push the question of narrative into the realm of ethics. MacIntyre, to his credit, recognizes the essentially narrative character of the human condition—that subjectivities are enmeshed in a complex polymythic world of human narrativity. Narrative is, according to this view, the most appropriate form of unity for human life in that narratives render human actions both intelligible and accountable (Patton 1986). But it is Paul Patton's criticism of MacIntyre that pushes the furthest, and in the right direction, by addressing the concept of a postmodern narrative ethics. Patton (1986: 136) argues that MacIntyre's account of modern narrative leaves out certain dimensions of modern subjectivity, that is, it leaves out the idea that subjects are "fragmented and dispersed across the range of social categories and institutional sites: male, female; sick, healthy; school, workplace and so on." According to Patton, MacIntyre's "undifferentiated and global notion of the modern self," leads him to call for essentially premodern forms of subjectivity.

While "recognizing that the unitary and socially embedded subjectivity implied by an Aristotelian conception of the virtues is only realizable within forms of community and social life incompatible with those of late capitalism" (p. 137), MacIntyre's diagnosis, argues Patton, locates the problem of modernity within subjectivity itself. Patton contrasts the analysis of MacIntyre with that of Foucault. I believe the comparison to be very instructive. Patton notes that in exploring how power works in modern society, Foucault directs his analysis at the institutions of surveillance and domination and their micropractices of power rather than, as in the case of MacIntyre, at the subjectivities which they effect. Foucault's particular starting point is consistent with my concern that narratives be situated ideologically, and not simply discursively. Foucault's notion of subjectivity is the antithesis of MacIntyre's modern self in that Foucault "presupposes an activist conception of the human subject" (p. 139). Patton is worth quoting at length on this observation:

> For Foucault, the human capacity for autonomous self-creation is not in doubt, but there are social and political limits to the exercise of that capacity. The political task which his work suggests is neither utopian nor nostalgic: it is the commitment to those movements in present society which are engaged in the attempt to push back those limits and to extend our sphere of freedom. (p. 139)

Narratives are not unitary: they are better understood as assemblages created within "the different kinds of segmentarity which divide up modern social life" (Patton 1986: 143). Rather than lament the loss of premodern forms of narrative subjectivity, I believe that it makes more political sense to live in the narrative reality of the present, to encourage the subversion of stratified, hierarchized, and socially calcified forms of subjectivity and to struggle against present forms of subjectification which thwart our experimentation with new narrative forms of desire and modes of being-in-the-world (cf. Patton 1986).

Narratives and Identity

Patrick Taylor (1989) maintains that narratives are fundamentally related to the organization of human experience. A narrative is, Taylor asserts,

> not merely a mental structure than can be imposed on reality; narrative is meaningful only to the extent that it captures the vitality and dynamic of social life. Narrative is transformed, its patterns are rearranged, its significance determined anew as the processes of history erupt into human experience. (p. xii)

As hegemonic inscriptions, narratives make legible lines of forces crisscrossing, cutting through, freezing, trapping, and repressing power. As the product of discursive formations and social practices located in material interests, identities are located in historically continuous and pragmatically dispersed networks of social power. Stuart Hall (1987: 46) notes that "every identity is placed, positioned, in a culture, a language, a history."

Our subjectivities need to be inscribed or encoded through narrative in order for us to act. These may be counternarratives or narratives of resistance or else narratives forged out of the magisterial enterprise of empire and colonialism; the point is that our identities take shape with the discursive contingency of arbitrary yet incomplete closures of meaning in the larger text of historical memory. In fact, Stuart Hall (1987: 44) describes identity as "formed at the unstable point where the unspeakable stories of subjectivity meet the narratives of history, of a culture." Hall goes on to make the important observation that identity is possible only within unfinished closures of meaning. He writes:

> all identity is constructed across difference and begins to live with the politics of difference. But doesn't the acceptance of the fictional or narrative status of identity in relation to the world also require as a necessity, its opposite—the moment of arbitrary closure? Is it possible for there to be action or identity in the world without arbitrary closure—what one might call the necessity to meaning of the end of the sentence? (p. 45)

Hall notes correctly that new conceptions of identity as discursive contingency require us to redefine the meaning of political activity. For instance,

Hall alerts us to "the politics of difference, the politics of self-reflexivity, a politics that is open to contingency but still able to act" (p. 45). He articulates a concept of identity that, in his own words, "isn't founded on the notion of some absolute, integral self and which clearly can't arise from some fully closed narrative of the self."

It is worth noting at this point the difference between Hall's concept of narrative and Jerome Bruner's (1991) account of *narrative accrual*. Narrative accrual, according to Bruner, refers to "a 'local' capacity for accruing stories of happenings of the past into some sort of diachronic structure that permits a continuity into the present—in short, to construct a history, a tradition, a legal system, instruments assuring historical continuity if not legitimacy" (pp. 20–21). In this view, narrative is a type of "cultural tool kit" that enables humans to work together through "the process of joint narrative accrual" (p. 20). But we need to follow Hall in ensuring that what we locally and communally 'accrue' is not monumentalized and sanctified simply because it has become part of a shared narrative archive. It is one thing to seek continuity as part of one's communal, civic, or national identity; it is quite another to fix identity in those narratives that will 'read' us in a distinctly totalizing way. Contained in all cultural narratives is a preferred way of reading them. We don't only live particular narratives but we inhabit them (as they inhabit us). The degree to which we resist certain narratives depends upon how we are able to read them.

Narrative as Text

As texts, identities cannot be fixed within closed systems of meanings (i.e., a closed pattern of signifiers and signified); consequently, there are no *true* identities—only identities that are open to inscription, articulation, and interpretation. Richard Rorty (1991: 10) recently noted that "'Truth' is not the name of a power which eventually wins through, it is just the nominalization of an approbative adjective." It is important to acknowledge that identities are never completed but always in the process of negotiation; they are continually struggled over within a polyvalent assemblage of discourses and through nomadic and atopic lines of flight. There is a compostability to identity formation, a malleability that is linked linguistically to the function of the signifier and the permutations of interpretive possibilities around which subjectivity pivots. The context of our identities does not determine how our identities are represented, but plays a part in their rhetorical inscription. For instance, we tend to view our identities in the context of romance, comedy, tragedy, satire, etc., or as conservative, liberal, or radical; but these contextual categories do not occur synchronically outside of history, but are in fact the result of struggles over meaning by various groups in the larger society.

Homi K. Bhabha locates identity in symbolic consciousness—in "that iterative temporality of the signifier" (1987: 6) that occupies "the discursive and affective conditions of a *claim* to selfhood." In other words, the idea of a true, timeless self is a fiction of discourse—a "demand for identification"—that gives the sign a sense of autonomy. Bhabha asserts that the space of enunciation gives rise to the process of doubling (splitting the difference between Self and Other)—or fixing cultural difference in a confinable, visible object when, in fact, *difference is always uncertain and undecidable*. Identity cannot be identified as presence since there is always a principle of undecidability—the double inscription of the moment of enunciation—that can neither negate or transcend difference.

While there is no clear-cut causal relationship between economic structures and psychological ones, I want to argue that new flexible forms of economic production, surveillance, and electronic strategies have produced dangerously "necessary" corresponding forms of subjectivity (Hammer and McLaren, 1992). The self-autonomous subject of liberal humanism lies in an unmarked grave, having been clubbed to death in the back alley of poststructuralist theory. So it is fairly safe now—if not commonplace—to make the statement that identities are not merely reflective of preconstituted social interests of which we are for the most part unaware. However, it is not so popular to make the observation of Terry Eagleton that "the relation between certain social locations, and certain political forms, is a 'necessary' one—which is not, to repeat, to assert that it is inevitable, spontaneous, guaranteed or God-given" (1991: 218). Because this observation appears to have lost favor with an entire generation of post-Marxist social theorists (and I'm referring here to 'ludic' and not 'critical' strands of postmodern social theory), and because I feel we ignore it at our peril, I shall quote Eagleton extensively:

> Ideology is never the mere expressive effect of objective social interests; but neither are all ideological signifiers "free-floating" in respect of such interests. . . . Ideology is a matter of "discourse" rather than of "language"—of certain concrete discursive effects, rather than of signification as such. It represents the points where power impacts upon certain utterances and inscribes itself tacitly within them. But it is not therefore to be equated with just any form of discursive partisanship, "interested" speech or rhetorical bias; rather, the concept of ideology aims to disclose something of the relation between an utterance and the material conditions of possibility, when those conditions of possibility are viewed in the light of certain power-struggles central to the reproduction (or also, for some theories, contestation) of a whole form of social life. (p. 223)

After Terry Eagleton, I want to make the claim that within identity formation certain human interests "become masked, rationalized, naturalized, universalized, legitimated in the name of certain forms of political power"

(1991: 202) and I believe that it is necessary for critical educators to focus on the *political effects* of discourses in the context of Western capitalist society.

I agree with poststructuralists on a number of crucial points: that language does not present us with a faded copy of some homogeneous and unchanging reality; that there exists "no privileged epistemological language which could allow us untroubled access to the real"; that "objects are internal to the discourses which constitute them" and that "language is not just some passive reflection of reality but actively constitutive of it." Nevertheless, I also believe, following Eagleton, that we need a concept of ideology to understand the relation between material situations and discursive formations because the Saussurean semiotic model of some poststructuralists—a model that essentially argues that the signifier produces the signified—is largely inadequate.

Here, too, like Eagleton, I follow Charles Sanders Pierce's pragmatic phenomenology of the sign rather than Saussure's model in stressing the importance of the interpretant or *habit* which is embodied (received and lived). We can shift the meaning of the interpretant by critical self-reflexivity. This rather crucial aspect enables the historical agent to transcend arborescent spirals of endless semiosis in order to effect acts of political *transgression*. It acknowledges also that we can have direct experience of the world but that knowledge about it is only possible in a secondary sense through semiotic systems. It also helps to highlight the idea that material practices are legitimated through the essentially "ideological" workings of discourse. This means that there is an extra-discursive (material) reality and one's location in that reality can cause certain readings of and social practices within the material world to be overcoded (Hammer and McLaren 1992).

I don't want to sound reductionist here by arguing that material location by, say, class or race *necessarily* furnishes an individual with some appropriate or ironclad set of political beliefs and desires. Eagleton rightly asserts there is no "internal relation between particular socio-economic conditions, and specific kinds of political or ideological positions" (Eagleton 1991: 210). Quite true. Nevertheless, what the 'ludic' postmodernists describe as 'pure contingency' or 'undecidability' doesn't "disconnect" discourses from their political effects. Certain subjectivities are surely reinforced by the promotional culture of markets and merchandise in race-, class-, and gender-specific ways so that one could safely say that *there exist generic as well as idiosyncratic relationships between identities and social determinants*. The militant stress that some poststructuralists place on particularism can't adequately explain the connections between forms of social consciousness and material conditions. Some relations are indeed "motivated" by narratives of class, race, ethnicity, and gender.

Market Identities in the "New Times"

I want to argue that there has occurred in these "new times" a particular zoning of subjective space, the segmentation and cleavage of identity, a retooling of subjective experience (personal genres of identification), many of which are reflective of a downgraded economy that exists in the twilight of modern Fordist production. These identities are partly the result of and partly constitutive of what Mayer (1991) calls "the eliminat[ion] of the achievements of the Fordist working class (social security, health insurance, and union representation," the growth of "part-time employment and short-term contracts" and "high levels of precarious and casualized jobs" which characterize shrinking local markets, the expansion of the urban informal sector, and the dynamics of "the advanced services and high-tech sector and the unregulated, labor-intensive informal sector." For instance, advertisers and marketers can break society down into segments or subgroups, each characterized by certain attitudes and behaviors and lifestyles. These are the collective wills fashioned by market demands of the dominant culture—inevitable correlates of particular forms of economic power.

The current move towards a post-Fordist economy—services, automation, data processing—has not fundamentally changed the nature of work as "old style 'industrialization' has invaded the big firms in the non-industrial sectors, with rhythm of work and rates of output submitted to impersonal, mechanical control" (Castoriadis 1992: 14–15). Hence, modernity is finished as far as it can be linked to capitalism's project of social and individual autonomy. Yet modernity remains more alive than ever as far as it embodies "the unlimited expansion of (pseudo) rational (pseudo) mastery" (p. 23). Of course, there is a cultural dimension to this crisis of industrial labor and this is the "ethicization of labor" or the "degree to which employment determines individuals biographically and shapes them in a way characteristic for the particular labor situation" (Honneth 1992: 32). The labor sphere has been drastically marginalized in the biographies of individual workers in terms of permitting them to act as moral agents within roles of self-confirmation. As Axel Honneth (1992) notes, the decline of values associated with and constituted by industrial labor, has also brought a chance for a greater pluralization of individual life-forms. However, *these life forms are not grounded in the appropriate cultural and ethical preconditions.* Honneth writes that

> Cultural everyday praxis is freed step by step from its received value commitments and traditions without them having already been replaced by encompassing orientation patterns, within which the individual subjects' attempts at self-realization could find intersubjective recognition. (p. 32)

Market identities or prepackaged aesthetic substitutes for socially depleted biographies are being accepted by workers as a means of filling up the social vacuum created by the absence of postindustrial forms of ethical life (p. 32). The sphere of labor (including schooling) joins that of leisure in having become colonized by electronic modes of information. Postmodern information technologies (i.e., computers) have brought about the displacement of use-value by sign-value as information has replaced the demand for labor (McLuhan 1973; Baudrillard 1975). Manufactured consumer needs have taken precedence over labor power while the commodity form has subsumed subjectivity and identity under the laws of capital accumulation and the regime of productivity. Subjectivities and identities of citizens have *been virtually reterritorialized by new postmodern electronic mediating devices of television, radio, film, and computers such that the stress on interpretation that was formerly linked to bourgeois individualism has given way to a simulated self that has become socially integrated though the politics of consumption with its surfeit of conservative ideologies.* Identity in postmodern times mirrors opinion polls and forms of organized resistance collapse into public apathy and mass inertia. The dominant strategy of resistance has become that of silence (Baudrillard 1975).

Marcy Darnovsky (1991) has made the important point that advertisers understand culture far better than its critics. She has analyzed their "new traditionalist" ads which both articulate and respond to audiences' fears and desires "more clearly and sympathetically" than the discourse of leftist intellectuals. Stuart Hall has also touched on this theme recently, arguing that "If 'post-Fordism' exists, then it is as much a description of cultural as of economic change" (1990: 128). There exists a certain limited democratization of culture in the contradictory and commodified landscape of popular pleasures. These are reflected in the world of consumption and style. Hall writes that

> Through marketing, layout and style, the "image" provides the mode of representation and fictional narrativisation of the body on which so much of modern consumption depends. Modern culture is relentlessly material in its practices and modes of production. And the material world of commodities and technologies is profoundly cultural. Young people, black and white, who can't even spell "postmodernism" but have grown up in the age of computer technology, rock-video and electronic music, already inhabit such a universe in their heads. (p. 128)

Of course, market identities are exactly the kind of identities that fit comfortably with the corporate vision that conservative educators have of citizenship and schooling with its emphasis on free market enterprise and consumer logic. This can been seen in President Bush's Education 2000 plan and Chris Whittle's plan for profit-making schools. The conservative educational agenda scorns the ideals of collective empowerment and social responsibility in the name of the economic realism. Narratives of identity produced through an emphasis on private education based on market imperatives are aimed at producing compliant workers and loyal consumers. This master narrative takes many forms and is largely a result of the political conservatism of the 1980s in which the "New Right constructed conceptions of who its ideal subjects were, and how they personify the sacred values of religion, hard work, health, and self-reliance" (Denzin 1991: 150). Norman K. Denzin describes the condition of late capitalism as one that perpetuates the "ancient narratives" and myths of the nuclear family, imperialism and rugged individualism in which "capitalism needs and uses anything and everything to perpetuate its hegemonic control over popular culture" (p. 151).

Denzin is worth quoting at length on this issue:

> Late capitalism's "both-and" logic constantly expands, like a rubber band, to fit all that has come before, turning everything, including lived experience, into a commodity that is bought and sold on the contemporary marketplace. This logic requires a positive nostalgia which infuses the past with high value; for if the past were worthless, it could not be sold in the present. Old is good. New is good. Old and new together are best. *This popular ideology scripts a politics which keeps ancient narratives alive.* (1991: 151, italics mine)

The New Right perpetuates its attack on difference, labor militancy, and the entire idea of a national school system by waging war on the very idea of the "public" as the enemy of profit-making private institutions, but in doing so it mistakes its own quest for power for a defence of freedom and masquerades its reactionary power as democratic populism. As conservative spokespersons for the educational New Right such as Diane Ravitch and Chester Finn rail against entrenched self-interest in patriotic hyperbole that is as self-congratulatory, self-indulgent, and self-glorifying as it is obscenely lacking in insight, they in fact are serving the interests of corporate capital and the status-quo distribution of power and wealth which, let's face it, is the central narrative undergirding conservative policy.

Postcolonial Narratives of Liberation:
Beyond Marketplace Identity

We can, I believe, free ourselves from the dead weight of dominant corporate consumer narratives. We can do this, I am convinced, by crossing cultural boundaries and negotiating new, hybrid identities. As an initial step towards creating emancipatory social practices in both private and public spheres, we can help our students bring to a halt the immutable constancy of imperial identities of the patriarchal family, the authoritarian state, and the narrative of the unthinking, obedient citizen of consumer society.

The construction of narrative identities of liberation must place a central emphasis on the meaning of difference. Angela Harris uses the term "multi-

ple consciousness" in order to capture "a world in which people are not oppressed only on the basis of gender, but on the bases of race, class, sexual
orientation, and other categories in inextricable webs" (1990: 587). The
complexity of such oppression suggests that experience needs to be explored
as multivocal—as that which cannot be described independently of other
facets of experience such as race, class, and sexual orientation. Consequently, as teachers and students we need to envision identity as a subjective formation which avoids assuming narrative forms based on race and gender essentialism (voices that monolithically claim to speak for all)—an essentialism which "forcibly" fragments experience in the name of a commonality,
that is, in the name of that which masquerades as normative experience.
There is no essential 'female' identity, of 'male' identity or 'American' identity. There is no universal narrative of citizenship that cannot or should not
be open to contestation among students.

In understanding how narratives of the self become constituted in contexts of colonialism, postcolonialism, and neocolonialism, teachers can develop a new politics of difference and identity and bring about a new sub-
ject-space of meaning construction and praxis. To reveal the fissures in the
continuity of the narrative self is to contest claims to domination by groups
on the basis of race, class privilege, and gender and other interests. For
teachers, the classroom can be transformed into a hybrid pedagogical space
where permission is not denied students who wish to narrate their own
identities outside of marketplace identities and the politics of consumerism,
a space where individual identities find meaning in collective expression and
solidarity with cultural others, where mimetic, Eurocentric times recedes
into the lived, historical moment of contemporary struggles for identity.
Here the imperatives of consumer culture and the hegemony of market
identities are challenged by narratives of identity that are underwritten by a
concern for liberation and social justice.

A pedagogy informed by a post-colonial narratology shifts the relation of
the social actor to the object of his or her knowledge and the problematic in
which identity is defined and struggled over. In this respect, a postcolonial
narratology encourages the oppressed to contest the stories fabricated for
them by "outsiders" and to construct counterstories that give shape and direction to the practice of hope and the struggle for an emancipatory politics
of everyday life. It is a pedagogy that attempts to exorcise from the social
body the invading pathologies of racism, sexism, and class privilege (Giroux
and McLaren 1986). It is a pedagogy that is able to rupture the dominant
narratives of citizenship and destabilize the pretensions to monologic identity that this narrative exhibits. A postcolonial narratology must trouble the
surface of the Western texts of identity such that the gaps and faults (failles)
produced can create an historically discontinuous subject and thus can help

to inhibit the resurfacing of colonialist discourses of the self (Giroux and McLaren 1991a.). In this sense, a postcolonial narratology bears some affinity to what Linda Hutcheon refers to as "narcissistic narrative" or "metafiction" in that the text of liberation is explicitly recognized as socially constructed and demands that the social actor be engaged "intellectually, imaginatively, and *affectively* in its co-creation" (1980: 7, emphasis mine).

For post colonial educators, this means raising the following questions about their pedagogies as part of a "critical narratology": What is the narrative schematization that orders their own lives and the lives of our students? Is it populated by bourgeois individualism and by the assumptions of capitalist social life and their social and cultural correlates? How may the practice of a pedagogy of liberation be constructed so that it is not recuperable within a scenario of white supremacist colonial desire? Following DeLauretis (1990: 144), we need to begin to rethink the identity of liberation as becoming "the subject of an unusual knowing, a cognitive practice, a form of consciousness that is not primordial, universal or coextensive with human thought . . . but historically determined and yet subjectively and politically assumed." Postcolonial educators need to help in the development of what Cornel West (1990: 93) calls "a new kind of cultural worker" capable of exercising "a politics of difference" that will enable students to "interrogate the ways in which they are bound by certain conventions and to learn from and build on these very norms and models" (p. 107). We need to situate pedagogy within a narratology that creates *histories of our own making, which fractures the philosophical time of Western concepts and which can surmount the categorical oppositions of philosophical logic* (Godzich 1990). In other words, Western cultural authority is not a stable system of reference since cultural difference (as distinct from cultural diversity) is always about how culture is enunciated—how culture is constructed in terms of a politics of signification. Any cultural identity must acknowledge its discursive embeddedness and address as well as its politics of location and place. The way identities are enunciated are always ambivalent and have no primordial origins that 'fix' them as Latino, as African-American, or as Anglo. This does not mean identities as ethnicities are unimportant. But it does suggest that they do not guarantee one's politics.

The Production of Border Identities

Border identities are narratives and counternarratives which we choose to enact (but as Marx reminds us, not in conditions of our own making) in the context of our everyday, mundane practical existence. Border identities are anchored in and are the outcome of those social practices that configure experience and shape affective investment in such experience *in relation to narratives of liberation* which challenge the market identities produced by the

New Right's narratives of consumer citizenship. This form of *auto-praxis* follows authorizing strategies which consist of naming oppression and forging identity through positive forms of subjectivity *signified by one's active participation in making one's own history*; similarly, the construction of border identities consists of renaming and reconstructing reality rather than engaging reality through the production of a negative subjectivity (in which case identity is constructed out of signifiers of lack and omission). Border identities are created out of empathy for others by means of a passionate connection through difference (McLaren 1988, 1992). Such a connection is furthered by a narrative imagination which enables critical linkages to be made between our own stories and the stories of cultural others (McLaren, 1993; Darder, 1992).

While it is important to recognize that subjectivities are culturally constructed and discursively interpreted, this observation is not meant to defend the cultural relativism surrounding the claim that any one identity is as important as any other. This is not the meaning of border identity. Nor is it simply a means of meeting the radical requirements of constructing one's identity in opposition to the *doxa* (the *déjà-dit* or *already said* of public consumer conventions) in order to form a narrative identity that is more enabling of social transformation. Rather, it is to fight against the foreshortening of the possibility of self and social transformation as co-implicated in the dialectic of freedom. That is, it is to fight against our failure to see our own reflection in the eyes of others. Border identity requires what Ramon Saldivar (1990: 175) calls a "dialectics of difference" which refers to the formation of subjectivities of resistance, that is, subjectivities that are able to resist "the absolutizing tendencies of a racist, classist, patriarchal bourgeois world that founds itself on the notion of a fixed and positive identity and on specified gender roles based on this positive fixation."

The work of D. Emily Hicks (1988) on "border writing" and Henry A. Giroux's (1992) concept of "border pedagogy" is suggestive of what I mean when I discuss the concept of "border identity." Hicks describes border writing as an "anti-centering strategy" in which border narratives are decentered so that "there is no identity between the reader and individual characters, but rather, an invitation to listen to a Voice of the Person which arises from an overlay of codes out of which characters and events emerge. . . ." (p. 51). She bases her concept of border writing on what she refers to as the heterogeneous border cultures of Latin America and their relationship to contemporary Latin American literature. She is also interested in exploring how the dominant cultures of Europe and the United States "are presented in their inter-action with Latin American culture" (p. 48). Her discussion of border writing draws upon writers whom she contends have actually prefigured recent forms of European postmodernist characteristics such as decentering the subject and appropriating images. She refers to, among others, the work of the Brazilian concrete poets and the artists of the *neo-gráfica* movement in Mexico. According to Hicks, border writing

> emphasizes the differences in reference codes between two or more cultures and depicts, therefore, a kind of realism that approaches the experience of border crossers, those who live in a bilingual, bicultural, biconceptual reality. I am speaking of cultural, not physical, borders: the sensibility which informs border literature can exist among guest workers anywhere, including European countries in which the country of origin does not share a physical border with the host country. (1988: 49)

The attributes that Hicks applies to border writing, I am applying to the concept of identity formation. Similarly, what Giroux (1992) has called border pedagogy can be utilized suggestively in the project of remaking identities. To engage in the project of creating border identities is a means of deconstructing and taking control of narratives of the self, while recognizing the multiplicity of languages or codes within a single language—i.e., the polylingualism in one's own language—as well as appreciating the meaning-tropes in other languages. In effect, it is a dialogue with oneself and the Other, one that contests and ruptures the one-dimensional monotopic narrative structure of dominant social texts based on market incentives and consumer logic and their relationships to readers. Border identities are identities in which readers and narrators are both one and the Other in the sense that the "border crosser is both 'self' and 'other'" (Hicks, 1988: 52). In other words, "The border crosser 'subject' emerges from double strings of signifiers of two sets of reference codes, from both sides of the border" (p. 52).

I am suggesting that teachers and students learn to re-present themselves through a form of border writing in which the narratives they construct for themselves in relation to the Other are effectively deterritorialized politically, culturally, and linguistically, so that the meaning-tropes through which subjectivity becomes constructed fails to dominate the Other. To construct border identities is to refuse to adopt a single perspective linked to cultural domination. Refusing "the metonymic reduction of reality to the instrumental logic of Western thought" (p. 56), is to *reterritorialize identity* in a way that holds out the possibility of "subverting the rationality of collective suicide" (p. 57).

A serious problem with forging an emancipatory pedagogy of border identity needs to be identified here. It stems from the failure of male critics to extricate themselves from their entrenchment in phallocentric discourses. Male critics are often reluctant to narrate the contingency of their own enunciative positions as masculine. Theorists need to specify their sexual locations and other sites of textual enunciation so that they do not mistakenly speak for others. Similarly, in the case of African-American communities, Cornel

West notes that "The modern Black diaspora problematic of invisibility and namelessness can be understood as the condition of *relative lack of Black power to present themselves to themselves and others as complex human beings, and thereby to contest the bombardment of negative, degrading stereotypes put forward by White supremacist ideologies*" (1990: 102). It is important that a project of liberation not constitute subaltern voices as simply the mirror image of the white, Western male sovereign subject. Euro-American liturgical calls for a common identity are camouflaged attempts to reclaim the past from those who threaten the image of what Americans currently represent and what they have been. Subaltern groups cannot be turned into living allegories of menace by naturalizing the difference between "us" and "them" but must speak through the codes of their race- class- and gender-specific struggles for voice and freedom. All groups require a narrative that recognizes, in the words of Stuart Hall, "that we all speak from a particular place, out of a particular history, out of a particular experience, a particular culture, without being contained by that position" (1988: 29). However, rather than searching for the origins of our identities as historical agents in struggle, we need to focus more on what we can achieve together. What we might become together takes precedence over who we are. In other words, before I speak in solidarity I should not demand that others present to me their identity papers. This is the politics of the border guard, not the border-crosser. Identities constructed in the act of solidarity will be provisional, and the alliances formed will be contingent on the strategies, negotiations, and translations that occur *in the act of struggle* for both a common ground of alliance-building (rather than a common culture) and a radical and transformative politics. It's more important to create identities out of strategies of resistance and the passion of struggle that a search for some primordial ground of being that will forever suture subjects to a narrative inevitability—to rerun identities in which subjectivity is primarily constituted through nostalgia and familiarity (cf. Grossberg, 1992).

Identity-formation needs to occur in what Homi Bhabha calls the "third space of translation." Translation requires that identities—especially cultural identities—be seen as "decentered structures" that are constituted only in relation to otherness. Through a displacement of origins, a creative liminality "opens up the possibility of articulating *different*, even incommensurable cultural practices and priorities" (1990a: 210–11). The "third space" refers to a condition of hybridity in which the essentialism of origins and the discourse of authenticity are challenged. Otherness always intervenes to prevent the subject from "fixing" itself in a closed system of meaning and keeps open "a new area of negotiation of meaning and representation." (211). This enables "new structures of authority, new political initiatives, which are inadequately understood through received wisdom."

The construction of border identities follows Joel Kovel's "philosophy of becoming." To identify with the processual social and material event of "becoming" is to align oneself explicitly with a narrative of freedom. In Kovel's words, it is "to speak of a practical wish to be free" and to commit to a philosophy "in which the self can become Other to itself, and from that position either remain alienated or transcend itself" (1991: 108). Kovel expands on this idea by proclaiming:

> I am a subject, not merely an object; and I am not a Cartesian subject, whose subjectivity is pure inwardness, but rather an expressive subject, a transformative subject; I am a subject, therefore, who needs to project my being into the world, and transform the world as an expression of my being; and finally, I will appropriate my being rather than have it expropriated. (p. 108)

The production of border identities has less to do with the search for self-knowledge as it has to do with what Foucault saw as "a method of self care" (McLaren, 1993). From the perspective of a postcolonial narratology, the question is whether or not we can forge border identities that can resist reinscription or reenthronment in the hegemonic mapping of nationalist, consumer-oriented culture. Will border identities simply become supplemental—an efflux of counterhegemonic discourses consumed rather than counterposed—conditional upon rather than resistant to the machineries of hegemonic state power? This question of incorporation—of reintegrating the oppressed into the world of unequal power relations—is a nagging one; yet it needs to be addressed. Capitalism thrives on the regulation and eventual assimilation of difference, after all. Difference becomes chartered in the service of capital so that the subjectivities of the citizenry can be emptied out as part of the rite of passage of becoming American. So the question remains, has the periphery become imperialized and if this is the case, what does it mean, in Giroux's (1992) important sense, to be a "border crosser?" Do border identities in this context mean simply a retooling of a consumerist ethics in the form of an aggressive individualism, a cult of hypermasculinity, of sales-motivated cultural ethics purveyed by an economy of "flexible specialization," of warrior-citizens bent on global domination? Or is it possible to dethrone mainstream pedagogical method in order to create cultural sites where counter-hegemonic subjectivities can be constructed that effectively destabilize the production of market identities?

Another issue is how to construct border identities that speak to the lived experiences of oppressed people—people who possess a natural suspicion of academics writing from the high-altitude vistas of Mount Olympus. The imperious call for a transcultural narrative identity that traverses particular identities constituted perhaps by a universal law of the unconscious parallels the corrosive call for a common culture and the collective de-ethnicization of the population. It is a vision snatched from the Eurocentric archives and dipped in the blood of imperialism, a vision sharing the conspiracy of civilization (McLaren and Leonard, 1993; McLaren, 1993). It is a vision both academics and activists must abandon.

Majority discourses narrativized under the auspices of whiteness monologically locate and contain minority subjects as 'ethnic' whereas white people are rarely accorded this status (hooks, 1992). By masking their own situatedness in forms of white ethnicity, white people universalize the Other as ethnic and themselves as existing metaphysically beyond all forms of ethnic signification. They thus remove themselves from the negative connotations of the term 'ethnic' that they themselves created. White culture unifies itself in its invisibility and avoids negative equivalences. White culture is thus able to occupy the position of the privileging signifier and position in a fixed relation of binary opposition people of color. One insidious irony is that white culture attempts to de-ethnicize America through its melting-pot ideology and yet it is camouflaging a form of re-ethnicizing the citizenry into the flat and barren identity of white middle class 'family values' America.

Critical pedagogy needs to construct a praxis of border identity in which binary systems of thought (e.g. White vs. Black) no longer organize one's politics. The challenge is to create what Trinh T. Minh-ha calls a "shifting multi-place of resistance" that "no longer simply thrives on alternate, homogenized strategies of rejection, affirmation, confrontation, and opposition well-rooted in a tradition of contestation" (1991: 220). She asserts that this "challenge has to be taken up every time a positioning occurs: for just as one must situate oneself (in terms of ethnicity, class, gender, difference), one also refuses to be confined to that location" (p. 229–30). Minh-ha's concept of multiculturalism is one that I have been attempting to chart out throughout this essay, one that neither endorses the idea of a juxtaposition of cultures nor "subscribes to a bland 'melting-pot' type of attitude that would level all differences" (232). Instead, Minh-ha locates multiculturalism "in the intercultural acceptance of risks, unexpected detours, and complexities of relation between break and closure" (p. 232). The idea here is to develop a strategy of identity that Marcos Sanchez-Tranquilino and John Tagg (referring to Chicano art) describe as "not of fixed difference, but of the transformation of languages and spaces of operation to evade both invisibility and assimilation" (1991: 104).

Gloria Anzaldúa has described the identity of *la mestiza* within *la cultura chicana* that captures this sense of ambiguity and transformation associated with the border identity. She writes that *la mestiza*

> can't hold concepts or ideas in rigid boundaries. The borders and walls that are supposed to keep the undesirable ideas out are entrenched habits and patterns of behavior; these habits and patterns are the enemy within.

Rigidity means death. Only by remaining flexible is she able to stretch the psyche horizontally and vertically. *La mestiza* constantly has to shift out of habitual formations; from convergent thinking, analytical reasoning that tends to use rationality to move towards a single goal (a Western mode), to divergent thinking, characterized by movement away from set patterns and goals and toward a more whole perspective, one that includes rather than excludes.

The new *mestiza* copes by developing a tolerance for contradictions, a tolerance for ambiguity. She learns to be an Indian in Mexican culture, to be Mexican from an Anglo point of view. She learns to juggle cultures. She has a plural personality, she operates in a pluralistic mode—nothing is thrust out, the good, the bad and the ugly, nothing rejected, nothing abandoned. Not only does she sustain contradictions, she turns the ambivalence into something else. (1987: 79)

Anzaldúa's project is a laudatory one, for she is genuinely trying to connect subaltern communities and critical theory. This is important because Western theories of identity are linked to the culture of whiteness in disabling ways. For instance, official Western discourses of identity exclude from the concept of 'citizen' everything which challenges its determination as an empty signifier, a marker of 'American' in which anything can be articulated with it that has sufficient authoritative exegesis. But before identities can be sutured to conventional meanings, they must first be cleansed of 'ethnic' significations. Anzaldúa's task is to unmask the pretensions of Western identity formations and to cut them at their joints. She accomplishes this by dismantling false images—"rechazamos esas falsas imágenes" (1990: xxvii) and formulating marginal theories. For Anzaldúa, marginal theories

are partially outside and partially inside the Western frame of reference (if that is possible), theories that overlap many "worlds." We are articulating new positions in these "in-between," Borderland worlds of ethnic communities and academies, feminist and job worlds.

. . . In our *mestizaje* theories we create new categories for those of us left out or pushed out of the existing ones. We recover and examine non-Western aesthetics while critiquing Western aesthetics; recover and examine non-rational modes and "blanked-out" realities while critiquing rational, consensual reality; recover and examine indigenous languages while critiquing the "languages" of the dominant culture. . . . If we have been gagged and disempowered by theories, we can also be loosened and empowered by theories (xxvi).

What Hall, hooks, Minh-ha, Giroux, Hicks, Anzaldúa and others are calling for is a borderization of identity, a rupturing of the unitary cohesiveness of the culture of terror we know as the politics of whiteness. It is an identity described with a forceful elegance by Sanchez-Tranquilino and Tagg:

> What we begin to make out is another narration of identity, another resistance. One that asserts a difference, yet cannot be absorbed into the pleasures of a global marketing culture. One that locates its different voice, yet will not take a stand on the unmoving ground of a defensive fundamentalism. One that speaks its location as more than local, yet makes no claim to universality for its viewpoint or language. One that knows the border and crosses the line. (1991: 105)

Guillermo Gómez-Peña echoes Anzaldúa in capturing the "multiple repertoires" or identity in a response to questions about his own nationality:

> Today, eight years after my departure [from Mexico], when they ask me for my nationality or ethnic identity, I can't respond with one word, since my 'identity' now possesses multiple repertoires: I am Mexican but I am also Chicano and Latin American. At the border they call me *chilango* or *mexiquillo*; in Mexico City it's *pocho* or *norteño*; and in Europe it's *sudaca*. The Anglos call me "Hispanic" or "Latino," and the Germans have, on more than one occasion, confused me with Turks or Italians. My wife Emilia is Anglo, but speaks Spanish with an Argentine accent, and together we walk amid the rubble of the Tower of Babel of our American postmodernity. (cited in Yudice, 1992, pp. 214–15)

However, as George Yudice points out, multiculturalism must move beyond a mere ethnocentric celebration of cultural transformism and the crossing of linguistic, political and ethnic borders. He cites remarks made by Néstor García Canclini in response to interviews he conducted with residents of Tijuana, Mexico:

> Other Tijuana artists and writers challenge the euphemistic treatment of the contradictions and uprooting. . . . They reject the celebration of migrations caused by poverty in the homeland and in the United States. (cited in Yudice, 1992, p. 215)

Yudice sounds a telling warning to U.S. critical multiculturalists when he suggests that we incur in our own brand of imperialism when we unwittingly "become a 'front' for our own integration into a global market in which the image—the politics of representation—supplants resources and services, shrinking at an ever faster pace." (1992: 213) We do this when we assume that we can show the rest of the world how to discover itself. When we suggest that multiple subject positions should be celebrated as the apogee of a new postmodern hybridity that escapes the fascist tendencies of militant particularisms, we need to be careful. Some people cross-borders willingly, some people are forced to cross them, and others are literally shot in their attempts at crossing. Yet at the same time there is a wonderful fecundity in the concept of the border-crosser, as Hicks and Giroux have singularly illustrated. It is an edifying metaphor for a critical multiculturalism that needs to be taken seriously. That is why we need to exercise caution in defining for cultural others what the *mestiza* identity should look like. For instance, it will be different for the exile, for the metropolitan 'professional' intellectual, and for the tourist. We need to map the different identifications constituted by border identities and appropriate the most critical elements and potentialities for both local and global struggles for liberation.

A critical narratology needs to be grounded in a politics of difference that is more than a salutary derangement of our enslavement to the habitual and the mundane. Critical narratology is a justificatory, defamiliarizing strategy but also a practice of hope. In Stuart Hall's terms (1990), I am speaking of fashioning a new collective will; of producing what Darnovsky (1991: 88) refers to as "self representations, forged self-consciously through confrontation . . . and negotiation." This has connections with Foucault's imperative of the practice of the self. We need new practices of identity that stem from new forms of subjectivity and historical agency (Giroux and McLaren 1991 1991a). I want to emphasize a particular claim here by Paul Raymond Harrison that the rationalist narrative be contested by "multiple voices of reason through story-telling" (1989: 64). Critical narratology must be made compatible with a nonreductionist and nonrationalist concept of culture. Like Mexican artist Frida Kahlo, who "saw herself literally on the borderline—between nature and culture, between the ancient earth of pre-Columbian America and 'Gringolandia'—a distatefully technological USA" (Lippard, 1987, p. 221), educators need to move between and within different zones of cultural semiosis. The absolutization of narrative through reductive notions of culture forecloses an exploration of "the complex and divergent character of our narrative condition in modernity, where we do not simply live in a narrated world, but many narrated words" (Harrison, 1989: 76). This idea is reflected in a number of the articles included in this present volume. For instance, Yvonna Lincoln calls for alternative research strategies that "will increasingly lean toward the constructivist, the critical, the feminist . . . and other standpoint methodologies" (p. 34). She further argues that teachers as researchers need to collaborate with the silenced in order to "tell the stories and present the narratives of nonmainstream 'border' individuals" (p. 35). In doing so, we need, as Ivor Goodson and Ardra L. Cole note, to pay more attention to the "micropolitical and contextual realities of school life" which "affect the lives and arenas in which personal practical and pedagogical knowledge are utilized" (p. 72). Attempting to utilize postmodern social theory and critical theory as a framework for understanding identity-formation, Bill Tierney situates identity within the context of "multiple selves" and "manifold narrative voices" in opening up to a critical understanding the many-sided histories of the silenced and oppressed.

Patricia J. Gumport reveals how a postmodernist perspective can shift our understanding of ourselves as researchers by revealing how identities are forged within shifting parameters of power. She underscores the important observation that the shaping and re-vision of identities is relational in nature and context-specific. Grace Mest Szepkouski stresses the importance of understanding the life-history research process as itself a potential narrative of liberation that can lead to greater self-knowledge and the development of more critical forms of historical agency. Andrew Gitlin sensitively articulates the story of "Beth," who undertakes a journey of profound self-realization. Gitlin underscores with his poignant contribution the relationship between personal narrative and the development of voice. And finally, Dan McLaughlin describes the process of personal narrative development that was undertaken by a group of Navajo public school teachers had enabled them to locate their own pedagogies as a form of cultural politics. Further analysis of this process led these teachers to develop an alternative K–6 language arts program.

Richard Harvey Brown echoes the concerns of these authors when he advises us to write our narratives of liberation, of disidentification, by authorizing "a new vision of ourselves and our world" (1987: 147). It is important that we "[summon] forth an alternative definition of the world and thereby [authorize] a new form of social existence." In Pêcheux's (1975) terms, we need to displace and transform the subject form of our narratives, and not just abolish it. Harold Rosen makes the persuasive point that all narratives *need to be retold*. He writes that "In some cultures there are privileged tales . . . which must be retold; but every authentic teller must turn them into internally persuasive discourse or be reduced to a mere reciter, an inflexible mimic" (1986: 235). According to Rosen, students need to liberate themselves from the authority of another's discourse while not necessarily rejecting the discourse itself. *The retelling of stories is what gives us our voice.* While all stories—even or perhaps especially those that are retold—recruit the desires of the Other in order to maintain narrative authority and contain their own "surreptitious menace" (p. 235), they can also counter "magisterial" narratives. Teachers and students need access to insurgent narratives that challenge phallocentric self-stories that leave out that which is contingent, irrational, or ambiguous. They need a language of narrative refusal that contests the conventional rules of self-fashioning within autobiographical identities encouraged and legimated within patriarchy (Smith 1987).

Teachers have a particular responsibility in constructing their narrative voice in the practice of pedagogy. They need to be aware of how history is represented or "inscribed" not only in their own voices, but the voices of their students (McLaren and Hammer 1989). Of course, the question is whether these voices serve to expedite the process of the legitimation of the hegemonic culture or contest it. Here the question of narrative closure becomes important (Kalogeras 1991). According to Kalogeras (1991: 31) narrative closure "predicates a central consciousness that represents the structures and processes of 'reality' as if they naturally wield a specific meaning. Hence, this meaning is promoted as "'found' rather than as 'constructed'." The issue here, of course, especially in the case of the representation of ethnic history, is to what extent the process of narrativization "entails a totalization that suppresses the discontinuities, gaps, and silences that constitute not only one's life but also one's ethnic history" (p.32). If teachers enacting their pedagogical duties serve to mediate between the host society and the ethnic cultures of their students, to what extent are the narratives that teachers use to mediate between dominant narratives and counternarratives, or narratives of difference, populated by imperial and corporate discourses of the host culture?

This question underscores the importance of inviting students themselves to become the mediators of their own narratives and assume narrative authority for their own lives by adopting a *metacultural* perspective in which they can become a critic of both cultures (cf. Kalogeras 1991). Of course, the underlying narrative and insurgent imaginations that invites them to assume the role of metacultural mediator is one that speaks the story of hope and liberation. Such a narrative must not invite premature closure on the meaning of emancipation or simply annex the ongoing struggle for liberty to an outworn Marxist tradition. It can be employed to meet such an objective by encouraging students to remain ruthlessly self-critical in examining their own assumptions and recognizing when a praxis of liberation unwittingly serves to re-contain oppression. A narrative of hope and liberation must additionally be analyzed in relation to the historical and cultural specificity of its production in the context of classroom relations and the larger social order to as to reveal both its enabling and disabling effects. Needed to be secured within this process is a narrative identity that is restless and not merely reactive, one that does not simply run counter to a Eurocentric identity as a type of endless return, because this would be tantamount to turning the act of resistance into a millenarianism in reverse that tries to invert the subject of modernity produced by the logic of possessive individualism (Saenz 1991). Required, too, is a loyalty to possibility, to forging alternative identities that are contemporaneous with modernity but that do not simply invert its normative truths (Saenz 1991).

The struggle is a proleptic one against the archival knowledge of Western colonialism, the inherited vocabulary of mainstream pedagogy, and a narratology populated by identity formations whose overall trajectory is a logocentric orientation of consciousness—one which history has shaped within particular economies of desire. We need to introduce to teachers narratives that are contrary politically to those prescribed by the dominant regime of truth, counternarratives underwritten by a politically inspired teleology whose narrative closures are always contingent and therefore always open to the creative and the new. As teachers, we need to become theorists of a resistance postmodernism that can help students make the necessary connections among their desires, their frustrations, and the cultural forms and social practices which inform them. Norman K. Denzin notes that theorists of postmodernism are inevitably *storytellers* who enable us to understand social life as a cultural plot. He reports that "Our most powerful effects as storytellers come when we expose the cultural plot and the cultural practices that guide our writing hands" (1991: 156). We need also to remember that the narratives we tell and retell in our classrooms are both reflective and constitutive of who we are and what we will become.

References

Appiah, Anthony. 1991. "Tolerable Falsehoods: Agency and the Interests of Theory." In *Consequences of Theory,* edited by Jonathan Arac and Barbara Johnson, 63–90. Baltimore: Johns Hopkins University Press.

Auni, Ora. 1991. "Narrative Subject, Historic Subject: *Shoah* and *La Place de l'Etoile.*" *Poetics Today* 12, no. 3: 495–516.

Anzaldúa, Gloria. 1990. "Haciendo caras, una entrada: An Introduction." In *Making Face, Making Soul: Creative and Critical Perspectives by Women of Color,* edited by Gloria Anzaldúa, xv–xxviii. San Francisco: Aunt Lute.

Anzaldúa, Gloria. 1987. *Borderlands/La Frontera: The New Mestiza.* San Francisco: Aunt Lute.

Baudrillard, Jean. 1975. *The Mirrors of Production.* St. Louis: Telos Press.

Bennett, Tony. 1986. "Texts in History: The Determinations of Readings and Their Texts." In *Post-Structuralism and the Question of History,* edited by D. Attridge, G. Bennington, and R. Young, 63–81. Cambridge: Cambridge University Press.

Bennett, Tony, and Wollacott, Janet. 1987. *Bond and Beyond: The Political Career of a Popular Hero.* New York: Methuen.

Bhabha, Homi K. 1987. "Interrogating Identity." In *The Real Me: Post-Modernism and the Question of Identity.* London: ICA Documents, vol. 6, 5–12.

Bhabha, Homi K. 1990. "Dissemination: Time, Narrative, and the Margins of the Modern Nation." In *Nation and Narration,* edited by Homi K. Bhabha, 291–322. London and New York: Routledge.

Bhabha, Homi K. 1990a. "Interview with Homi Bhabha." In *Identity: Community, Culture, Difference,* edited by Jonathan Rutherford, 207–221. London: Lawrence and Wishart.

Bhabha, Homi K. 1988. "The Commitment to Theory." *New Formations*, 5: 5–23.

Brown, Richard Harvey. 1987. *Society as Text: Essays on Rhetoric, Reason and Reality*. Chicago: University of Chicago Press.

Bruner, Jerome. 1991. "The Narrative Construction of Reality." *Critical Inquiry* 18, no 1: 1–78.

Cascardi, Anthony. 1990. "Narration and Totality." *The Philosophical Forum* 21, no 33: 277–294.

Castoriadis, Cornelius. 1992. "The Retreat from Autonomy: Post-Modernism as Generalized Conformism." *Thesis Eleven* 31: 14–23.

Clegg, Stewart R. 1989. *Frameworks of Power*. Newbury Park, Calif.: Sage Publications.

Connerty, J. P. 1990. "History's Many Cunning Passages: Paul Ricoeur's *Time and Narrative*." *Poetics Today* 2, no 2: 383–403.

Coste, Didier. 1989. *Narrative as Communication*. Minneapolis: University of Minnesota Press.

Darder, Antonia. 1992. *Culture and Power in the Classroom*. South Hadley, Mass.: Bergin and Garvey.

Darnovsky, Marcy. 1991. "The New Traditionalism: Repackaging Ms. Consumer." *Social Text* 9, no. 4: 72–91.

DeLauretis, Teresa. 1990. "Eccentric Subjects: Feminist Theory and Historical Consciousness." *Feminist Studies* 15, no. 1: 15–50.

Denzin, Norman K. 1991. *Images of Postmodern Society: Social Theory and Contemporary Cinema*, Newbury Park, Calif.: Sage Publications.

Eagleton, Terry. 1981. *Walter Benjamin*, London: Verso Press.

————. 1991. *Ideology: An Introduction*, New York: Verso Press.

Feldman, Allen. 1991. *Formations of Violence: The Narrative of the Body and Political Terror in Northern Ireland*, Chicago: University of Chicago Press.

Felski, Rita. 1989. "Feminism, Postmodernism, and the Critique of Modernity." *Cultural Critique* 13: 33–56.

Fuss, Diana. 1989. *Essentially Speaking: Feminism, Nature, and Difference*. New York: Routledge.

Game, Ann. 1991. *Undoing the Social: Towards a Deconstructive Sociology*. Toronto, Ontario and Buffalo, N.Y.: University of Toronto Press.

Gergen, Kenneth J. 1991. *The Saturated Self: Dilemmas of Identity in Contemporary Life*. New York: Basic Books.

Giroux, Henry. 1992. *Border Crossings*. New York: Routledge.

Giroux, Henry, and McLaren, Peter. 1986. "Teacher Education and the Politics of Engagement: The Case for Democratic Schooling." *Harvard Educational Review* 56, no. 3: 213–38.

―――. 1990. "Leon Golub's Radical Pessimism: Towards a Pedagagy of Representation." *Exposure* 28, no 12: 18–33.

―――. 1990a. "Radical Pedagogy as Cultural Politics: Beyond the Discourse of Critique and Anti-Utopianism." In *Theory/Pedagogy/Politics,* edited by D. Morton and M. Zavarzadeh, 152–86. Urbana and Chicago: University of Illinois Press.

Godzich, Wlad. 1990. "Foreword: The Time Machine." In *Narrative as Communication,* edited by Didier Coste, ix–xvii. Minneapolis: University of Minnesota Press.

Grossberg, Lawrence. 1992. *We Gotta Get Out of This Place: Popular Conservatism and Postmodern Culture*. New York and London: Routledge.

Guattari, Felix, and Negri, Tony. 1990. *Communists Like Us: New Spaces of Liberty, New Lines of Alliance*. Columbia University: Semio Text(e).

Hall, Stuart.1987. "Minimal Selves." In *The Real Me: Post-Modernism and the Question of Identity*. London: ICA Documents, vol. 6, 44–46.

―――. 1988. "New Ethnicities." In *Black Film/British Cinema*. London: ICA Documents, vol. 7, 27–31.

―――. 1990. "The Meaning of New Times." In *New Times: The Changing Face of Politics in the 1990s,* edited by Stuart Hall and Martin Jacques, 116–34. New York: Verso.

―――1991. "Ethnicity: Identity and Difference." *Radical America* 23, no 4: 9–20.

Hammer, Rhonda, and McLaren, Peter. 1992. "The Spectacularization of Subjectivity: Media Knowledges, Global Citizenry and the New World Order." *Polygraph* 5: 46–66.

―――. 1992. "Le Paradoxe de l'image: Connaissance médiatique et déclin de la qualité de la vie." *Anthropologie et Sociétés,* 16, 1: 21–39.

Haraway, Donna. 1990. *Primate Visions: Gender, Race, and Nature in the World of Modern Science*. New York: Routledge.

Harding, Sandra. 1991. *Whose Science? Whose Knowledge?* Ithaca, N.Y.: Cornell University Press.

Harris, Angela. 1990. "Race and Essentialism in Feminist Legal Theory." *Stanford Law Review* 42: 581–616.

Harrison, Paul Raymond. 1989. "Narrativity and Interpretation: On Hermeneutical and Structuralist Approaches to Culture." *Thesis Eleven* 22: 61–78.

Heath, Stephen. 1990. "The Ethics of Sexual Difference." *Discourse* 12: no. 2: 128–53.

Hicks, Emily D. 1988. "Deterritorialization and Border Writing." In *Ethics/Aesthetics: Post-Modern Positions,* edited by Robert Merrill, 47–58. Washington: Maisonneuve Press.

Honneth, Axel. 1992. "Pluralization and Recognition: On the Self-Misunderstanding of Postmodern Social Theorists." *Thesis Eleven* 31: 224–33.

hooks, bell. 1992. *Black Looks: Race and Representation.* Boston: South End Press.

hooks, bell. 1989. *Talking Back: Thinking Feminist/Thinking Black.* Boston: South End Press.

Hutcheon, Linda. 1980. *Narcissistic Narrative: The Metafictional Paradox.* London: Methuen.

Jay, Martin. 1982. "Anamnestic Totalization." *Theory and Society* 11: 1–15.

Kalogeras, Yiorgos D. 1991. "Historical Representation and the Cultural Legitimation of the Subject in Ethnic Personal Narratives." *College Literature* 18, no 3: 30–43.

Kearney, Richard. 1987. "Ethics and the Postmodern Imagination." *Thought,* 62, no. 244: 39–58.

Kemp, Peter T. 1989. "Toward a Narrative Ethics: A Bridge between Ethics and the Narrative Reflection of Ricoeur." In *The Narrative Path: The Later Works of Paul Ricoeur,* edited by Peter T. Kemp and David Rasmussen, 65–87. Cambridge: The MIT Press.

Kovel, Joel. 1991. *History and Spirit: An Inquiry into the Philosophy of Liberation.* Boston: Beacon Press.

Lippard, Lucy R. 1987. "Feminist Space: Reclaiming Territory." In *The Event Horizon,* edited by Lorne Falk and Barbara Fischer, 215–37. Toronto: The Coach House Press and Walter Phillips Gallery.

Lyotard, Jean François. 1973. *Des Dispositits Pulsionnels.* Paris: Union Générale d'Editions.

MacIntyre, Alistair. 1981. *After Virtue.* London: Duckworth.

McGovern, Arthur F. 1981. *Marxism: An American Christian Perspective.* Maryknoll, New York: Orbis Books.

McLaren, Peter. 1988. "Schooling the Postmodern Body: Critical Pedagogy and the Politics of Enfleshment," *Journal of Education,* 170, no. 3: 58–83.

———, 1992. "Collisions with Otherness: Travelling Theory, Post-Colonial Criticism, and the Politics of Ethnographic Practice—The Mission of the Wounded Ethnographer." *International Journal of Qualitative Studies in Education* 5, no. 1: 77–92.

———. 1993. "Multiculturalism and the Postmodern Critique: Towards a Pedagogy of Resistance and Transformation." *Cultural Studies* 7, no. 1: 118–146.

McLaren, Peter, and Hammer, Rhonda. 1989. "Critical Pedagogy and the Postmodern Challenge." *Educational Foundations* 3, no. 3: 29–62.

McLaren, Peter, and Leonard, Peter. 1993. "Absent Discourses: Paulo Freire and the Dangerous Memories of Liberation." In *Paulo Freire: A Critical Encounter,* edited by Peter McLaren and Peter Leonard. New York: Routledge.

McLuhan, Marshall. 1973. *Understanding Media.* London: Abacus.

Mayer, Margit. 1991. "Politics in the Post-Fordist City." *Socialist Review,* 21, no. 1: 105–124.

Minh-ha, Trinh T. 198 "Difference: 'A Special Third World Women Issue'." *Feminist Review* 25: 5–22.

———. 1989. *Woman, Native, Other: Writing Post-coloniality and Feminism.* Bloomington, Ind.: Indiana University Press.

———. 1991. *When the Moon Waxes Red: Representations, Gender and Cultural Politics.* New York: Routledge.

Mort, Frank, and Green, Nicholas. 1988. "You've Never Had It So Good—Again." *Marxism Today* (May): 30–33.

Ogbu, John. 1990. "Minority Education in Comparative Perspective." *Journal of Negro Education* 59: no. 1: 45–57.

Patton, Paul. 1986. "Ethics and Post-Modernity." In *Futur*Fall: Excursions into Post-Modernity,* edited by E.A. Grosz, Terry Threadgold, David Kelly, Alan Cholodenko, and Edward Colless, 128–45. Sydney, Australia: Power Institute of Fine Arts, University of Sydney.

Pêcheux, Michel. 1982. *Language, Semantics, and Ideology: Stating the Obvious.* Trans. by Harbaas Nagpal. London: Macmillan.

Pecora, Vincent P. 1991. "Nietzsche, Genealogy, Critical Theory." *New German Critique* 53: 104–30.

Perez, Rolando. 1990. *On An(archy) and Schizoanalysis.* Brooklyn, N.Y.: Autonomedia.

Polan, Dana. 1986. "Brief Encounters: Mass Culture and the Evacuation of Sense." In *Studies in Entertainment,* edited by Tania Modleski, 167–87. Bloomington: Indiana University Press.

Przybylowicz, Donna. 1987. "Contemporary Issues in Feminist Theory." In *Criticism without Boundaries,* edited by Joseph A. Buttigieg, 129–59. Notre Dame: University of Notre Dame Press.

Ricoeur, Paul 1984. *Time and Narrative.* Chicago: University of Chicago Press.

Rigney, Ann. 1991. "Narrativity and Historical Representation." *Poetics Today* 12, no. 3: 591–605.

Rorty, Richard. 1991. "Feminism and Pragmatism." *Radical Philosophy* 59: 3–14.

Rosen, Harold. 1986. "The Importance of Story." *Language Arts* 63, no. 3: 226–37.

Saenz, Mario. 1991. "Memory, Enchantment and Salvation: Latin American Philosophies of Liberation and the Religions of the Oppressed." *Philosophy and Social Criticism* 17, no. 2: 149–73.

Saldivar, Ramon. 1990. *Chicano Narrative: The Dialectics of Difference*. Madison, Wis.: University of Wisconsin Press.

Sanchez-Tranquilino, Marcos and Tagg, John. 1991. "The Pachuco's Flayed Hide: The Museum, Identity and Buenas Garras." In *Chicano Art: Resistance and Transformation, 1965–1985*, edited by Richard Griswold del Castillo, Teresa McKenna, and Yvonne Yarbro-Bejarano, 97–108. Los Angeles: Wight Art Gallery, University of California.

Sawicki, Jana. 1991. *Disciplining Foucault: Feminism, Power, and the Body*. New York: Routledge.

Smith, S. 1987. *A Poetics of Women's Autobiography: Marginality and the Fictions of Self-Representations*. Bloomington, Ind.: Indiana University Press.

Spivak, Gayatri Chakravorty. 1990. "The Making of Americans, the Teaching of English, and the Future of Culture Studies." *New Literary History* 21, no. 4: 781–98.

Taylor, Patrick. 1989. *The Narrative of Liberation*. Ithaca, N.Y.: Cornell University Press.

West, Cornel. 1990. "The New Cultural Politics of Difference." *October* 53: 93–109.

White, Hayden. 1987. *The Content of the Form*. Baltimore: Johns Hopkins University Press.

Witkowski, Lech. 1990. "Education and the Universal Challenge of Border." Paper presented at the 2nd International Symposium for Universalism. Max-Planck Institut für Bildungsforschung, 1–41.

Yudice, George. 1992. "We Are Not the World." *Social Text* 31/32: 202–16.

Coda:
Toward the Pathway of a True Human Being

Daniel McLaughlin

It was an ordinary, typically busy Tuesday morning at the university. I got a call from the Indian Drug and Alcohol Recovery Center, on whose board I serve, reminding me of the meeting with auditors that afternoon. It was meant to be an important gathering. The regional office was not happy with the center's progress in recuperating from virtual insolvency during the past eighteen months. Bureaucrats had come with clipboards, calculators, and hard questions.

I drove downtown to the center, across from the park and the railway station, in view of dozens of homeless individuals, some of whom were gathered in quiet, animated clusters; some of whom, I noticed, were American Indians; others of whom wove about in a daze. I arrived at the center to find the auditors closeted with the director in her office, no doubt poring over policies and spreadsheets. Most of the center's staff and the other board members were in the cafeteria. They were sitting around a circle of chairs: counselors, cooks, and maintenance staff; lawyers, activists, doctors, and educators. Most were Indian. Many were recovering alcoholics. Waiting. It was not clear what for. Perhaps for the auditors. Perhaps our session with them would commence after theirs with the director was finished.

Fifteen or twenty minutes passed before the medicine man entered. His hair was untied. It fell to his waist. His ribbon shirt, moccasins, and drum produced a quick effect, as if to say, "The meeting of bureaucrats can wait; there are other matters to attend to." Slowly, deliberately, he fixed the drum, wetting and tightening the leather. Several more minutes passed. The small talk among staff and board members gradually petered out. The auditors would wait. We would not see them at all that day. The floor was now the medicine man's.

"Often we forget to step back from our running around, to think about the important things," he began. "What's most important is to remember what it is to be a true human being." He asked us to stand. After pausing and clearing his throat, he drummed. Then he sang. We were fixed in the circle listening and thinking for some time before he stopped, allowed us to sit, and told us a story.

> I had problems growing up. . . . When I was a young man, I got married, had a couple of kids, but I ran around. You couldn't tell me what to be or what to do. Those were the days of Red Power and Coors beer and getting as much as you can as fast as you can. Along the way, I almost lost everything. . . . One time, though, I left the reservation to visit a dear friend. He lived near the mountains near Douglas, Arizona. He knew that I needed help. He told me, "Go into the mountains. Hear them. Stay there and fast. Sing and pray on your own. . . ." That's what I did . . . . I took a few belongings and went deep into the wilderness and stayed there for four days. Without food . . . I began to see and to hear. I heard the animals. I heard the plants, the trees, the insects. . . . And I heard once again the stories that my grandfather told me—Apache stories, stories of the holy people . . . stories about living a true life. . . . I came down from those mountains, and I was on a road back. . . . I'm here today to remind all of us to see and to hear so that we do things in true ways. . . .

Here, then, as a coda to analyses of personal narratives for school change, is my story about a medicine man's story about stories. The medicine man's retrieval of stories and subsequent pathway of hope bring us full circle. They underscore what all of the authors in this volume have argued, that the development and critical analysis of personal histories with those who have been silenced and denied access in schools in particular and in society as a whole represent ways of creating coherence, attaching meaning, caring, wrestling with new questions, resisting, contesting inequities, and propounding change. They permit new perspectives on how we view our life circumstances. They connect us to organizational life and to the world at large and allow for the critical examination of these interpenetrations. In so doing, we understand in fundamentally new ways ourselves and others who have been traditionally denied, marginalized, and kept quiet.

The naming of silenced lives offers these possibilities; but, as each of the authors in this book has emphasized, simple naming is not enough. Actual empowerment requires more than making an individual aware of his or her life situation. It begins with recovering the past, as Michèle Foster demonstrated with her analysis of interviews with African-American teachers. As Andrew Gitlin and Beth Myers described, it entails a twofold process of developing voice: first, doing so as a form of publicly speaking out, then doing so as form of protest against marginalizing, silencing arrangements in schools in particular and in society as a whole. To paraphrase Patricia Gumport, it requires using the narratives to invite *critical engagement,* to enable others to decide for themselves whether the politics of knowledge and truth may not only be engaged and scrutinized, but also renegotiated, reorganized, and retold. Margaret LeCompte reminds us that such engagement, for educational researchers, is not a "quiet academic pursuit." It requires genuine participant observation, long-term commitment, collaboration, problem solving, resistance, and risk. An informant's newfound voice may not always be welcome, as Grace Mest Szepkouski described. Rather than empower, such voice may serve to raise a fruitless false consciousness, adding to rather than resolving the complexities of teacher empowerment and ensuring more stringent oppression.

At a minimum, as Peter McLaren asserted, critical engagement for university-based researchers begins with the need to reinvent research conditions that prize abstraction over narrative, theory over practice, and researcher over the researched. As difficult and as rife with contradictions as it occasionally may be, we must enable our research subjects and colleagues to deal with us on an equal footing, as Ivor Goodson, Ardra Cole, and William Tierney argued. As Yvonna Lincoln described, we must consider how we teach, what assumptions about research and practice we hold, what questions we ask, what answers we find, and how we define the anthropological "other" and ourselves, to devise teaching, research, and authoring strategies that help students and objects of our efforts to discover and affirm their own stories, theories of themselves, and theories of the world, and that help them and others to challenge the oppressive structures that create conditions for silencing, as I attempted to point out.

This is what the medicine man understood from his four days on the mountain. Hear the power that sedimented, forgotten stories hold. Learn from them, and reinvent your life pathway accordingly. For in the telling and careful hearing of them begins the journey of a true human being.

Index

Contributors

Margaret LeCompte is Associate Professor of Sociology and Education at the University of Colorado at Boulder. Specializing in ethnographic research methodology and research on school reform, dropouts, and sociocultural processes in schooling, she currently studies school restructuring on the Navajo reservation. Her books include *Ethnography and Qualitative Design in Educational Research, The Way Schools Work, Giving Up on School: Teacher Burnout and Student Dropouts* and *The Handbook of Qualitative Research in Education.*

Yvonna S. Lincoln is Professor of Higher Education at Texas A & M University. She is the editor or co-author of four books and over forty chapters and articles which relate to her interests in the problems of "normal science" for higher-education research and policy.

Andrew Gitlin is Professor of Educational Studies, University of Utah. He has taught and published in the areas of curriculum, critical theory, and teacher education. His major areas of interests include the effects of school structure on teachers' work, evaluation, school reform, and alternative research methods. His most recent books include *Teacher Evaluation: Educative Alternatives* co-authored with J. Smyth and *Teachers Voices for School Change: An Introduction to Educative Research.*

Beth Myers taught in the Salt Lake City schools for seven years prior to receiving her master's degree from the University of Utah in 1989. She is co-author of *Teachers' Voices for School Change.* Feminist issues, and those related to race and class, are her major areas of interest. She and her husband, a pediatrician, have one daughter.

Ardra Cole is an Assistant Professor in the Focus on Teaching Program, Department of Applied Psychology, The Ontario Institute for Studies in Education (OISE), Toronto, Canada. Her research, writing, and teaching fall into two main areas: teacher education and development with a particular emphasis on preservice and beginning teachers; and qualitative approaches to educational research. She has published several articles in both of these areas and is co-author, with J. Gary Knowles, of a forthcoming book, *Through preservice teachers' eyes: Exploring field experience through narrative and inquiry.*

Ivor Goodson is a Professor of Education and Honourary Professor of Sociology at the University of Western Ontario. He also runs the Research Unit on Classroom Learning and Computer Use in Schools (RUCCUS) where he is directing a range of projects pursuing his longstanding interest in curriculum and culture. He is currently a Visiting Professor at King's College London and is Frederica Warner Scholar at the University of Rochester. He is the author of many books, most recently *The Making of Curriculum* (1988), with Rob Walker *Biography, Identity and Schooling* (1991) and *School Subjects and Curriculum Change* (1993). He is the founding editor of the *Journal of Education Policy* and a national editor of *Qualitative Studies in Education.*

Daniel McLaughlin is a former classroom teacher, school principal, and university professor. At present, he works with program and curriculum development at Kayenta Public School District on the Navajo Reservation. His main areas of interest include curriculum, critical literacy, and American Indian education. He is the author of *When Literacy Empowers: Navajo Language in Print* and editor of the *Journal of Navajo Education.*

William G. Tierney is Associate Professor and Senior Research Associate in the Center for the Study of Higher Education at Pennsylvania State University. He has recently published an ethnographic case study of Native American college students, *Official Encouragement, Institutional Discouragement,* and a book about higher education, *Building Communities of Difference.*

Patricia J. Gumport is an Assistant Professor of Education at Stanford University. She is also Deputy Director of the Stanford Institute for Higher Education Research. She has written about the dynamics of knowledge change in higher education organizations, including curricula, academic vocations, and research training practices. Her current research focuses on the contested terrain of academic program reduction.

Michèle Foster is Associate Professor of African-American and African Studies and Education at the University of California-Davis. A 1989–90 Spencer Postdoctoral Fellow, she received the 1992 Early Career Achievement Award awarded by the Committee on the Status and Role of Minorities in Educational Research of the American Educational Research Association.

Grace Mest Szepkouski is an Assistant Professor of Education, Special Education Program, at Seton Hall University. Her current research activities involve a partnership with The Arc of Somerset County, N.J. (formerly The Association for Retarded Citizens) assessing "quality of life" issues by asking adults with retardation what they think about their community residences.

Peter McLaren is a former teacher activist and union journalist. He is currently Renowned Scholar in Residence and Director of the Center for Education and Cultural Studies, Miami University, where he is also Associate Professor of Educational Leadership. He is the author of *Schooling as a Ritual Performance; Life in Schools,* and co-editor (with Henry Giroux) of *Critical Pedagogy, the State, and Cultural Struggle.* Three of his most recent books include *Paulo Freire: A Critical Encounter* (edited with Peter Leonard); *Critical Literacy: Politics, Praxis, and the Postmodern* (edited with Colin Lankshear); and *Postmodernism, Postcolonialism, and Pedagogy* (editor). He is a frequent speaker in Europe, Latin America, and in his native Canada.